Lecture Notes in Computer Science 16228

Founding Editors

Gerhard Goos
Juris Hartmanis

The series Lecture Notes in Computer Science (LNCS), including its subseries Lecture Notes in Artificial Intelligence (LNAI) and Lecture Notes in Bioinformatics (LNBI), has established itself as a medium for the publication of new developments in computer science and information technology research, teaching, and education.

LNCS enjoys close cooperation with the computer science R & D community, the series counts many renowned academics among its volume editors and paper authors, and collaborates with prestigious societies. Its mission is to serve this international community by providing an invaluable service, mainly focused on the publication of conference and workshop proceedings and postproceedings. LNCS commenced publication in 1973.

Markus Wagner · Man Zhang
Editors

Search-Based Software Engineering

17th International Symposium, SSBSE 2025 Seoul, South Korea, November 16, 2025 Proceedings

Editors
Markus Wagner
Monash University
Clayton, VIC, Australia

Man Zhang
Beihang University
Beijing, China

ISSN 0302-9743 ISSN 1611-3349 (electronic)
Lecture Notes in Computer Science
ISBN 978-3-032-24838-1 ISBN 978-3-032-24839-8 (eBook)
https://doi.org/10.1007/978-3-032-24839-8

This Springer imprint is published by the registered company Springer Nature Switzerland AG
The registered company address is: Gewerbestrasse 11, 6330 Cham, Switzerland

Preface

Message from the General Chair

Welcome to the proceedings of the 17th Symposium on Search-Based Software Engineering, SSBSE 2025, held in Seoul, South Korea on 16 November 2025. This year SSBSE was co-located with the 40th IEEE/ACM International Conference on Automated Software Engineering, ASE 2025. SSBSE is a premier symposium dedicated to presenting and discussing novel ideas on formulating software engineering problems as search and optimization problems and to advancing computational and machine-intelligence techniques for solving these problems. This symposium provides a forum for the community to explore how these ideas can be effectively applied to evolve software engineering practice toward greater automation and intelligence.

We would like to thank the Technical Program Chairs, Markus Wagner and Man Zhang, for their dedication in making this symposium successful. We thank our track chairs for their great work: Aitor Arrieta and Seongmin Lee (RENE/NIER track), Vincenzo Riccio, Carol Hanna, and Mijung Kim (Challenge track), and Mitchell Olsthoorn and Matteo Biagiola (Hot-off-the-Press track). We thank the Steering Committee for their continuous support and guidance. We also thank Tao Yue for delivering the insightful keynote. Finally, we thank our sponsor, the Software Disaster Research Center at Kyungpook National University, South Korea for their support, and we thank the Organizing Team of ASE 2025 for providing a great venue and excellent services.

November 2025

Shin Hong

Message from the Program Chairs

SSBSE welcomes, but is not limited to, contributions on novel applications of SBSE, theoretical analyses of search algorithms in SE, rigorous empirical evaluations of SBSE approaches, and experience reports from industry. In SSBSE 2025, the venue was organized into four tracks: Research, Challenge, Hot off the Press (HOP), and Replications and Negative Results and New Ideas and Emerging Results (RENE/NIER).

In addition to the Research Track, the Challenge Track invited SBSE researchers to apply their tools, techniques, and algorithms to resolve challenge cases in real-world software systems. The goal was to produce insightful and interesting results that may advance the state of the art and inspire future SBSE research. The Hot-off-the-Press (HOP) track offered the opportunity to SBSE researchers to present their recent work to the SSBSE community, and submit summaries within the proceedings of SSBSE. The Hop track invited SSBSE researchers to submit summaries of their recent work published in top-tier journals and conferences and present these highlights to the SSBSE community. RENE/NIER offered the opportunity to SBSE researchers to submit research that replicates previous studies, reports negative results, or presents new ideas that could benefit from community discussion in the field of SBSE. This year's submissions demonstrated that search approaches are increasingly being combined with or applied to advanced techniques, such as machine learning, large language models (LLMs), and quantum annealing, to address a wide range of problems, including software testing, software operations, and configurations.

In SSBSE 2025, the Research track received 14 submissions, which were evaluated through a double-anonymous review process to ensure unbiased assessment. Each submission was assigned three to five reviewers and was evaluated through a comprehensive review process. As a result, 7 of the 14 submissions (50%) were accepted in the Research Track. The Challenge Track received 5 submissions, of which 4 (80%) were accepted. The HOP Track accepted both of its submissions (100%), while the RENE/NIER Track accepted 1 of 3 submissions (33%). Overall, SSBSE 2025 accepted 14 out of 24 papers (58%). The decisions on the papers were based solely on the Program Committee's assessment of each paper's content and quality, with no consideration of quotas.

Many colleagues contributed to the organization of SSBSE 2025 and the preparation of the proceedings. The HOP Track was co-chaired by Mitchell Olsthoorn (Delft University of Technology, Netherlands) and Matteo Biagiola (University of St. Gallen and Università della Svizzera italiana, Switzerland). The RENE/NIER Track was co-chaired by Aitor Arrieta (Mondragon University, Spain) and Seongmin Lee (University of California, Los Angeles, USA). The Challenge Track was organized by Vincenzo Riccio (University of Udine, Italy), Carol Hanna (University College London, UK), and Mijung Kim (Ulsan National Institute of Science and Technology, South Korea). As part of the Challenge Track, in collaboration with the University College London CREST Centre, they also organized a Collaborative Jam Session open to the public, held from September 1st to 2nd, 2025, at King's College London. Through this preface, we express our thanks to the co-chairs and Program Committee members of all tracks, as well as to the authors of all submissions, for their valuable contributions to SSBSE 2025.

Last but not least, we would like to thank all members of the SSBSE community for attending and participating in SSBSE 2025. We hope you had a wonderful time in Seoul and enjoyed the program. For those who could not attend, the proceedings are available for your reference.

November 2025

Man Zhang
Markus Wagner

Organization

General Chair

Shin Hong	Chungbuk National University, South Korea

Research Track Chairs

Man Zhang	Beihang University, China
Markus Wagner	Monash University, Australia

Hot-off-the-Press Track Chairs

Mitchell Olsthoorn	Delft University of Technology, Netherlands
Matteo Biagiola	University of St. Gallen and Università della Svizzera italiana, Switzerland

RENE/NIER Track Chairs

Aitor Arrieta	Mondragon University, Spain
Seongmin Lee	University of California, Los Angeles, USA

Challenge Track Chairs

Vincenzo Riccio	University of Udine, Italy
Carol Hanna	University College London, UK
Mijung Kim	Ulsan National Institute of Science and Technology, South Korea

Steering Committee

Shaukat Ali	Simula Research Laboratory and Oslo Metropolitan University, Norway
Andrea Arcuri	Kristiania University College and Oslo Metropolitan University, Norway
Gordon Fraser	University of Passau, Germany
Giovani Guizzo	University College London, UK
Phil McMinn	University of Sheffield, UK
Justyna Petke	University College London, UK
Federica Sarro	University College London, UK
Silva Regina Vergilio	Federal University of Paraná, Brazil
Shin Yoo	Korea Advanced Institute of Science & Technology, South Korea

Research Track Committee

Man Zhang	Beihang University, China
Markus Wagner	Monash University, Australia
Shaukat Ali	Simula Research Laboratory and Oslo Metropolitan University, Norway
Paolo Arcaini	National Institute of Informatics, Japan
Andrea Arcuri	Kristiania University College and Oslo Metropolitan University, Norway
Aitor Arrieta	Mondragon University, Spain
Matteo Biagiola	University of St. Gallen and Università della Svizzera italiana, Switzerland
Thiago Ferreira	University of Michigan - Flint, USA
Gordon Fraser	University of Passau, Germany
Gregory Gay	Chalmers University of Technology and University of Gothenburg, Sweden
Lars Grunske	Humboldt-Universität zu Berlin, Germany
Fitsum Kifetew	Fondazione Bruno Kessler, Italy
Inmaculada Medina-Bulo	Universidad de Cádiz, Spain
Manuel Núñez	Universidad Complutense de Madrid, Spain
José Miguel Rojas	University of Sheffield, UK
Silvia Regina Vergilio	Federal University of Paraná, Brazil
Marcio Barros	Federal University of the State of Rio de Janeiro, Brazil
Xavier Devroey	University of Namur, Belgium
Thomas Vogel	Humboldt-Universtität zu Berlin, Germany

Shin Yoo	Korea Advanced Institute of Science & Technology, South Korea
Giovani Guizzo	Brick Abode, Brazil
Fuyuki Ishikawa	National Institute of Informatics, Japan
Mitchell Olsthoorn	Delft University of Technology, Netherlands
Aymeric Blot	University of Rennes, IRISA/INRIA, France
Justyna Petke	University College London, UK
Brad Alexander	University of Adelaide, Australia
Sungmin Kang	National University of Singapore, Singapore
Max Hort	Simula Research Laboratory, Norway
Jifeng Xuan	Wuhan University, China
Alina Geiger	Johannes Gutenberg University Mainz, Germany
Francisco Chicano	University of Málaga, Spain
Carol Hanna	University College London, UK

Hot-off-the-Press Track Committee

Mitchell Olsthoorn	Delft University of Technology, Netherlands
Matteo Biagiola	University of St. Gallen and Università della Svizzera italiana, Switzerland
Xavier Devroey	University of Namur, Belgium
Gregory Gay	Chalmers University of Technology and University of Gothenburg, Sweden
Fabrizio Pastore	University of Luxembourg, Luxembourg
Donghwan Shin	University of Sheffield, UK

RENE/NIER Track Committee

Aitor Arrieta	Mondragon University, Spain
Seongmin Lee	University of California, Los Angeles, USA
Mingfei Cheng	Singapore Management University, Singapore
Liping Han	Nanjing University of Posts and Telecommunications, China
Sungmin Kang	National University of Singapore, Singapore
Chengjie Lu	Simula Research Laboratory and University of Oslo, Norway
Alberto Martin-Lopez	Università della Svizzera italiana, Switzerland
Aurora Ramírez	University of Córdoba, Spain
Vincenzo Riccio	University of Udine, Italy
José Raúl Romero	University of Córdoba, Spain

Miriam Ugarte	Mondragon University, Spain
Pablo Valle	Mondragon University, Spain

Challenge Track Committee

Carol Hanna	University College London, UK
Mijung Kim	Ulsan National Institute of Science and Technology, South Korea
Vincenzo Riccio	University of Udine, Italy
Antony Bartlett	TU Delft, The Netherlands
Christian Birchler	Zurich University of Applied Sciences & University of Bern, Switzerland
Xingcheng Chen	Technical University of Munich & fortiss GmbH, Germany
Francesca Da Ros	Università degli Studi di Udine, Italy
Patric Feldmeier	University of Passau, Germany
Sophie Fortz	King's College London, UK
Gregory Gay	Chalmers University of Technology and University of Gothenburg, Sweden
Sungmin Kang	National University of Singapore, Singapore
Jinhan Kim	Università della Svizzera italiana, Switzerland
Stephan Lukasczyk	JetBrains Research, Germany
Maryam Maryam	University of Udine, Italy
Eñaut Mendiluze Usandizaga	Simula Research Laboratory, Norway
Pablo Valle	Mondragon University, Spain
Giordano d'Aloisio	University of L'Aquila, Italy

Keynote

Classical, Quantum, Hybrid, and Beyond: The Changing Landscape of SBSE

Tao Yue

Beihang University, China

Abstract. This talk reviews recent developments in Search-Based Software Engineering (SBSE) and examines how enduring challenges such as testing, configuration, and optimisation interact with emerging quantum, hybrid, and quantum-inspired techniques. The talk is based on two recent surveys (arXiv:2510.27113, 2506.16878). It highlights how these new computational paradigms influence problem formulation and expose both confusion and insight when familiar SBSE tasks meet unfamiliar machines.

The talk outlines several 'go beyond' directions: scaling problems and datasets to more realistic and demanding scenarios; exploring multiple solution strategies and tuning them effectively; and improving encodings, constraint handling, and hybrid quantum–classical workflows, including decomposition and pre/post-processing. It also emphasizes extending quantum-inspired algorithms using ideas from broader optimisation traditions. A further theme is the need for clearer, standardized cost and quality metrics, given the very different resource models of classical, quantum, and hybrid environments. Finally, the talk stresses awareness of the gap between benchmark results and real-world feasibility, especially considering hardware limits, noise, qubit counts, and the complexity of encoding SE problems into QUBO or Ising models. Overall, the talk shows how evolving computational paradigms are reshaping SBSE's assumptions and opening new avenues for responsible, evidence-driven progress.

SSBSE Summary of BQTmizer: A Tool for Test Case Minimization with Quantum Annealing

Xinyi Wang[1,2], Shaukat Ali[1,3], and Paolo Arcaini[4]

[1] Simula Research Laboratory, Oslo, Norway
{xinyi,shaukat}@simula.no
[2] University of Oslo, Oslo, Norway
[3] Oslo Metropolitan University, Oslo, Norway
[4] National Institute of Informatics, Tokyo, Japan
arcaini@nii.ac.jp

Abstract. Quantum computing has shown great potential in a wide range of applications across various fields, including search-based software engineering. Quantum annealing (QA) is a promising quantum algorithm specifically designed for solving combinatorial optimization problems, offering a quantum approach to searching for optimal solutions. In this paper, we designed a quantum-classical hybrid tool, *BQTmizer* , to solve large-scale real-world test case minimization problems. *BQTmizer* aims to select the smallest number of test cases among an existing test suite, while satisfying all test objectives. We demonstrated the performance of *BQTmizer* on two open-source industrial datasets. Results show that *BQTmizer* can effectively and efficiently reduce the number of selected test cases on large-scale datasets. This paper summarises: "X. Wang, S. Ali and P. Arcaini, BQTmizer: A Tool for Test Case Minimization With Quantum Annealing, in IEEE Software, vol. 42, no. 5, pp. 51-57, Sept.-Oct. 2025, doi: https://doi.org/10.1109/MS.2025.3546511."

Keywords: Quantum optimization · Quantum annealing · Test Case Minimization · search-based software engineering

1. Summary of BQTmizer

Quantum computing can solve complex problems that are hard to solve by classical algorithms. Quantum optimization algorithms like *quantum annealing* (QA) are search algorithms that have demonstrated promising results in various fields, including software engineering, finance, etc. They can solve optimization problems more efficiently than classical state-of-the-art search algorithms.

In [2], we used QA to tackle test case minimization (TCM), which aims to select the smallest subset of tests that ensures high coverage, high fault detection, and reduced execution time. To handle the large-scale industrial data with the current quantum hardware, we proposed a hybrid quantum-classical framework that combines QA with bootstrap sampling, used for problem decomposition.

In [1], to automate this approach for the convenience of developers, who integrate it with other testing techniques in real-world software development, we develop the hybrid framework *BQTmizer* based on the D-Wave platform.

BQTmizer **Description.** The architecture of *BQTmizer* is shown in Fig. 1. To use *BQTmizer* , the users should provide all input information to configure the search-based optimization process, including the dataset of test cases, test case properties (effectiveness and cost ones), weights of the weighted single-objective fitness function, sub-problem size for decomposition, etc. Then, *BQTmizer* will solve the TCM problem by the following steps: (i) it calculates the number of subsets to sample as M ; (ii) a bootstrap sampling strategy is used to decompose the original TCM problem; it randomly selects subsets until a total of M subsets are generated; (iii) a QUBO formulation of TCM is constructed for each subset of test cases (each subset is a sub-problem); (iv) the search algorithm QA is run to solve each sub-problem individually by D-Wave Advantage system; *BQTmizer* merges all subsolutions to obtain the final solution of the search problem. After execution, *BQTmizer* outputs four files: (1) *result.csv* with the selected test cases; (2) *summary.csv* with overall fitness, total execution time, and average qubits for each sub-problem; (3) *sample_info.zip* tracking fitness evolution; and (4) log.csv with sub-problem logs.

xxx

Validation. We evaluate *BQTmizer* on two real-world industrial datasets (89 and 1941 test cases). For the small dataset, it selects 8 test cases in 0.14 secs, while for the larger one, it selects 253 test cases in 4.4 secs. This indicates that the cost scales roughly linearly with dataset size, offering a significant speed advantage over classical search methods like simulated annealing.

Interest to the SSBSE Audience. In this work, we show how quantum computing (quantum annealing in particular) can be used to efficiently and effectively solve test case minimization, a typical SBSE problem. This is of interest to the SSBSE community that must handle computationally expensive problems, that could benefit from the application of quantum computing.

Acknowledgments. The work is supported by the Qu-Test project (Project #299827) funded by the Research Council of Norway and Simula's internal strategic project on quantum software engineering. X. Wang is supported by Simula's internal strategic project on quantum software engineering. S. Ali is supported by Oslo Metropolitan University's Quantum Hub. P. Arcaini by the ASPIRE grant No. JPMJAP2301, JST.

References

1. Wang, X., Ali, S., Arcaini, P.: BQTmizer: A tool for test case minimization with quantum annealing. IEEE Software **42**(5), 51–57 (2025). https://doi.org/10.1109/MS.2025.3546511
2. Wang, X., Muqeet, A., Yue, T., Ali, S., Arcaini, P.: Test case minimization with quantum annealers. ACM Trans. Softw. Eng. Methodol. **34**(1) (2024). https://doi.org/10.1145/3680467

SSBSE Summary of Search-Based Repair of DNN Controllers of AI-Enabled Cyber-Physical Systems Guided by System-Level Specifications

Deyun Lyu[1], Zhenya Zhang[1,2], Paolo Arcaini[1], Fuyuki Ishikawa[1], Thomas Laurent[3], and Jianjun Zhao[2]

[1] National Institute of Informatics, Tokyo, Japan
{lyudeyun,arcaini,f-ishikawa}@nii.ac.jp,
zhang@ait.kyushu-u.ac.jp

[2] Kyushu University, Fukuoka, Japan
zhao@ait.kyushu-u.ac.jp

[3] SFI Lero and School of Computer Science and Statistics, Trinity College Dublin, Dublin, Ireland
tlaurent@tcd.ie

Abstract. In an *AI-enabled CPS*, a *DNN* serves as controller of the physical system. Despite extensive training, a DNN may still produce wrong decisions, causing safety risks. DNN repair is a search-based approach that can be potentially used to perform targeted improvement of the DNN controller. However, existing DNN repair methods rely on ground-truth labels for each inference, which are unavailable in AI-enabled CPSs. Instead, system-level specifications can be used to detect wrong behaviours. Based on this intuition, we propose a novel search-based repair approach guided by system-level specifications. It takes as input a specification, a test suite with passing and failing tests (i.e., satisfying/violating the specification), and some faulty DNN weights; given these inputs, it searches for alternative weight values to improve the performance of the DNN controller. We also introduce a heuristic that accelerates the search. Experiments on real-world AI-enabled CPSs show that the approach effectively repairs their controllers. This abstract summarises: "D. Lyu, Z. Zhang, P. Arcaini, F. Ishikawa, T. Laurent, J. Zhao. Search-Based Repair of DNN Controllers of AI-Enabled Cyber-Physical Systems Guided by System-Level Specifications. In GECCO 2024."

Keywords: DNN repair · DNN controllers · Cyber-physical systems

1 Summary of ContrRep

Cyber-physical systems (CPSs) are increasingly using deep neural networks (DNNs) as controllers, leading to the emergence of *AI-enabled CPSs*. Despite their advantages, DNN controllers can be faulty and lead to system failures. *DNN repair* is an emerging search-based approach that modifies a DNN with the goal to improve its performance.

However, existing DNN repair techniques mainly target classification problems and rely on ground-truth labels, which are unavailable for DNN controllers; indeed, the correctness of an individual control decision cannot be directly determined. Instead, system-level specifications can be used: satisfaction implies correct behaviour of the DNN controller, while violation indicates a wrong a control decision.

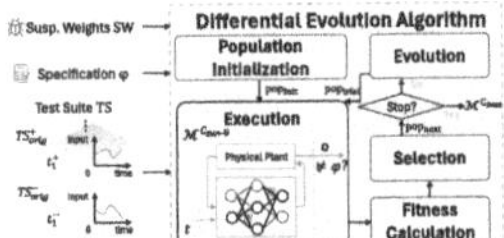

Fig. 1. ContrRep

Based on this intuition, we propose ContrRep [1], a search-based approach to repair DNN controllers of AI-enabled CPSs, guided by system-level specifications (see Fig. 1). ContrRep takes as input the original system $M^{C_{orig}}$ with its DNN controller C_{orig}, a system-level specification φ written in Signal Temporal Logic (STL), a test suite *TS* with failing and passing tests (i.e., violating and satisfying φ), and faulty weights *SW* identified by fault localisation. The search-based repair (implemented in Differential Evolution) searches for an alternative setting of *SW* that improves the performance of the DNN controller; specifically, the fitness function aims to maximize the number of failing tests that are fixed and the passing ones that are not broken. As running all tests for a candidate solution is computationally costly, we introduce ContrRep$_{\text{FAST}}$, which leverages STL robust semantics to prioritize test evaluation in the fitness computation: failing tests are evaluated from high to low robustness until one fails, and passing tests from low to high robustness until one passes, so reducing the number of system executions.

Experiments. We evaluate ContrRep on four AI-enabled CPSs, addressing three questions: **RQ1** How is the repair performance of ContrRep? **RQ2** Does ContrRep$_{\text{FAST}}$ reduce the execution time of the search-based repair approach? Does it affect the repair performance? **RQ3** To what extent does ContrRepfix failing tests and break passing tests? The results show that [(i)] ContrRep improves the performance of DNN controllers; ContrRep$_{\text{FAST}}$ speeds up the search, with a small impact on repair effectiveness; break rates of originally passing tests and repair rates of originally failing tests vary, with harder benchmarks showing higher break and lower repair rates.

Interest to the SSBSE Audience. The work shows the application to search-based repair (a typical SBSE activity) to a new relevant domain, namely AI-enabled CPSs. Moreover, it provides a novel solution to reduce the cost of fitness evaluation, a typical issue occurring in search-based repair.

Acknowledgments. Work supported by Engineerable AI Techniques for Practical Applications of High-Quality Machine Learning-based Systems Project (Grant Number JPMJMI20B8), JST-Mirai. Z. Zhang and J. Zhao are supported by JSPS KAKENHI Grant No. JP23H03372. Z. Zhang is also supported by JSPS KAKENHI Grant No. JP23K16865. P. Arcaini is supported by the ASPIRE grant No. JPMJAP2301, JST.

Reference

1. Lyu, D., Zhang, Z., Arcaini, P., Ishikawa, F., Laurent, T., Zhao, J.: Search-based repair of DNN controllers of AI-Enabled Cyber-Physical Systems guided by system-level specifications. In: Proceedings of the Genetic and Evolutionary Computation Conference, pp. 1435–1444. GECCO'24, Association for Computing Machinery, New York, NY, USA (2024). https://doi.org/10.1145/3638529.3654078

Contents

Research Track

RENE/NIER Track

Challenge Track

Research Track

Constraint-Guided Unit Test Generation for Machine Learning Libraries

Lukas Krodinger[1(✉)], Altin Hajdari[1], Stephan Lukasczyk[1,2], and Gordon Fraser[1]

[1] University of Passau, Passau, Germany
lukas.krodinger@uni-passau.de
[2] JetBrains Research, Munich, Germany

Abstract. Machine learning (ML) libraries such as PyTorch and TensorFlow are essential for a wide range of modern applications. Ensuring the correctness of ML libraries through testing is crucial. However, ML APIs often impose strict input constraints involving complex data structures such as tensors. Automated test generation tools such as Pynguin are not aware of these constraints and often create non-compliant inputs. This leads to early test failures and limited code coverage. Prior work has investigated extracting constraints from official API documentation. In this paper, we present PynguinML, an approach that improves the Pynguin test generator to leverage these constraints to generate compliant inputs for ML APIs, enabling more thorough testing and higher code coverage. Our evaluation is based on 165 modules from PyTorch and TensorFlow, comparing PynguinML against Pynguin. The results show that PynguinML significantly improves test effectiveness, achieving up to 63.9 % higher code coverage.

Keywords: Test Generation · Python · API Constraints

1 Introduction

Machine learning (ML) libraries such as PyTorch[1] and TensorFlow,[2] are used in many real-world applications and downloaded thousands of times each day.[3] To ensure that these libraries work as intended, developers typically write unit tests. However, manually creating effective unit tests is a tedious and time-consuming task [19]. Thus, automated unit test generation tools have been introduced. Prominent examples of existing tools include Randoop [15] and EvoSuite [5] for Java or Pynguin [9] for Python. These tools typically analyse a *subject under test* (SUT), such as a Java class or Python module, and use meta-heuristic search algorithms to generate tests. The goal is to create inputs

[1] https://pytorch.org/, last accessed 2025-07-29.
[2] https://tensorflow.org/, last accessed 2025-07-29.
[3] https://pypistats.org/packages/pytorch and https://pypistats.org/packages/tensorflow, last accessed 2025-07-29.

M. Wagner and M. Zhang (Eds.): SSBSE 2025, LNCS 16228, pp. 3–18, 2026.
https://doi.org/10.1007/978-3-032-24839-8_1

```
def glu(
    input: Tensor, dim: int = -1
) -> Tensor:
    if input.dim() == 0:
        raise RuntimeError()
    # Logic of the function ...
```

(a) Simplified code of the PyTorch API `torch.nn.functional.glu`.

```
import torch.nn.functional as F

@mark.xfail(strict=True)
def test_case_0():
    none_type_0 = None
    F.glu(none_type_0)
```

(b) Typical test generated by PYNGUIN with non-compliant input parameters.

Fig. 1. Example of a failing test case due to missing input constraints.

```
import numpy
import torch
import torch.nn.functional as F

def test_case_0():
    var_0 = [
        [15.06, 1038.1, 1695.079, -97.7],
        [12.06, 0.1179, 16.6, 32.23]
    ]
    var_1 = "float32"
    var_2 = numpy.array(object=var_0, dtype=var_1)
    var_3 = torch.tensor(data=var_2)
    F.glu(var_3)
```

Fig. 2. Compliant test generated by PYNGUINML using API constraints.

that trigger the SUT's routines (i.e., functions, methods, and constructors) in a manner that maximizes a fitness metric, most commonly branch coverage.

However, many ML libraries require specific input constraints, which current test generation tools do not consider [23,26]. Inputs must follow a particular structure, such as a `list`, `tuple`, or `tensor` and they must satisfy certain properties like a specific data type or shape. The most popular language for ML applications is Python, yet Python's state-of-the-art test generation tool PYNGUIN is not aware of these constraints. Thus, many generated test cases include API calls with non-compliant inputs, which often trigger early failures. This results in low code coverage. For example, consider Fig. 1a, which shows a simplified version of the PyTorch API `torch.nn.functional.glu`, which calls the `dim()` method on the parameter `input`, assuming it is a valid tensor. An example test case generated by PYNGUIN (Fig. 1b) calls this function with `None` as input, which is not a valid tensor and causes an exception to be raised. As PYNGUIN generates test suites where all test cases pass by construction, it marks this test with `@mark.xfail(strict=True)` from PYTEST, which results in the test case to expect the exception and thus pass. However, the test does not reach the core logic of the function and contributes little to code coverage.

To address this problem, we leverage API constraints previously extracted from the documentation [24] of libraries to guide test generation. These constraints specify the expected structure and properties of input arguments, such as *data type*, tensor *shape*, or *dimension* values. By incorporating this information into the test generation process, we can create compliant inputs that satisfy these constraints. This enables deeper parts of the API code to be reached during testing. We implement our approach, PYNGUINML, as an extension of PYNGUIN.

Figure 2 shows a test case generated by PYNGUINML for the `glu` function from Fig. 1a. The API constraints for the `glu` function tell PYNGUINML that a tensor is required as well as its expected *dimension*, *shape*, and *data type*. PYNGUINML generates a nested list that adheres to these structural properties and assigns the correct NUMPY data type as a string. It then converts the list to a NUMPY array and finally to a PYTORCH tensor. The generated input satisfies the API's requirements, thus executing the SUT beyond input validation.

To evaluate our approach, we identified 165 modules from PYTORCH and TENSORFLOW for which API constraint data is available. We compare PYNGUINML to PYNGUIN and to the existing MUTESTER [14] tool that also uses API constraints. Our evaluation focuses on two key metrics: code coverage and the number of compliant test cases, i.e., test cases where input parameters do not violate the documented API constraints. We make the following contributions:

- We propose PYNGUINML, an extension of PYNGUIN that incorporates constraints from the documentation of libraries into the test generation process.
- We introduce new statement types tailored to ML-specific needs, such as nested lists with valid shapes, enum values, and unsigned integers.
- We evaluate PYNGUINML compared to PYNGUIN and MUTESTER on 165 modules from PYTORCH and TENSORFLOW.

Our evaluation shows that PYNGUINML significantly improves test generation for Python ML libraries compared to PYNGUIN and MUTESTER.

2 Background

Our work is based on unit test generation for Python and is tailored to libraries with extensive API documentation, specifically machine learning (ML) libraries.

2.1 Machine Learning Libraries in Python

Machine Learning (ML) is the foundation for many applications, such as image classification, natural language processing, and recommendation systems. To facilitate ML development open-source libraries like TENSORFLOW and PYTORCH provide standardized APIs that simplify complex algorithms. To ensure correct usage of these APIs, ML libraries provide detailed documentation. A key part of the API documentation defines constraints for input parameters. The two main categories are: (1) the required data structures and (2) the properties of these data structures. Firstly, parameters must follow specific data structures, which includes built-in types such as `int`, `str`, or `list` and library-specific types like TENSORFLOW's `tf.Tensor`[4] or PYTORCH's `torch.Tensor`.[5]

[4] https://tensorflow.org/api_docs/python/tf/Tensor, last accessed 2025-08-21.
[5] https://pytorch.org/docs/stable/tensors.html, last accessed 2025-08-21.

If the input does not match the expected type, the API function typically raises an error during input validation. Secondly, these data structures must satisfy several specific properties, so-called constraints. One property of the constraints is the *data type*, like `float` or the library-specific `torch.float32`. Another property is the *shape*, which defines the dimensions as a tuple of integers indicating the size along each axis. A tuple's length corresponds to the *dimension* of the tensor; e.g., a shape of `(3, 4)` describes a 2-dimensional tensor. A valid value *range* defines the allowable set of values for a parameter, e.g., restricting a `float` to the interval `[0, 1]` or a string to a predefined list of supported values.

While these ML constraints are crucial for correct API usage and essential for automated test generation, they are often not explicitly defined in the code but rather documented informally using different formats and conventions across libraries. The constraints must be extracted and normalized into a consistent, standardized form. This poses several challenges that were addressed in prior work [14,20,24]. We use previously extracted constraints [24] for the ML libraries TensorFlow and PyTorch for evaluating our approach.

2.2 Unit Test Generation for Python

Creating effective test suites is critical for reducing the risk of software failures. However, manually creating test cases is often time-consuming and labour-intensive. To alleviate this burden, numerous automated techniques for unit test generation have been proposed [6]. Some approaches use random test generation, sometimes enhanced by feedback from previous executions to inform subsequent test creation [16]. Besides that, search-based software engineering (SBSE) methods, such as evolutionary algorithms, have been employed to optimize test cases with respect to a specified fitness function [21], such as branch coverage. For an in-depth discussion of search-based test generation and the underlying algorithms, we refer to the extensive literature on this topic [3,18].

Pynguin [9] is a state-of-the-art test-generation framework designed for the Python programming language. It incorporates multiple SBSE test-generation strategies, including feedback-directed random test generation [16] and the DynaMOSA [17] evolutionary algorithm. Pynguin aims to generate test cases that yield high coverage values. To achieve this, it analyzes the SUT and collects all public classes, functions, and methods and saves all their lines or branches (depending on the configuration) as targets for the test generation. Upon creating test cases for a focal method that has at least one parameter, Pynguin needs to generate arguments to call the method with. It randomly generates objects for built-in types, collections, and classes defined in the SUT. For assembling objects of user-defined classes, Pynguin tries using constructors or factory methods. If the selected constructor requires more than one parameter, Pynguin repeats the process recursively (up to a pre-defined maximum recursion depth) until all parameters are satisfied. During this process, Pynguin does not consider API constraints defined in the API documentation which leads to non-compliant inputs. In turn, the generated tests execute less of the SUT's code, which reduces the effectiveness of the generated tests.

2.3 MuTester

MuTester [14] is a test generation tool based on Pynguin that, similarly to our approach, enhances test generation for ML libraries. MuTester uses signature definition constraints mined from the method signature using a regular expression based string analyzer, API constraints mined from API documentation, and concrete input values mined from example code snippets. During test generation, MuTester iteratively matches candidate methods to sequence patterns by checking for usage patterns based on the API constraints. It further searches past executions for matching inputs or generates new ones based on the mined constraints if none are found. In contrast to MuTester, PynguinML does not use mined constraints from signatures. Type hints in the source code, which are used by Pynguin if available, already provide the same information. Furthermore, PynguinML does not use mined constraints from example code snippets, but instead focuses on constraints mined from API documentation.

3 Test Generation Using API Constraints

To address the limitations of test generation for libraries with API constraints—especially Machine Learning (ML) libraries—we extend Pynguin [9] by integrating API constraints into input generation, which we call PynguinML. Before generating tests, PynguinML analyzes the module under test to identify used APIs based on the module and API name and loads the corresponding constraints. Each constraint file describes input requirements for a specific API. These files specify properties per parameter, including:

- **dtype**: the expected data type (e.g., `torch.float32`),
- **ndim**: required number of dimensions (rank),
- **tensor_t**: whether the input must be a tensor,
- **structure**: required container types (e.g., `list` or `tuple`),
- **range**: valid intervals for numeric parameters,
- **enum**: allowed values for categorical parameters.

When loading the constraints in the initial setup phase, a validation process removes invalid ones. This includes syntactically incorrect entries, undefined types, or constraints that are logically contradictory, such as specifying a negative integer as *dimension* or an invalid numeric *range*, e.g., `[1, 0]`.

The constraints guide the input generation of PynguinML to generate compliant inputs and sequences. For primitives, e.g. `float`, PynguinML extends existing Pynguin mechanisms by applying constraints such as `range`. For example, a `float` parameter with a `range` of `[0.0, 1.0]` results in a random `float` within this `range`. To support further constraints, PynguinML introduces additional statements: (1) an *enum* statement for parameters with `enum` values, selecting from the predefined set of allowed values; (2) an *unsigned-integer* statement for `dtype` constraints that specify unsigned integer types, generating non-negative integers; and (3) a *nested-list* statement for `dtype` constraints that specify tensors. This *nested-list* serves as a library-independent representation of tensors, which PynguinML uses in the following pre-defined sequence of statements tailored towards ML libraries to generate a compliant tensor:

1. Generate a *nested-list* with a shape, as defined by the `ndim` constraint.
2. Create a string statement storing the desired NumPy `dtype`.
3. Construct a `numpy.ndarray` from the list and `dtype`.
4. Convert the array into a library-specific tensor using a user-defined function (e.g., `torch.tensor` or `torch.from_numpy`).

The new statements require modifications to the evolutionary algorithm used by PynguinML. To prevent invalid test cases, we do not allow crossover operations within tensor-generation sequences. If a crossover point occurs inside such a sequence, PynguinML discards the subsequent statements of the sequence and replaces them with a newly generated sequence. We added mutation functionality for the new statements: a *nested-list* mutates its elements while preserving its *shape*, an *enum* selects a different allowed value, and an *unsigned integer* always mutates to a new non-negative value. If a mutation deletes a tensor creation statement, any subsequent dependent statements are also deleted.

While these modifications help producing compliant parameters when calling functions, achieving high code coverage also requires non-compliant inputs. For example, input validation code that performs checks on the parameters passed into a function can only be properly tested when also allowing for non-compliant parameter values (i.e., negative tests). Consequently, when generating parameters for a function for which API constraints are available, PynguinML makes a probabilistic choice of whether to produce a compliant parameter, or whether to fall back to Pynguin's standard object generation mechanisms, which will likely lead to non-compliant parameters suitable for testing input validation.

4 Evaluation

We extended Pynguin with support for API constraints as described in Sect. 3. To evaluate the effectiveness of our extension, PynguinML, we ask:

RQ1 Branch Coverage: *To what extent does* PynguinML *improve code coverage compared to* Pynguin *and* MuTester*?*

We conjecture that the API constraints lead to more compliant inputs. We define a test case as *compliant* if it does not include an API call with inputs that violate the constraints specified in the API documentation. To evaluate the impact of more compliant test cases, we ask:

RQ2 Compliant Tests: *How many more compliant test cases does* PynguinML *generate compared to* Pynguin*?*

4.1 Evaluation Setup

Subjects. We evaluate our approach on ML libraries for which constraint data is available [24], specifically PyTorch and TensorFlow. The provided constraints correspond to TensorFlow v2.1.0 and PyTorch v1.5.0. However, we use TensorFlow v2.8.0 and PyTorch v1.13.0 in our evaluation, as these versions are compatible with Python 3.10, which is required by Pynguin. Although DocTer [24] provides constraints for MXNet as well, we exclude MXNet from our evaluation because it does not support Python 3.10 and is retired. Among all importable, non-test and non-`__init__.py` modules (2 134 for PyTorch and 1 277 for TensorFlow), we selected those modules for which we have a constraint for at least one API within the module, resulting in 53 modules from PyTorch and 112 modules from TensorFlow, for a total of 165 modules.

Experiment Settings. PyTorch and TensorFlow use Python's *foreign function interface* (FFI) to call low-level functions in C or C++ for performance reasons. These functions can lead to low-level errors, such as *segmentation faults*, which cannot be caught by Python's exception handling and instead cause the Python interpreter to crash, which in turn terminates Pynguin. We therefore configure Pynguin to execute the test cases in separate subprocesses rather than only in separate threads. This comes with the drawback of a performance overhead. To compensate for this, we set the *search time* to 900 s rather than previously used 600 s [8–11,25]. Additionally, we set the newly introduced *maximum tensor dimension* and the *maximum size per shape dimension* to 5. This is sufficient for most ML APIs and helps balance memory usage. All other configuration options use the default settings of Pynguin. We execute both PynguinML and Pynguin on each subject 20 times. We use a Docker container to isolate the executions from their environment based on Python 3.10.16 and execute all runs on dedicated servers, each equipped with an AMD EPYC 7443P CPU and 256 GB RAM. We only assign a single CPU core and 8 GB of RAM to each run to simulate an environment closer to real-world operation conditions.

Experiment Procedure. As a basis for answering all research questions, we execute both PynguinML and Pynguin on all 165 subject modules. For every successful run, we collect the achieved branch coverage and the generated test cases. We use the collected coverage data to answer RQ1 by comparing between Pynguin and PynguinML. We also compare our findings with those from MuTester, but as their replication package is incomplete, we were unable to re-run MuTester ourselves. We therefore compare the numbers reported in the MuTester paper with a re-run of PynguinML for 300 s (as was done for MuTester) for a fair comparison. To address RQ2 we inspect a subset of the generated tests by first randomly sampling 10 modules per ML library, and then randomly selecting one test file (out of 20 repetitions) per tool for each of these modules. All test cases violating documented API constraints are then manually classified individually by two of the authors of the paper. Further details on our setup and analysis scripts can be found in our replication package [7].

Evaluation Metrics. To assess by how much PYNGUINML improves over PYNGUIN, we compute the relative coverage [2] as a percentage. Given the coverage of a subject s in an execution e, denoted by $\text{cov}(s, e)$, we refer to the best coverage on s in any execution by $\max(\text{cov}(s))$ and to the worst coverage on s in any execution by $\min(\text{cov}(s))$. We define relative coverage $\text{cov}_r(s, e)$ as

$$\text{cov}_r(s, e) = \frac{\text{cov}(s, e) - \min(\text{cov}(s))}{\max(\text{cov}(s)) - \min(\text{cov}(s))}.$$

In case $\min(\text{cov}(s)) = \max(\text{cov}(s))$, i.e., minimum and maximum coverage for a subject s are equal, we define the relative coverage $\text{cov}_r(s, e) = 100\%$ [3].

To evaluate if one configuration performs better than another configuration, we use the Mann-Whitney U-test [12] with $\alpha = 0.05$. Additionally, we compute the Vargha and Delaney effect size $\hat{A}_{12}$ [22] to investigate the difference in the achieved overall coverage between two configurations. These metrics do not make assumptions on the data distribution, are in line with recommendations for assessing randomized algorithms [1], and were used in previous work [8–11,25].

We analyse whether a test case is compliant per module, with Cohen's Kappa coefficient κ measuring inter-rater agreement in manual validation [4].

4.2 Threats to Validity

Internal Validity. There are several threats regarding the comparison with MUTESTER: First, we use a newer version of PYNGUIN than the one used in the original MUTESTER study. Our version may include performance improvements that impact coverage and test generation behaviour. We did this to allow for the usage of subprocess-execution. Second, the usage of subprocess-execution allows isolating crashes during test execution. While this is necessary for stability when testing ML libraries, it introduces additional overhead. However, when not using it the results for PYNGUIN and PYNGUINML can only be better due to omitting the performance overhead. Third, the exact configuration, module selection, and constraints used by MUTESTER are not publicly available, and thus the experiments might have been executed under different conditions. We did everything possible to make comparability as good as possible.

Besides the comparison with MUTESTER other threats are regarding the manual analysis of compliant test cases. The manual analysis introduces a risk of human error, as determining whether inputs violate constraints requires interpreting API documentation. To mitigate this, we determine the violations two times independently, and only consider those as compliant where both agree.

External Validity. Our evaluation focuses on two widely used ML libraries: PYTORCH and TENSORFLOW. While these libraries differ in implementation, they share a similar structure and design commonly found in many ML

Table 1. Number of modules where PYNGUINML (treatment) performed (significantly) better, equal or (significantly) worse than PYNGUIN (control) and the Vargha and Delaney $\hat{A}_{12}$ effect size.

Library	Better (Sig)	Equal	Worse (Sig)	$\hat{A}_{12}$
PYTORCH	30 (19)	6	15 (3)	0.631
TENSORFLOW	78 (58)	11	19 (6)	0.697
Total	**108 (77)**	**17**	**34 (9)**	**0.675**

frameworks. Therefore, we expect PYNGUINML to generalize well to other ML libraries with similar characteristics. However, the results may not generalize to libraries outside the ML domain, where APIs and usage patterns differ considerably. Additionally, our evaluation is limited to modules for which constraints were available, because the replication package for DOCTER does not include the code for HTML scraping [24]. Therefore, the results may not generalize to ML libraries or APIs where constraint information is incomplete or less accurate.

Furthermore, our evaluation of compliant test cases is based on a limited sample of 10 randomly selected modules per library, which may not fully capture the diversity of APIs in PYTORCH and TENSORFLOW.

Construct Validity. Our approach relies on API constraints extracted by prior work [24], which may not always be fully accurate or up to date. The constraint versions differ from the versions we use for test generation (see Sect. 4.1). While some APIs may have changed, the APIs are generally stable enough for relatively small version gaps. Furthermore, the constraints were extracted with an accuracy of approximately 85.4 % [24], i.e., some rules may be incorrect or missing. This can lead to false assumptions such as incorrectly rejecting compliant inputs or accepting non-compliant ones. Despite these limitations, we chose these constraints as they are publicly available and were used in prior work [24].

4.3 RQ1: Branch Coverage

To answer RQ1, we compare the development of coverage over time (Fig. 3): PYNGUINML achieves higher branch coverage on both ML libraries than PYNGUIN. The relative coverage of PYNGUINML overall is 63.9 %. For both ML libraries, PYNGUINML starts with a higher initial coverage and maintains a clear lead throughout the generation process (Fig. 3). On PYTORCH, PYNGUINML gains coverage more quickly in the early phase, while on TENSORFLOW, it keeps a more consistent advantage from PYNGUIN for the entire search time. This shows that PYNGUINML not only starts efficiently, but consistently outperforms PYNGUIN. These observations are also confirmed statistically as shown in Table 1. On 108 (77 significant) modules, PYNGUINML achieves a (significantly) higher branch coverage than PYNGUIN, while on 34 (9 significant) modules PYN-

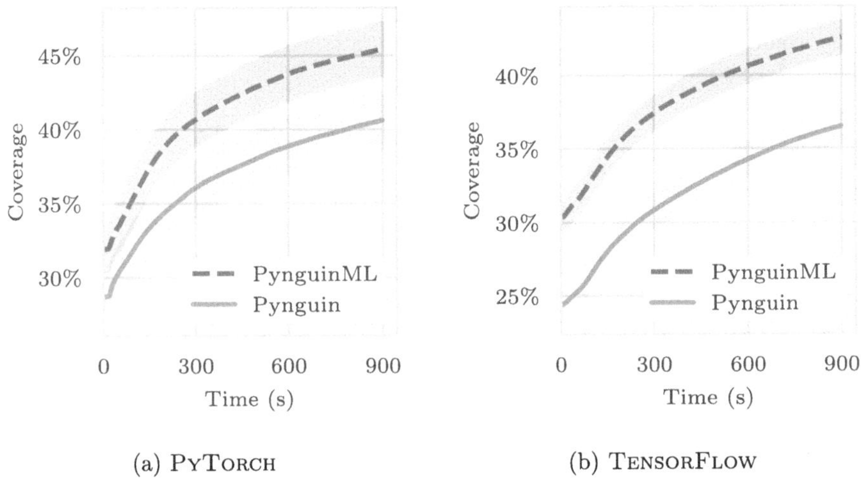

(a) PyTorch (b) TensorFlow

Fig. 3. Development of the coverage over time for Pynguin and PynguinML.

guin achieves a (significantly) higher branch coverage than with PynguinML. The Vargha and Delaney $\hat{A}_{12}$ effect size confirms a mean positive effect of 0.675.

While for average coverage (over time) PynguinML outperforms Pynguin, we want to further analyse how the coverage distribution differs across different modules. Figure 4 depicts coverage values over the full range of 0 % to 100 %. We observe that PynguinML tends to achieve higher and more concentrated coverage values. Its distribution is denser around the mid-to-high range, suggesting more consistent performance across modules. In contrast, Pynguin shows a wider spread, particularly towards lower coverage values and most notably for TensorFlow. Overall, PynguinML not only increases average coverage compared to Pynguin, but it produces better results across different modules.

Table 2. Mean branch coverage of Pynguin, MuTester, PyEvosuite and PynguinML on PyTorch and TensorFlow in %. We weighted average values by the number of modules/code examples per library.

Library	Pynguin	PynguinML	PyEvosuite	MuTester
PyTorch	36.1	40.8	27.8	33.0
TensorFlow	30.8	36.3	24.1	29.1
Average	**33.4**	**38.6**	**26.3**	**31.4**

We are further interested in how PynguinML performs compared to other state-of-the-art tools. Since MuTester [14] also employs a constraint-based strategy to improve test generation for ML libraries, we compare PynguinML with MuTester. Table 2 shows the mean branch coverage achieved by Pynguin, MuTester, PyEvosuite, and PynguinML across both ML libraries.

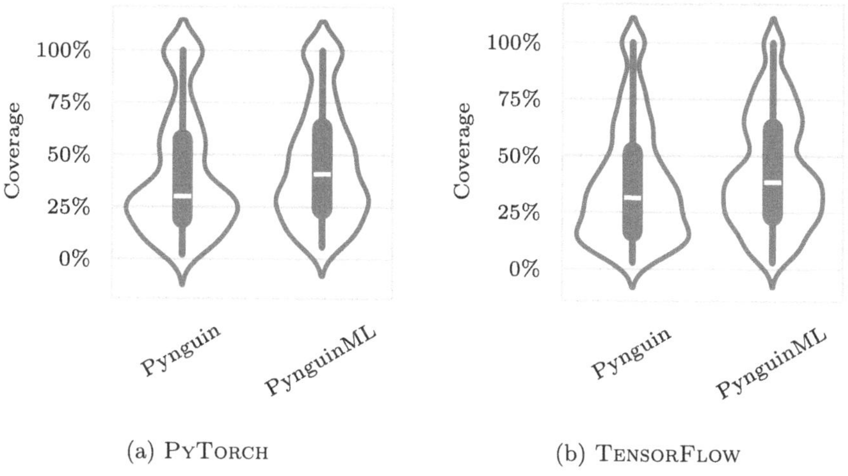

(a) PyTorch (b) TensorFlow

Fig. 4. Coverage distributions for Pynguin and PynguinML.

PyEvosuite refers to the baseline Pynguin used in the MuTester study [14], which in fact is a version of Pynguin. Pynguin achieves 33.4 %, while PynguinML achieves 38.6 % branch coverage on average across both libraries. Despite not using subprocess-execution, which avoids a performance overhead, MuTester achieves 31.4 % on average, which is lower than PynguinML. PyEvosuite achieves 26.3 % on average, which is lower than Pynguin.

Summary (RQ1: Branch Coverage)

In our experiments, PynguinML achieves higher branch coverage than Pynguin and MuTester.

Discussion. Our results show that incorporating API constraints extracted from the documentation of ML libraries significantly improves branch coverage compared to unconstrained test generation. Test cases generated by PynguinML are more likely to pass internal API validation checks, which enables them to reach code branches that Pynguin's test cases often miss. We conclude that the increased coverage is due to the tensor-aware PynguinML generation loop that leverages the API constraints.

Despite these improvements, the achieved branch coverage remains modest, with PynguinML reaching on average 38.6 %. Figure 3 shows that the search has not converged after 900 s which suggests that running the search longer achieves higher coverage. This is particularly relevant for ML libraries, where many modules are large and internally complex. For example, the `torch.nn.functional.interpolate` API has a cyclomatic complexity of 38, which, according to McCabe's metric [13], indicates high structural complexity and thus greater testing difficulty. Moreover, the `torch.nn.functional` module alone comprises more than 80 APIs and over 5 000 lines of code, emphasizing the challenges of covering all branches even when using API constraints. We conclude that the limited improvement in coverage may be due to the complexity of the modules under test, which might require even more sophisticated input generation strategies to achieve more substantial coverage gains.

Another limiting factor is the required use of subprocess-execution, which introduces considerable execution overhead. Testing such complex modules effectively would likely require substantially more than 900 s of generation time, but longer time budgets are impractical in real-world development workflows. Future work should therefore investigate more efficient alternatives to subprocess-execution that can accelerate test generation while preventing low-level crashes.

In our experiments, the baseline PYNGUIN achieves higher branch coverage than PYEVOSUITE in MUTESTER's evaluation. This may be because MUTESTER used an older PYNGUIN version or due to differences in the evaluated modules—MUTESTER does not specify them—or in constraint accuracy (they extracted their own, we used a set from prior work [24]).

4.4 RQ2: Compliant Tests

Table 3 shows the number of total, compliant, and non-compliant test cases generated by PYNGUIN and PYNGUINML. With PYNGUIN, 75 of 114 test cases for PYTORCH and 107 of 154 test cases for TENSORFLOW are compliant. With PYNGUINML, 80 of 124 test cases for PYTORCH and 121 of 180 test cases for TENSORFLOW are compliant. Thus, PYNGUINML on average generates more compliant test cases in the same amount of time than PYNGUIN. Interestingly, PYNGUINML also generates more *non-compliant* test cases than PYNGUIN: 36 against 30 for PYTORCH and 45 against 42 for TENSORFLOW. This can be explained by the generally higher code coverage achieved by PYNGUINML which leads to overall more test cases in the same time.

Table 3. Generated, compliant (Comp.) and non-compliant (Non-Comp.) test cases from PYNGUIN and PYNGUINML for 10 randomly selected modules per ML library and the inter rater agreement as Cohen's κ.

Library	Pynguin			PynguinML			Cohen's κ
	Generated	Comp.	Non-Comp.	Generated	Comp.	Non-Comp.	
PYTORCH	114	75	30	124	80	36	0.760
TENSORFLOW	154	107	42	180	121	45	0.720
Total	**268**	**182**	**72**	**304**	**201**	**81**	**0.730**

Summary (RQ2: Compliant Tests)

PYNGUINML generates both more compliant and more non-compliant test cases in the same amount of time as PYNGUIN.

Discussion. Our results demonstrate that using API constraints from ML library documentation during test generation increases the number of both compliant and non-compliant test cases. By leveraging expected parameter and tensor constraints, PYNGUINML produces more compliant inputs than PYNGUIN, which lets execution pass input checks and exercise deeper code paths.

At the same time, PYNGUINML deliberately produces more non-compliant test cases resulting in similar overall percentages of compliant tests for PYNGUINML (0.266 %) and PYNGUIN (0.269 %), with a slight edge to PYNGUIN. Our configuration intentionally allows a probability of generating arbitrary, potentially non-compliant parameters (25% in our experiments). Such non-compliant test cases are beneficial because they probe input validation logic and error-handling routines that would remain untested if using only compliant inputs. The additional non-compliant test cases may result from the generation of tensor-based inputs that violate constraints and from crossover and mutation of compliant and non-compliant test cases. Overall, compliant and non-compliant test cases serve complementary roles: Compliant test cases verify that the SUT behaves as expected, whereas non-compliant test cases evaluate its robustness. Combined, they enable comprehensive testing of the SUT. Thus, unlike MUTESTER [14], we do not aim to reduce the number of non-compliant test cases.

We further observe that both PYNGUIN and PYNGUINML generate more test cases for TENSORFLOW than for PYTORCH. This difference may reflect variations in library structure, the number of available APIs, the strictness of internal input checks, and the coverage and accuracy of extracted constraints. Such differences suggest that the effectiveness of constraint-guided test generation can depend on the characteristics of the target library.

5 Related Work

Previous research explored mining constraints from documentation and using them to improve automated testing. We used the constraints mined for the DOCTER [24] tool, a framework for testing API functions using fuzzing [24]. DOCTER uses the mined and pre-processed constraints to generate compliant and non-compliant test inputs for the SUTs. While their approach uncovered numerous bugs and inconsistencies, fuzzing does not generate unit tests, which are necessary for regression testing and continuous integration.

MUTESTER [14] overcomes this limitation by extending the unit-test generator PYNGUIN [10] with API constraints, similar to our approach, PYNGUINML. MUTESTER applies linguistic rules and frequent itemset mining, achieving improvements in code coverage by 15.7% to 27.0% and reducing non-compliant tests by 19.0 % across ML frameworks like TensorFlow and PyTorch. However, the provided source code for MuTester[6] is incomplete. This makes using their framework or replication of their experiments impossible. Nevertheless, the results reported in their work serve as a baseline for comparison which we used to show that PynguinML outperforms MuTester in terms of code coverage. PynguinML is publicly available to support reproducibility [7].

6 Conclusions and Future Work

In this paper, we introduced PynguinML, an extension of the automated unit test generator Pynguin, designed to improve test generation for ML libraries by leveraging API constraints extracted from documentation. We evaluated PynguinML on two ML frameworks, PyTorch and TensorFlow, and compared it against the baseline Pynguin and the related tool MuTester. Our evaluation showed that PynguinML outperforms Pynguin and MuTester. PynguinML achieves up to 63.9 % higher branch coverage than Pynguin.

Although PynguinML improves over Pynguin, many branches remain uncovered due to the complexity of the SUTs. Future work should focus on efficiently generating tests for such complex APIs. Besides ML libraries, PynguinML's flexible architecture allows integrating constraints from other domains, like databases or web APIs. Mining documentation to extract machine-readable constraints is practical for well-structured libraries but might be challenging for smaller or less-documented ones. By adapting type mappings and defining domain-specific requirements, PynguinML can be extended to other domains.

Acknowledgments. This work was partially supported by the German Research Foundation (DFG) under grant FR 2955/5-1 (TYPES4STRINGS: Types For Strings).

Data Availibility Statement. We provide additional artefacts consisting of PynguinML, datasets, result data and analysis scripts to Zenodo to allow for future use and replication [7].

Disclosure of Interests. The authors have no competing interests to declare that are relevant to the content of this article.

References

1. Arcuri, A., Briand, L.C.: A hitchhiker's guide to statistical tests for assessing randomized algorithms in software engineering. Softw. Test. Verification Reliab. **24**(3), 219–250 (2014)
2. Arcuri, A., Fraser, G.: Parameter tuning or default values? An empirical investigation in search-based software engineering. Empir. Softw. Eng. **18**(3), 594–623 (2013)

[6] https://zenodo.org/records/7987893, last accessed 2025-08-21.

3. Campos, J., Ge, Y., Albunian, N.M., Fraser, G., Eler, M., Arcuri, A.: An empirical evaluation of evolutionary algorithms for unit test suite generation. Inf. Softw. Technol. **104**, 207–235 (2018)
4. Cohen, J.: A coefficient of agreement for nominal scales. Educ. Psychol. Measur. **20**(1), 37–46 (1960)
5. Fraser, G., Arcuri, A.: EvoSuite: automatic test suite generation for object-oriented software. In: Proceedings of ESEC/FSE, pp. 416–419. ACM (2011)
6. Fraser, G., Rojas, J.M.: Software testing. In: Cha, S., Taylor, R.N., Kang, K.C. (eds.) Handbook of Software Engineering, pp. 123–192. Springer (2019)
7. Krodinger, L., Hajdari, A., Lukasczyk, S., Fraser, G.: Constraint-guided unit test generation for machine learning libraries (2025). https://doi.org/10.5281/zenodo.16920814
8. Lemieux, C., Inala, J.P., Lahiri, S.K., Sen, S.: CodaMosa: escaping coverage plateaus in test generation with pre-trained large language models. In: Proceedings of ICSE, pp. 919–931. IEEE (2023)
9. Lukasczyk, S., Fraser, G.: Pynguin: automated unit test generation for Python. In: Proceedings of ICSE Companion, pp. 168–172. ACM/IEEE (2022)
10. Lukasczyk, S., Kroiß, F., Fraser, G.: Automated unit test generation for Python. In: Proceedings of SSBSE. LNCS, vol. 12420, pp. 9–24. Springer (2020)
11. Lukasczyk, S., Kroiß, F., Fraser, G.: An empirical study of automated unit test generation for Python. Empir. Softw. Eng. **28**(2), 36 (2023)
12. Mann, H.B., Whitney, D.R.: On a test of whether one of two random variables is stochastically larger than the other. Ann. Math. Stat. **18**(1), 50–60 (1947)
13. McCabe, T.J.: A complexity measure. IEEE Trans. Software Eng. **2**(4), 308–320 (1976)
14. Narayanan, A., Harzevili, N.S., Wang, J., Shi, L., Wei, M., Wang, S.: Automatic unit test generation for deep learning frameworks based on API knowledge. CoRR (2023)
15. Pacheco, C., Ernst, M.D.: Randoop: feedback-directed random testing for Java. In: Proceedings of OOPSLA Companion, pp. 815–816. ACM (2007)
16. Pacheco, C., Lahiri, S.K., Ernst, M.D., Ball, T.: Feedback-directed random test generation. In: Proceedings of ICSE, pp. 75–84. IEEE Computer Society (2007)
17. Panichella, A., Kifetew, F.M., Tonella, P.: Automated test case generation as a many-objective optimisation problem with dynamic selection of the targets. IEEE Trans. Software Eng. **44**(2), 122–158 (2018)
18. Panichella, A., Kifetew, F.M., Tonella, P.: A large scale empirical comparison of state-of-the-art search-based test case generators. Inf. Softw. Technol. **104**, 236–256 (2018)
19. Runeson, P.: A survey of unit testing practices. IEEE Softw. **23**(4), 22–29 (2006)
20. Shi, J., et al.: ACETest: automated constraint extraction for testing deep learning operators. In: Proceedings of ISSTA, pp. 690–702. ACM (2023)
21. Tonella, P.: Evolutionary testing of classes. In: Proceedings of ISSTA, pp. 119–128. ACM (2004)
22. Vargha, A., Delaney, H.D.: A critique and improvement of the cl common language effect size statistics of McGraw and Wong. J. Educ. Behav. Stat. **25**(2), 101–132 (2000)
23. Wang, S., Shrestha, N., Subburaman, A.K., Wang, J., Wei, M., Nagappan, N.: Automatic unit test generation for machine learning libraries: how far are we? In: Proceedings of ICSE, pp. 1548–1560. IEEE (2021)
24. Xie, D., et al.: DocTer: documentation-guided fuzzing for testing deep learning API functions. In: Proceedings of ISSTA, pp. 176–188. ACM (2022)

25. Yang, R., Xu, X., Wang, R.: LLM-enhanced evolutionary test generation for untyped languages. Autom. Softw. Eng. **32**(1), 20 (2025)
26. Zhang, J.M., Harman, M., Ma, L., Liu, Y.: Machine learning testing: survey, landscapes and horizons. IEEE Trans. Software Eng. **48**(2), 1–36 (2022)

KrakQL: LLM-Guided Blind Introspection of GraphQL Schemas

Marcello Maugeri[1(✉)], Abenezer Angamo[2], and Giampaolo Bella[1]

[1] University of Catania, Catania, Italy
marcello.maugeri@phd.unict.it, giampaolo.bella@unict.it
[2] Addis Ababa, Ethiopia

Abstract. *GraphQL APIs* provide a single endpoint for data access in distributed web applications. Clients retrieve only the data they need in one request by querying a structured *schema*. *Introspection queries* allow clients and developers to retrieve the schema programmatically. However, the schema reveals valuable information (such as available fields and type relationships) that could benefit attackers. For this reason, production environments typically disable introspection.

Tools such as CLAIRVOYANCE use *blind introspection*, a technique that retrieves the schema by combining brute forcing with GraphQL's field suggestion feature, which suggests corrections for misspelt or similar fields. However, retrieval quality, measured by schema coverage, depends on the wordlist used. In our benchmark of 7 open-source projects, CLAIRVOYANCE covered roughly 35% of the schemas on average, even when using the best available GraphQL-specific wordlist.

In this paper, we propose KRAKQL: an LLM-guided, novelty-search-based schema retriever that leverages the partially discovered schema to propose context-aware candidate fields and arguments. We demonstrate that KRAKQL outperforms CLAIRVOYANCE with 140% improvement in average coverage, 134× fewer HTTP requests, and a 93× higher success rate, all at a negligible token cost. Finally, we release KRAKQL to support reproducibility and enable further research.

Keywords: GraphQL API · Search-based Software Testing · Blind Introspection · Black-box Testing · Large Language Models

1 Introduction

GraphQL APIs provide a unified endpoint to query data from multiple data points, ultimately solving the over-/under-fetching problem of RESTful. Since its release in 2015 by Facebook – now Meta – which uses it in both Facebook and Instagram, GraphQL has been adopted by a wide range of services, including automotive companies like Audi, e-commerce platforms like Shopify, and version control systems such as GitHub and GitLab [6].

A. Angamo—Independent Research.

M. Wagner and M. Zhang (Eds.): SSBSE 2025, LNCS 16228, pp. 19–33, 2026.
https://doi.org/10.1007/978-3-032-24839-8_2

As the adoption increases, the necessity of testing methodologies and tools has become paramount. In the literature, existing testing tools focus on detecting faults [3] and Denial-of-Service (DoS) attacks [9]. However, to generate valid test cases, every tool requires prior knowledge of the schema, which is usually extracted by a GraphQL feature called *introspection*. Unfortunately, for security reasons, the schema is usually hidden in production to enable a form of *security by obscurity*, which hinders the usability of such tools [12].

CLAIRVOYANCE stands out as a potential solution to this problem, providing a way to retrieve a GraphQL schema by leveraging the *field suggestion* feature from GraphQL and a wordlist for guesses. However, CLAIRVOYANCE falls short for three reasons: *field suggestion* can be disabled, it supports a specific response format which could differ in some backend implementations, and, finally, it heavily relies on a wordlist.

In this paper, we propose KRAKQL, a GraphQL blind introspection tool that leverages Large Language Models (LLMs) to generate context-aware candidate names. Unlike CLAIRVOYANCE's exhaustive wordlist approach, KRAKQL employs a multi-agent system with a novelty-based scheduler to guide schema discovery.

To evaluate KRAKQL, we selected 7 GraphQL open-source servers supporting field suggestions and Apollo Server-compatible error formats. These were chosen from BENGQL[1] [1]: a benchmark framework for GraphQL apps. We find that KRAKQL not only increases coverage by 140% compared to CLAIRVOYANCE but also reduces the number of requests by 134× and achieves a 93× higher success rate, all at a total LLM cost of merely $4.50 with GPT-5-nano. We release KRAKQL's source code and extend BENGQL with our evaluation scripts to enable reproducibility and foster future research in GraphQL security testing.

The paper is organised as follows: Sect. 2 provides background on GraphQL, presenting blind introspection as a search-based problem. Section 3 presents KRAKQL's architecture. Section 4 evaluates our approach against CLAIRVOYANCE, answering our research questions. Section 5 reviews related work. Section 6 discusses limitations and threats to validity. Finally, Sect. 7 concludes. Our contributions can be summarised as follows:

- We design KRAKQL, an LLM-guided tool that generates context-aware candidates using a multi-agent architecture and novelty-based scheduling;
- We demonstrate KRAKQL's effectiveness with 140% improvement in coverage and 134× reduction in requests compared to the state-of-the-art;
- We release KRAKQL as open-source and provide evaluation scripts extending BENGQL for reproducibility.

[1] https://github.com/marcellomaugeri/BenGQL.

2 Background

2.1 A Primer on GraphQL APIs

GraphQL exposes application data through a single HTTP endpoint – typically on the */graphql* path – that serves structured responses following a *schema*. The schema defines *types*, *fields*, and *arguments*, which together constrain both the shape of queries and the structure of results.

Listing 1.1. Excerpt of a fruit catalogue schema.

```
type Query {    fruit(id: ID!): Fruit    }
type Fruit {
  id: ID
  scientific_name: String /* other fields omitted */
}
```

For example, in Listing 1.1, `Query` is the *root* type for queries. By standard, root types are `Query` for data fetching, `Mutation` to update existing data, and `Subscription` to receive real-time updates. In the example, the field `fruit` takes one argument `id` of type `ID` – the exclamation mark denotes the argument to be mandatory – and returns an object of type `Fruit`. The `Fruit` type is an `Object` type that declares fields such as `id` and `scientific_name`, which are respectively of the `Scalar` types `ID` and `String`. Notably, the fields of an object type may themselves be other object types, but at the lowest level, these fields resolve to scalar types, which represent primitive leaf values.

As a result, a client can therefore request these two fields as follows:

Listing 1.2. Querying a single fruit by id and selecting two fields.

```
query { fruit(id: 6) {
        id
        scientific_name
    }
}
```

A conforming server returns a JSON object whose structure corresponds to the selection set:

Listing 1.3. Expected response structure for the query above.

```
{"data": [
      "fruit": {
        "id": "3",
        "scientific_name": "Musa x Paradisiaca"
      }
}}
```

If a client requests a field that is not declared in the schema, the server usually responds with an error rather than silently ignoring it. This feature becomes central to the blind introspection discussed later.

2.2 Introspection

GraphQL includes a built-in *introspection* feature that exposes schema metadata through special fields, typically prefixed by __. When enabled, a client can recover types, fields, and arguments programmatically. For example, the following query lists the field names of the Fruit type:

Listing 1.4. Manual introspection when enabled.

```
query {
  __type(name: "Fruit") {
    name
    fields {
      name
    }
  }
}
```

In this way, tools such as ROVER[2] are able to retrieve the entire schema and present it in *Schema Definition Language* (SDL).

However, in many production environments, introspection is disabled to reduce information disclosure. When introspection is unavailable, it is still possible to glean information indirectly from *field suggestion* feedback produced by GraphQL validators when a request includes an unknown field or a valid field is misspelt. For example, the following misspelt request:

```
query {
  fruit(id: "3") {
    scientificName #Misspelt
  }
}
```

may yield an error resembling:

Listing 1.5. Illustrative error with suggestion (format varies by server).

```
{"errors": [{
    "message": "Cannot query field \"
       scientificName\" on type \"Fruit\". Did you
        mean \"scientific_name\"?"
}]}
```

This indirect feedback, combined with the success or failure of probe queries, forms the basis of the *blind introspection* technique, which attempts to reconstruct the schema even when direct introspection is disabled.

[2] https://www.apollographql.com/docs/rover/commands/graphs.

2.3 Blind Introspection as a Search-Based Formulation

Blind introspection can be formulated as a *discrete optimisation problem* over a *parametrised graph* where nodes are the types, edges are fields and edge attributes are the arguments. Specifically, at any given point, the tester has a partial schema $\hat{S}$ – initially containing only the known root types – and must decide which candidate field or argument names to probe next. From now on, we will assume that the field suggestion feature is enabled on the GraphQL target endpoint.

Search Operations. The discovery process consists of two operations:

- *Field probing*: Testing whether a name n is a valid field of type T
- *Argument probing*: Testing whether a name n is a valid argument of field F

Type name inference is trivial, as types are often revealed when field suggestion is enabled, making field and argument discovery the core challenge.

Contextual Search Space. While all fields and arguments are GraphQL names, hence they match the `[a-zA-Z][a-zA-Z0-9_]*` regex, the search space is not simply the set of all possible names. Instead, it is a *context-dependent space* where each probe operates within a specific scope:

$$\mathcal{S} = \bigcup_{T \in \text{Types}} \mathcal{S}_T^{\text{fields}} \cup \bigcup_{F \in \text{Fields}} \mathcal{S}_F^{\text{args}}$$

where:

- $\mathcal{S}_T^{\text{fields}}$ is the space of potential field names for type T
- $\mathcal{S}_F^{\text{args}}$ is the space of potential argument names for field F

Critically, a name n might be valid in one context but invalid in another. For example, `"id"` might be:

- A valid field of type `Fruit`;
- An invalid field of type `Query`;
- A valid argument for field `fruit`;
- An invalid argument for field `scientific_name`.

This contextual nature means the search problem is not finding valid names from a global dictionary, but discovering the correct name-context pairs (n, c) where c specifies the scope (type or field) in which n is valid.

Binary Fitness Function. When probing a name n in context c, three outcomes are possible:

1. The name is rejected as invalid;
2. The name triggers a suggestion mechanism, revealing the correct name;
3. The name is valid and accepted.

We define a binary fitness function that captures information gain:

$$f(n, c) = \begin{cases} 0 & \text{if the probe is rejected (case 1)} \\ 1 & \text{if the probe yields information (cases 2 or 3)} \end{cases}$$

This binary formulation reflects that both suggestions and valid names represent successful information discovery. Conversely, rejected probes provide no information about what the correct name might be. This binary fitness function poses blind introspection as a *flag problem*, inheriting all its limitation, as there is no actual measure at runtime to guide the search.

Objective. The blind introspection problem has two objectives:

1. *Maximise schema coverage*: Find $\hat{S}$ that maximises coverage of the actual schema S;
2. *Minimise query cost*: Limit the total number of probes required, ultimately minimising the total requests to the endpoint.

Clairvoyance systematically probes fields and arguments taken from a wordlist W. However, crafting a context-aware wordlist is a time-consuming task, whereas using a generic wordlist results in excessive requests with low success rates. KrakQL leverages LLMs to address this limitation by providing candidate names tailored to the specific context as presented in the following section.

3 KrakQL

3.1 Architecture Design

KrakQL extends Clairvoyance's architecture with two novel components: a multi-agent system for context-aware name generation and a novelty-based scheduler for exploration strategy. Figure 1 illustrates the architecture, with our contributions marked in yellow.

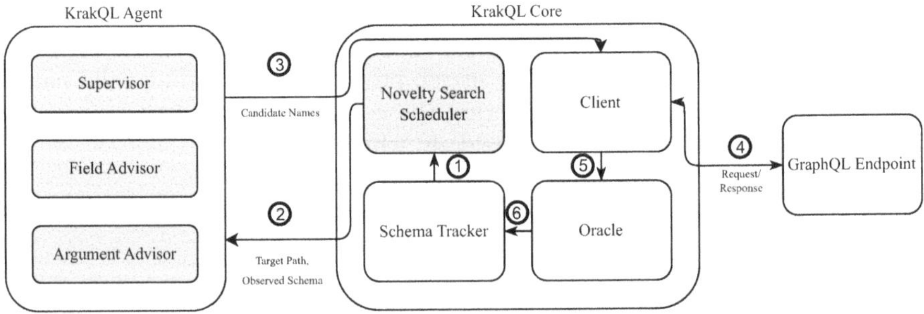

Fig. 1. Architecture Diagram of KrakQL (novel contribution is marked in yellow)

The *KrakQL Agent* consists of a multi-agent system where the *Supervisor* invokes the correct sub-agent. Based on the *target path*, it delegates to either the *Field Advisor* (when probing fields in a type) or the *Argument Advisor* (when probing arguments in a field). These advisors leverage LLM capabilities and the observed schema context to generate semantically appropriate candidate names.

The *KrakQL Core* contains four components. The *Novelty Search Scheduler*, detailed in Sect. 3.2, determines which document path to explore next: either a type where fields should be probed or a discovered field where arguments should be probed. The *Schema Tracker* maintains the data structure representing the currently observed schema $\hat{S}$. The Client sends batches of 64 candidate names to the target *GraphQL Endpoint*, matching CLAIRVOYANCE's default batch size. Lastly, the *Oracle* analyses responses using predefined regular expressions to identify valid fields, arguments, and field suggestions. *Schema Tracker*, *Client*, and *Oracle* are inherited from CLAIRVOYANCE with minor modifications.

The discovery workflow operates as follows:

① The Novelty Search Scheduler selects the target path to probe, choosing either a type for field discovery or a field for argument discovery.
② The observed schema $\hat{S}$ and target path are passed to the KrakQL Agent.
③ The Supervisor calls the appropriate sub-agent (Field Advisor or Argument Advisor), which returns a batch of 64 candidate names.
④ The Client sends this batch to the GraphQL endpoint, receiving a response containing one or more error messages.
⑤ The Oracle analyses the response using regular expressions to extract valid names and field suggestions, which may include multiple suggestions per error.
⑥ The Oracle updates the Schema Tracker with discovered elements, and the process returns to step (1).

3.2 Novelty Search Scheduler

The *Novelty Search Scheduler* guides the blind introspection process by prioritising exploration paths likely to yield new schema information. Unlike CLAIRVOYANCE's sequential approach, our scheduler dynamically balances breadth (discovering new types) and depth (exploring fields and arguments) based on empirical feedback.

Novelty Scoring. Each type and field in the partial schema $\hat{S}$ is assigned a novelty score $\nu \in \mathbb{R}_{\geq}0$. For types $T_i \in \hat{S}$, the novelty score $\nu(T_i)$ represents the likelihood of discovering new fields in T_i. For fields $F_j \in T_i$, the score $\nu(F_j)$ indicates the potential for finding arguments of F_j. Initially, all elements receive a default score $\nu_0 = 1.0$.

Selection Strategy. At each iteration, the scheduler selects the element with the highest novelty score:

$$e^* = \arg\max_{e \in \hat{S}} \nu(e)$$

where e can be either a type or a field. The `get_by_novelty()` method performs this selection by comparing all known types and fields holistically, prioritising types in case of ties.

Exploration Actions. Based on the selected element's kind, the scheduler triggers one of two actions:

- Type exploration: If e^* is a type, probe for its constituent fields to broaden schema knowledge
- Field exploration: If e^* is a field, probe for its arguments to deepen understanding of query parameters

Score Updates. After each probing action, the novelty score is updated based on the outcome. Let d be a boolean value indicating whether something new was discovered during the exploration:

$$\nu(e) \leftarrow \begin{cases} \max 1.0, \nu(e) + \alpha & \text{if } d = \textit{true}, \\ \max 0.0, \nu(e) - \beta & \text{if } d = \textit{false}, \end{cases}$$

where $\alpha = 0.1$ is the reward factor and $\beta = 0.05$ is the decay factor. These parameters were selected to achieve termination within reasonable time bounds but can be adjusted. In fact, increasing α or decreasing β encourages more exhaustive exploration at the cost of additional requests.

Termination. The exploration loop continues until either: (1) the time budget is exhausted, or (2) $\max_{e \in \hat{S}} \nu(e) \geq 0$.

Comparison with Clairvoyance. Clairvoyance employs a depth-first systematic exploration starting from the root types (Query, Mutation, and Subscription). The algorithm begins with Query and sends the entire wordlist W in batches of 64 (by default) to probe for fields. For each discovered field $f \in$ Query, it immediately probes for arguments by sending the complete wordlist again. Only after exhausting all discovered fields in Query does it proceed to the next type.

When a field or argument is discovered, both Clairvoyance and KrakQL infer the associated type from the response. For instance, discovering a field `user: User` adds the `User` type to the schema for future exploration. Clairvoyance then continues its depth-first traversal, selecting the next type without fields and repeating the exhaustive wordlist probing.

In contrast, our novelty-based scheduler adapts the exploration order based on discovery success. This dynamic prioritisation, combined with context-aware name suggestion from the *KrakQL Agent*, reduces the total number of requests while maintaining comparable coverage.

4 Evaluation

4.1 Experimental Setup

To evaluate the efficacy of LLM-guided versus wordlist-based search, we compare KrakQL against Clairvoyance. We selected 7 open-source GraphQL applications from BenGQL with field suggestion enabled and Apollo Server-compatible error format, ensuring consistent suggestion parsing required by both tools as discussed in Sect. 6. Unfortunately, because Clairvoyance assumes these strict requirements, we could not select more than 7 of the 24 applications available in BenGQL.

Clairvoyance was provided with the most extensive public wordlist, consisting of 100,000 GraphQL names built from over 60,000 public schemas[3], while KrakQL employs GPT-5-nano as the underlying LLM.

Both tools were configured with a batch size of 64 names per request and a time budget of 3 h, sufficient to allow natural termination in most cases (excluding *payload* case study) whilst avoiding excessive token consumption. To account for LLM non-determinism [2], we executed KrakQL five times per case study.

4.2 Research Questions

We structure our evaluation around three research questions that capture the trade-offs between wordlist-based and LLM-guided approaches:

RQ1: What absolute schema coverage do the approaches achieve? We measure the percentage of fields, arguments, and types discovered by each tool compared to the ground truth schema obtained via introspection.

RQ2: What is the discovery efficiency of LLM-guided over wordlist-based search? We analyse the success rate per batch, measuring how many new schema elements each 64-name batch discovers. Due to Clairvoyance's asynchronous batch processing and depth-first strategy versus our novelty-based scheduling, we focus on per-batch metrics rather than temporal comparisons.

RQ3: What are the economic trade-offs of using LLMs? We quantify the token consumption and associated costs, analysing whether the improved discovery rate justifies the computational expense.

We acknowledge that Clairvoyance's asynchronous nature provides a speed advantage, but our focus is on discovery effectiveness rather than wall-clock time.

4.3 Results

RQ1: Schema Coverage. Table 1 presents the detailed schema coverage with mean values across the five runs, while Table 2 summarises the statistical analysis and relative performance.

KrakQL achieves superior overall coverage on 5 of 7 targets, with a mean of 8.2% compared to 3.2% for Clairvoyance, representing a 2.6× improvement.

[3] https://github.com/Escape-Technologies/graphql-wordlist/blob/main/wordlists/100k/overallWordlist-100k.txt.

This advantage is most pronounced in field discovery, where KRAKQL discovers 679 fields (7.9%) versus 160 fields (1.9%) for CLAIRVOYANCE, representing an increase of roughly 325%. Consequently, the number of types discovered is also higher, as types are inferred by probing the field type.

A paired Wilcoxon signed-rank test on per-target average coverage yields $p = 0.156$ ($\alpha = 0.05$), which does not reach conventional statistical significance. However, the Vargha-Delaney $\hat{A}_{12}$ effect size of 0.63 indicates KRAKQL outperforms CLAIRVOYANCE 63% of the time, demonstrating practical value despite limited statistical power. KRAKQL demonstrates reasonably stable performance with mean coefficient of variation of 8.8% across targets, with only payload exhibiting higher variability (CV = 34.9%) due to its extreme scale (10,968 total elements). Notably, while CLAIRVOYANCE would require a new wordlist to discover more, KRAKQL could be used in a continuous setting by disabling the termination condition.

Interestingly, argument discovery presents the only area where CLAIRVOYANCE maintains an advantage, discovering 108 arguments (23.5%) versus 80 arguments (17.4%) for KRAKQL. We hypothesise this stems from the nature of LLM-generated candidates versus wordlist entries. Due to the small model size, the chosen model tends to generate semantically coherent names (e.g., `userId`, `userName`) rather than action-oriented patterns common in GraphQL arguments (e.g., `orderBy`, `filterBy`, `createInput`). The wordlist, compiled from thousands of schemas, naturally contains these action-oriented patterns that trigger field suggestions more effectively. Future work could address the argument discovery gap through improved prompt engineering, explicitly instructing the model to generate action-oriented naming, or by switching to a larger model.

Table 1. Detailed schema coverage comparison

Target	Clairvoyance				KrakQL (across 5 runs)			
	Types	Fields	Arguments	Overall	Types	Fields	Arguments	Overall
countries	**6/6 (100%)**	**25/45 (56%)**	3/7 (43%)	**34/58 (59%)**	5.0/6 (83%)	22.0/45 (49%)	3.0/7 (43%)	30.0/58 (52%)
dvga	5/14 (36%)	8/53 (15%)	0/33 (0%)	13/100 (13%)	**13.0/14 (93%)**	**42.0/53 (79%)**	**7.0/33 (21%)**	**62.0/100 (62%)**
fruits-api	**5/5 (100%)**	23/32 (72%)	**25/26 (96%)**	**53/63 (84%)**	4.4/5 (88%)	22.6/32 (71%)	22.4/26 (86%)	49.4/63 (78%)
payload	57/2542 (2%)	56/8066 (1%)	**46/360 (13%)**	159/10968 (1%)	**136.4/2542 (5%)**	**422.2/8066 (5%)**	18.4/360 (5%)	**577.0/10968 (5%)**
react-ecommerce	**8/8 (100%)**	5/163 (3%)	**13/13 (100%)**	26/184 (14%)	7.6/8 (95%)	**52.4/163 (32%)**	11.2/13 (86%)	**71.2/184 (39%)**
react-finland	15/19 (79%)	17/150 (11%)	**9/9 (100%)**	41/178 (23%)	**19.0/19 (100%)**	**85.0/150 (57%)**	6.2/9 (69%)	**110.2/178 (62%)**
rick-and-morty	7/8 (88%)	26/52 (50%)	12/12 (100%)	45/72 (62%)	**8.0/8 (100%)**	**32.6/52 (63%)**	12.0/12 (100%)	**52.6/72 (73%)**
Total	103/2602 (4.0%)	160/8561 (1.9%)	**108/460 (23.5%)**	371/11623 (3.2%)	**193.4/2602 (7.4%)**	**678.8/8561 (7.9%)**	80.2/460 (17.4%)	**952.4/11623 (8.2%)**

RQ2: Discovery Efficiency. Table 3 presents the discovery efficiency of both approaches, measured as the success rate per batch of 64 candidate names. These metrics count valid discoveries per batch, not unique fields or arguments, meaning the same element may be counted multiple times if discovered in different batches. Notably, KRAKQL employs a counter-based mechanism preventing it from suggesting names already proposed in the same context. This is limited to the top 10 most frequent names proposed to avoid excessive token consumption.

The aggregated results demonstrate extreme efficiency improvements. Our approach requires only 2,327 total batches (2,000 for fields, 327 for arguments)

Table 2. Statistical analysis and relative improvement (KrakQL: n = 5 runs per target). SD: standard deviation. CV: coefficient of variation. All data are shown in percentage.

Target	Clairvoyance Overall	KrakQL (n = 5)		Relative Improvement
		Mean ± SD	CV	
countries	58.6%	51.7 ± 4.6%	8.9%	−11.8 ± 7.9%
dvga	13.0%	62.0 ± 0.0%	0.0%	+376.9 ± 0.0%
fruits-api	84.1%	78.4 ± 3.7%	4.7%	−6.8 ± 4.4%
payload	1.4%	5.3 ± 1.8%	34.9%	+262.9 ± 126.7%
react-ecommerce	14.1%	38.7 ± 0.9%	2.4%	+173.8 ± 6.6%
react-finland	23.0%	61.9 ± 0.7%	1.1%	+168.8 ± 2.8%
rick-and-morty	62.5%	73.1 ± 1.1%	1.5%	+16.9 ± 1.8%
Mean	**36.7%**	**53.0 ± 10.0%**	**8.8%**	**+140%**

compared to CLAIRVOYANCE's 311k batches, a roughly 134× reduction in HTTP requests while achieving superior coverage.

The per-batch success rates reveal the magnitude of improvement: KRAKQL achieves 0.93% success rate for field discovery versus less than 0.01% for CLAIRVOYANCE, yielding a 93× improvement. This higher success rate indicates that KRAKQL's context-aware generation produces valid names far more frequently than random selection from a wordlist.

The efficiency gain is most pronounced in the `payload` case study, where KRAKQL discovers 560 elements with just 292 batches (3.27% success rate for fields) compared to CLAIRVOYANCE's 237 elements across 88k batches. It is important to note that arguments have not been probed as this is the only case study where the time budget was expired.

These efficiency improvements have critical practical implications. The 99.3% reduction in network traffic minimises server load, reduces detection risk, and enables testing within rate-limited environments.

Table 3. Discovery efficiency: Elements found per batch (KrakQL: mean of n = 5 runs, batch size = 64 names)

Target	Clairvoyance						KrakQL					
	Fields			Arguments			Fields			Arguments		
	Found	Batches	Rate	Found	Batches	Rate	Found	Batches	Rate	Found	Batches	Rate
countries	40	19k	<0.01%	6	38k	<0.01%	35	125	0.44%	3	24	0.19%
dvga	12	2k	0.01%	9	11k	<0.01%	50	339	0.23%	7	44	0.25%
fruits-api	30	6k	<0.01%	25	13k	<0.01%	28	113	0.39%	22	23	1.54%
payload	56	2k	0.06%	181	86k	<0.01%	542	259	3.27%	18	33	0.87%
react-ecommerce	17	3k	<0.01%	13	27k	<0.01%	74	262	0.44%	11	80	0.22%
react-finland	59	8k	0.01%	9	70k	<0.01%	139	265	0.82%	6	78	0.12%
rick-and-morty-api	32	6k	<0.01%	12	22k	<0.01%	45	165	0.42%	12	44	0.42%
Total	246	45k	<0.01%	255	266k	<0.01%	913	2k	0.93%	80	327	0.38%

Table 4. Token consumption and costs for KRAKQL with GPT-5-nano

Target	# Calls	Total Input	Total Output	Avg Input	Avg Output	Cost ($)
countries	166	0.1M	1M	652	6,308	0.42
dvga	417	0.3M	1.9M	875	4,767	0.81
fruits-api	161	0.1M	0.5M	709	4,080	0.27
payload	320	1M	1.3M	3,022	4,235	0.59
react-ecommerce	358	0.3M	2M	1,003	5,536	0.81
react-finland	404	0.5M	2M	1,181	5,154	0.86
rick-and-morty	266	0.2M	1.7M	785	6,564	0.71
Total	2,092	2.5M	10,4M	1,242	5,189	4.47

RQ3: Economic Trade-Offs. Table 4 presents the token consumption and associated costs for KRAKQL across all experiments using GPT-5-nano.

The economic analysis reveals that KRAKQL discovered approximately 50% of the schemas across all targets with a total cost of $4.5. This translates to less than $0.005 per discovered element – a negligible cost for security testing scenarios. The experiments ran for up to 3 h without parallel requests, demonstrating that comprehensive schema discovery is achievable within a single workday's budget for medium-sized schemas.

5 Related Work

5.1 Testing of GraphQL APIs

GraphQL testing research has been conducted to achieve different tasks. Vargas et al. [15] proposed deviation testing to identify anomalies in schema serving, while Karlsson et al. [7] introduced property-based testing to create generators to produce type-safe queries.

EVOMASTER [3] advanced the field through evolutionary algorithms, supporting both white-box testing with code instrumentation and black-box testing with random search. The focus is to optimise for code coverage, HTTP status diversity, and fault detection.

GRAPHQLER [14] focuses exclusively on black-box security testing by constructing a dependency graph from the schema to infer relationships among mutations, queries, and objects. This context-aware approach achieved 35% higher coverage than EVOMASTER in black-box mode.

WENDIGO [9] applies Deep Reinforcement Learning to evolve increasingly resource-intensive queries, identifying denial-of-service vulnerabilities with minimal requests.

Unfortunately, all these approaches require schema knowledge: property-based testing and WENDIGO need it as input, EVOMASTER fetches it via introspection, and GRAPHQLER reconstructs it using CLAIRVOYANCE when introspection is disabled. This universal dependency underscores the importance of efficient blind introspection techniques.

5.2 LLM-Enhanced Search-Based Approaches

LLMs have been integrated into search-based software engineering to address various challenges, from test generation to API exploration.

For API and web testing, Castagnaro *et al.* [4] achieved 969% improvement over wordlists in directory brute-forcing by using LLMs to predict paths based on learned patterns. ARAT-RL [8] applied Reinforcement Learning to prioritise REST API operations, demonstrating adaptive exploration's superiority over static approaches. LogiAgent [16] employed multiple LLM agents collaboratively, discovering 234 logical issues across 12 systems through coordinated Test Scenario Generation, Request Execution, and Response Validation.

In fuzzing, SearchSYS [5] pioneered LLM-seeded fuzzing, eliminating manual seed creation and discovering 21 bugs in *gem5* by generating intelligent starting points. A similar approach is leveraged in ChatAFL [10] which employs LLM in protocol fuzzing to generate sequences of messages.

In evolutionary algorithms, Language Model Crossover (LMX) [11] uses LLMs as variation operators in evolutionary algorithms, prompting them with parent genotypes (code, equations, or text) to generate offspring that combine parental traits through few-shot learning. Sartaj et al. [13] provide a comprehensive roadmap for integrating foundation models into search-based software engineering.

6 Discussion

6.1 Potential Improvements

KrakQL, inheriting code from Clairvoyance, suffers from the same limitations. The primary limitation stems from the oracle's reliance on predefined regular expressions tailored to Apollo Server's error format. Consequently, it may fail to parse semantically equivalent error messages with different formatting, breaking the feedback loop essential for blind introspection.

As a consequence, it misses potential nuances of the same exact information like field suggestion or wrong field, breaking the effectiveness of the oracle. A related limitation arises from the algorithm's assumptions about GraphQL server behaviour, expecting field suggestions when probe names are similar to valid fields, and consistent type information during type probing. In practice, GraphQL implementations exhibit varying levels of runtime feedback that current approaches do not fully exploit.

Future work could address these limitations by introducing an *Oracle Adapter* agent that dynamically adjusts regex patterns based on observed response formats, making the approach more robust across diverse GraphQL implementations.

6.2 Threat to Validity

A potential threat to validity arises from using open-source applications in our benchmark: their schemas may be present in the LLM's training data. This raises the question of whether the model is recalling rather than inferring field names, potentially inflating KrakQL's performance. However, we argue this reflects realistic conditions since production APIs are rarely truly secret: client code is often public, API documentation is widely available, and network traffic can be observed. Furthermore, the LLM must still correctly map suggestions to the specific context discovered during runtime probing. Nevertheless, we acknowledge that evaluation against schemas created post-training would provide stronger evidence of the approach's generalisation capability.

7 Conclusion

We presented KrakQL, a novel approach to GraphQL blind introspection that leverages Large Language Models to generate context-aware candidate names. By formulating blind introspection as a contextual search problem and introducing a multi-agent architecture with novelty-based scheduling, we transform what was traditionally an exhaustive brute-force process into an intelligent, guided exploration.

Our evaluation on seven real-world GraphQL applications demonstrates that KrakQL achieves 140% better coverage than the state-of-the-art Clairvoyance whilst requiring 134× fewer requests. This dramatic efficiency improvement makes comprehensive schema discovery practical even for production systems with strict rate limiting. The total cost of $4.5 for discovering approximately 50% of schemas proves that LLM-guided approaches are economically viable for security testing.

While our approach inherits some limitations from Clairvoyance, particularly the dependency on Apollo Server error formats, it establishes that LLM-guided testing is both practical and effective. Future work should explore prompt engineering for better argument discovery, adaptation to diverse GraphQL implementations and levels of feedback, and application of similar techniques to other API discovery challenges.

Acknowledgement. We want to thank the *GARR Consortium* for providing us with the test infrastructure. This work acknowledges support from: Italian PNRR 2022 SERICS Spoke 6, Task 1.2, Project "SCAI—Supply Chain Attack Avoidance".

Data Availibility Statement. The artifact, consisting of KrakQL source code, BenGQL integration and results is available on https://github.com/marcellomaugeri/KrakQL.

References

1. Angamo, A., Maugeri, M.: Bengql: an extensible benchmarking framework for automated graphql testing. In: Proceedings of the 40th IEEE/ACM International Conference on Automated Software Engineering (2025)

2. Arcuri, A., Briand, L.: A practical guide for using statistical tests to assess randomized algorithms in software engineering. In: Proceedings of the 33rd International Conference on Software Engineering (2011). https://doi.org/10.1145/1985793.1985795
3. Belhadi, A., Zhang, M., Arcuri, A.: Random testing and evolutionary testing for fuzzing GraphQL APIs. ACM Trans. Web **18**(1) (2024). https://doi.org/10.1145/3609427
4. Castagnaro, A., Conti, M., Pajola, L.: Offensive AI: enhancing directory brute-forcing attack with the use of language models. In: Proceedings of the 2024 Workshop on Artificial Intelligence and Security, AISec 2024, pp. 184–195. Association for Computing Machinery, New York, NY, USA (2024). https://doi.org/10.1145/3689932.3694770
5. Dakhama, A., Even-Mendoza, K., Langdon, W.B., Menéndez, H.D., Petke, J.: Enhancing search-based testing with LLMs for finding bugs in system simulators. Autom. Softw. Eng. **32**(2), 1–45 (2025)
6. GraphQL Foundation: Graphql landscape (2025). https://landscape.graphql.org/. Accessed 22 Aug 2025
7. Karlsson, S., Čaušević, A., Sundmark, D.: Automatic property-based testing of GraphQL APIs. In: 2021 IEEE/ACM International Conference on Automation of Software Test (AST), pp. 1–10. IEEE (2021)
8. Kim, M., Sinha, S., Orso, A.: Adaptive rest API testing with reinforcement learning. In: 2023 38th IEEE/ACM International Conference on Automated Software Engineering (ASE), pp. 446–458. IEEE (2023)
9. McFadden, S., Maugeri, M., Hicks, C., Mavroudis, V., Pierazzi, F.: Wendigo: deep reinforcement learning for denial-of-service query discovery in GraphQL. In: 2024 IEEE Security and Privacy Workshops (SPW), pp. 68–75 (2024). https://doi.org/10.1109/SPW63631.2024.00012
10. Meng, R., Mirchev, M., Böhme, M., Roychoudhury, A.: Large language model guided protocol fuzzing. In: Proceedings of the 31st Annual Network and Distributed System Security Symposium (NDSS), vol. 2024 (2024)
11. Meyerson, E., et al.: Language model crossover: variation through few-shot prompting. ACM Trans. Evol. Learn. Optim. **4**(4) (2024). https://doi.org/10.1145/3694791
12. Why You Should Disable GraphQL Introspection In Production: Khalil Stemmler (2024). https://www.apollographql.com/blog/why-you-should-disable-graphql-introspection-in-production/. Accessed 22 Aug 2025
13. Sartaj, H., Ali, S.: Search-based software engineering in the landscape of AI foundation models (2025). https://arxiv.org/abs/2505.19625
14. Tsai, O., et al.: Graphqler: enhancing graphql security with context-aware API testing (2025). https://arxiv.org/abs/2504.13358
15. Vargas, D.M., et al.: Deviation testing: a test case generation technique for GraphQL APIs. In: 11th International Workshop on Smalltalk Technologies (IWST), pp. 1–9 (2018)
16. Zhang, K., et al.: Logiagent: automated logical testing for rest systems with LLM-based multi-agents (2025). https://arxiv.org/abs/2503.15079

LLM-Guided Fuzzing for Pathological Input Generation

Didier Ishimwe(✉) and Thanhvu Nguyen

George Mason University, Fairfax, VA 22030, USA
{dishimwe,tvn}@gmu.edu

Abstract. Pathological inputs can trigger worst-case algorithmic behavior, leading to excessive resource consumption and revealing performance bottlenecks. Generating such inputs is difficult because they follow highly specific patterns that random testing or traditional fuzzing rarely uncovers. Existing fuzzing techniques either rely on domain-specific knowledge, which limits generality, or apply mutations on binary representations of inputs that produce predominantly invalid inputs.

We present PathoGen, a feedback-driven fuzzing framework that integrates LLMs into evolutionary search to efficiently discover pathological inputs. By leveraging LLMs for candidate generation, PathoGen achieves high-quality input without requiring domain-specific knowledge, such as handcrafted grammars. An adaptive prompt template mechanism ensures robustness during input generation, while convergence tracking by input size directs computational resources toward those most likely to expose worst-case behaviors.

Evaluation across textbook algorithms and real-world applications shows that PathoGen uncovers expected theoretical complexity bounds, induces significant slowdowns in practical systems, and outperforms existing domain-independent fuzzers in efficiency and input validity while performing comparably to domain-specific fuzzers within their specialized domains.

Keywords: Complexity Analysis · Performance Testing · Fuzzing · Large Language Models

1 Introduction

Reasoning about a program's worst-case complexity is crucial for applications such as performance analysis, optimization validation, and security assessment [3,14]. Because programs can exhibit vastly different resource usage on typical versus worst-case inputs, generating *pathological inputs* (those that trigger worst-case algorithmic behaviors [12]) is essential for accurate complexity analysis. These inputs help validate theoretical bounds, reveal performance bottlenecks, expose excessive resource usage [6], and highlight potential DoS attack vectors [15,33].

M. Wagner and M. Zhang (Eds.): SSBSE 2025, LNCS 16228, pp. 34–49, 2026.
https://doi.org/10.1007/978-3-032-24839-8_3

Pathological inputs often follow highly specific patterns that traditional random or mutation-based fuzzing is unlikely to discover, and they can reveal previously unanticipated worst-case runtime behaviors that are costly and difficult to detect. They typically manifest as nonfunctional defects, causing excessive resource consumption rather than outright crashes, leading to silent failures that escape conventional detection. To mitigate these challenges, companies including Amazon have adopted automated complexity analysis to catch performance regressions early in development [22,32]. Nevertheless, systematically identifying pathological inputs remains a difficult problem, as programs are complex and may rely on inaccessible library code, while pathological inputs vary widely across domains without a universal pattern [26].

To address the challenge of identifying worst-case performance behaviors, prior work has explored two main directions: automated complexity analysis and input generation. Automated complexity analyses aim to formally infer asymptotic bounds on resource usage [4,10]. While these approaches provide sound bounds, they do not generate concrete inputs that both witness the tightness of the bound and help developers debug unexpected performance issues [26].

In contrast, automated input generation, uncovers inputs that maximize resource consumption during execution. These techniques operate by exploring the input space through fuzzing [12] or synthesis [26,28], using runtime feedback as a guide to identify inputs that trigger worst-case behaviors. Some focus on domain-specific strategies tailored to structured inputs [13,15,28], while others aim for domain-independent solutions that can apply across a range of applications [20].

Existing input generation techniques face notable limitations. Domain-specific approaches achieve high precision by relying on program analysis and other domain-specific knowledge to guide exploration. For example, they may use handcrafted grammars [28], code vulnerability patterns discovered through static analysis [2,14,29], or symbolic execution to explore program paths [17]. However, these approaches restrict the programming languages and input formats that they can support. In contrast, domain-independent techniques apply mutations to byte-level input representations [12,20]. Such byte-level manipulation often produces a high proportion of invalid inputs (up to 80% for regular expressions [20]), wastes computational resources, and ignores program semantics, thereby limiting the discovery of deep performance bottlenecks that depend on subtle control-flow patterns [12].

In this paper, we present `PathoGen` (Pathological Input Generation), a fuzzing approach for discovering inputs that trigger worst-case resource usage. `PathoGen` enhances evolutionary fuzzing with Large Language Models (LLMs), allowing it to generate syntactically valid, diverse inputs without relying on handcrafted grammars or binary encodings. Input candidates are generated, executed, and scored by resource cost, with high performers guiding subsequent generations. Input generation is driven by autoprompting [30], where LLM prompts initialized with user-provided input specifications (e.g., natural language description) are iteratively refined using runtime feedback. `PathoGen` introduces per-size convergence tracking: it simultaneously generates pathological inputs for a set of input sizes, monitoring whether further generations at each size improve resource usage scores. Once a size converges, it is pruned from the search space. This allows smaller sizes to converge early while exploration continues for larger ones, eliminating wasteful search and scaling efficiently to realistic input lengths. The campaign terminates when every considered size converges or the budget is exhausted.

We evaluate `PathoGen` on a broad suite of benchmarks and demonstrate its effectiveness in generating pathological inputs for both classical algorithms and real-world applications. For textbook algorithms, `PathoGen` consistently produces inputs that realize the expected worst-case complexity. Compared to domain-independent complexity fuzzers such as `Slowfuzz` [20], `PathoGen` discovers pathological inputs more quickly and with substantially fewer invalid cases. At the same time, it narrows the performance gap with domain-specific fuzzers by achieving comparable slowdowns in their target domains, including regular expressions (`Revealer` [15]) and Java programs (`Acquirer` [14]), thus bringing domain-independent fuzzing much closer to domain-specific approaches in practice. Overall, these results highlight `PathoGen`'s advancement of domain-independent performance fuzzing through LLM-guided, feedback-driven input generation.

In summary, this paper makes the following contributions:

- We present `PathoGen`, a domain-independent fuzzer that integrates LLMs into a feedback-driven evolutionary loop, eliminating the need for handcrafted grammars or binary encodings. `PathoGen` is publicly available at https://github.com/dynaroars/pathogen
- A novel per-size convergence mechanism for efficiently discovering pathological inputs across input sizes.
- An extensive evaluation showing that `PathoGen` surpasses existing domain-independent fuzzers in efficiency and input validity, while achieving performance comparable to domain-specific fuzzers on both classical algorithms and real-world applications.

2 Overview

2.1 Large Language Models

Recent advances in machine learning have driven the widespread adoption of LLMs for both natural language and code-related tasks. Instruction-tuned LLMs, such as GPT-4, demonstrate strong abilities to follow complex instructions, reason over structured text, and understand code [16]. LLMs are adapted to tasks through two main paradigms: fine-tuning, which updates model weights using task data but demands significant resources, and prompting, which steers model outputs through carefully designed inputs [21]. Prompting has become the dominant, lightweight approach, with autoprompting [30] iteratively refining prompts for better output.

LLMs have shown promise in software engineering tasks such as program synthesis [25], testing [1,8,23,30,31], and formal methods [9]. `PathoGen` builds on this trend by embedding LLMs directly into the fuzzing loop, replacing traditional mutation and crossover operators with the goal of maximizing resource usage. This integration leverages LLMs emergent structural and semantic awareness to generate higher-quality inputs more efficiently, expanding applicability, reducing invalid or redundant cases, and improving discovery of worst-case behaviors compared to mutation-based fuzzers.

2.2 Illustrative Example: Quicksort

```
def qsort(arr):
    if len(arr) <= 1:
        return arr
    p = arr[0]
    l, r= [], []
    for x in arr[1:]:
        if x < p:
            l.append(x)
        else:
            r.append(x)
    return qsort(l) + [p] + qsort(r)
```

(a) **Quicksort implementation**

Fuzzing progress tracking

Iter	Active Sizes	Batch	Status
1	[4, 7, 16, 32]	16	All active
5	[7, 16, 32]	12	4: converged
12	[16, 32]	8	8: converged
18	[32]	4	16: converged
25	[ ]	0	All converged

Per-size evolution example

Size 4	Best Input	Score
Iter 1	[3, 1, 2, 5]	32
Iter 2	[1, 2, 5, 3]	45
Iter 3-5	[1, 2, 3, 5]	45

(b) **per-size convergence tracking**

System: Generate pathological inputs to maximize instruction count, focusing on constructs that increase runtime (e.g., nested loops, recursion, edge cases).
Target Program: `{program_code}`
Input Format: `{input_description}`
Size: `{size_description}`
Output: Raw inputs only, one per line; no explanations or extra text.

User: Generate `{batch_size}` inputs for sizes `{target_sizes}`, producing `{k}` inputs per size.
Strictly follow the input format above. Each input should aim to outperform the current best example at its size in terms of instruction count when executed on the target program
Current Best: `{best_inputs}`
Output: Raw inputs only, one per line; no explanations or extra text.

(c) **LLM prompt structure**

Fig. 1. Illustrative example of pathological input generation for `quicksort`

To demonstrate our approach, we use the widely studied `quicksort` algorithm, a standard benchmark in performance and complexity analysis [4,10,14,17,28] due to its simple control flow, basic data types, and well-understood semantics. It offers a clean setting to isolate performance behaviors without the confounding influence of complex control structures or data representations.

Identifying pathological inputs for `quicksort` is challenging due to its sensitivity to implementation details, such as pivot selection. In our implementation (Fig. 1a), choosing the first element as the pivot yields worst-case $O(n^2)$ behavior. Despite its simplicity, several complexity analysis tools report incorrect or overly conservative bounds: `TiML` [27] infers $O(n^3)$, `Chora` [4] reports $O(n2^n)$, and `Dynaplex` [10] incorrectly infers $O(n)$. By contrast, recent pathological input generation tools produce inputs that trigger the $O(n^2)$ worst-case behavior: `Singularity` [28], using handcrafted grammars, and `Acquirer` [14], guided by statically detected vulnerable code patterns.

Motivated by the need to systematically discover pathological inputs across a range of sizes, we frame the problem as a per-size search: given a program, the goal is to identify inputs of varying sizes that induce high resource consumption, such as instruction count. To address this, `PathoGen` employs an adaptive evolutionary fuzzing strategy guided by LLMs, simultaneously exploring multiple input sizes. For a range of sizes, `PathoGen` tracks convergence per size and removes those that reach optimal resource usage, focusing computation on sizes with remaining improvement potential. The algorithm terminates when all sizes have converged or the fuzzing budget is exhausted.

Let us use Fig. 1 to illustrate how `PathoGen` discovers pathological inputs for the `quicksort` example. The fuzzing campaign begins with a system prompt (Fig. 1c). The LLM's system prompt captures information that persists across iterations, such as the programs source code (Fig. 1a), the expected input specification, the meaning of input *size*, the objective to maximize instruction count, and the expected LLM output format. The input specification can range from a natural language description (e.g., list of integers) to a more complex Python object. The more precise the input specification, the better the LLM can generate valid inputs. At each iteration, `PathoGen` uses a user prompt (Fig. 1c) to instantiate multiple target sizes, the batch size (e.g., 16 inputs), and the number of inputs per size ($k = 4$). Each size maintains independent state tracking with the current best score and convergence monitoring, as shown in Fig. 1b.

As the campaign progresses, sizes that fail to improve after a threshold number of iterations are removed from the active set. In this example, size 4 failed to improve its score from iteration 2 to 5, leading `PathoGen` to consider it converged, reducing the batch size from 16 to 12 inputs. The LLM user prompt (Fig. 1c) is continuously updated with the best performing inputs and their scores for each active size, enabling targeted refinement. This process continues until all sizes converge to their optimal instruction counts or until the fuzzing budget is exhausted, systematically discovering pathological inputs across the size spectrum. This performance-driven feedback loop allows `PathoGen` to efficiently generate pathological inputs.

3 Proposed Approach

`PathoGen` combines evolutionary fuzzing with LLM-guided input generation to discover pathological inputs that trigger worst-case performance behaviors in programs. Within the evolutionary framework, the LLM replaces traditional crossover and mutation operations, generating candidates guided by concrete resource usage metrics. This LLM-driven generation allows convergence to be reached faster, but at different rates for different input sizes. To avoid wasteful computation on sizes that have already converged, `PathoGen` introduces per-size adaptive convergence tracking, which simultaneously monitors multiple input sizes and dynamically reallocates computational effort by pruning sizes that have reached optimal performance. The remainder of this section details the system architecture and its core components, including the fuzzing loop, prompt structure, input evaluation, and candidate refinement strategy.

We frame the pathological input generation as a per-size optimization problem: given a program and a resource metric, the goal is to find inputs of varying sizes that maximize the programs' measured resource usage under that metric. Because the input space is too large for exhaustive exploration, we adopt an adaptive evolutionary strategy in which an LLM generates candidate inputs for multiple target sizes simultaneously, guided by dynamically structured prompts and performance feedback. As sizes converge to their optimal resource usage, they are pruned from the search space, concentrating computation on sizes with remaining improvement potential. The system requires three user-provided inputs: (i) the target program, given as source code or an executable, (ii) an input specification defining format and size, and (iii) a resource metric such as instruction count.

3.1 Prompt Architecture

The effectiveness of LLM-guided input generation depends critically on well-structured prompts that provide clear guidance, context, and feedback to the LLM. `PathoGen` employs a multi-template prompt system tailored to different phases of the fuzzing workflow. This subsection outlines the prompt architecture, input specification, and template parameterization that enable systematic pathological input discovery.

`PathoGen` uses three prompt templates, each serving a distinct role:

1. *System prompt*: establishes persistent context and behavioral guidelines across iterations.
2. *Generation prompt*: provides iteration-specific objectives and feedback.
3. *Error-recovery prompt*: handles LLM induced failures and guides corrective behavior.

System Prompt. The system prompt defines the foundational context shared across all fuzzing iterations. It includes the target program, the fuzzing objective, the input specification, precise input size semantics with examples, and output formatting rules. The prompt also highlights algorithmic complexity triggers, such as nested loops, recursion depth, and costly edge cases, to steer the LLM toward pathological inputs rather than arbitrary ones.

Generation Prompt. The generation prompt encodes iteration-specific instructions and performance feedback. It specifies the number of inputs to produce (batch size), distributes them across active target sizes, and includes the best-performing inputs per size with their scores. By explicitly requiring the LLM to outperform current best examples *at the same size*, the prompt enforces competitive refinement without allowing trivial escalation through larger inputs.

Error-Recovery Prompt. When an input fails validation, `PathoGen` issues a recovery prompt containing the rejected examples and error details. This corrective feedback reinforces input requirements and supplies both valid and invalid examples, enabling the LLM to adapt its generation strategy and reduce repeated errors. Although modern LLMs follow instructions reliably, they may still produce invalid or unexpected outputs, making structured prompts essential for robustness.

Input Specification. Users provide structured input specifications in `YAML`. Each specification defines: (i) a description of the input domain and constraints (natural language or code), (ii) a size-calculation method (e.g., list length or byte count), and (iii) valid and invalid examples. For example, a quicksort specification defines inputs as "comma-separated integers enclosed in square brackets, with `[5, 2, 8, 1, 9]` as a valid example and `"2, 3, 5"` as invalid". The specification also includes a size function (e.g., Python code), ensuring precise mapping between inputs and target sizes. Explicit size definitions are crucial to avoid ambiguity in per-size optimization, especially since algorithmic complexity analysis often depends on different notions of *size* even for similar input domains. For instance, Karatsuba multiplication and Fibonacci programs both take integers as input, but their complexity sizes correspond to the number of digits and the integer value, respectively [7].

Template Parameterization. All prompts support dynamic parameterization through runtime placeholders, such as `target_sizes` in Fig. 1c for coordinating per-size search and `num_inputs` in Fig. 1c for adaptive batch sizing. Because templates are parameterized in this way, users can modify them to tailor prompts to specific domains, e.g., by supplying pathological patterns relevant to the program under analysis, while still providing the same runtime parameters. This flexibility allows the same template structure to support diverse input domains, from integer lists in sorting algorithms to class definitions, while maintaining consistent semantics and feedback.

3.2 Fuzzing Algorithm

`PathoGen` proceeds in four phases: initialization, evaluation, iterative fuzzing with error handling, and termination, as summarized in Algorithm 1.

Initialization. The algorithm begins by initializing the active size set, best seeds, error and convergence trackers, and prompt (line 1). Active sizes are spaced using an inverse-logarithmic scale to emphasize medium to large inputs, where algorithmic complexity behaviors are more likely to emerge. For each

Algorithm 1. `PathoGen`: Pathological Input Generation

```
Require: Program (P), InputSpec, Resource metric (R), Budget
 1: Seeds, Trackers, ActiveSizes, Prompts ← initialize_state(P, InputSpec, R)
 2: while Budget > 0 and ActiveSizes ≠ ∅ do
 3:     Candidates ← generate_candidates(ActiveSizes)
 4:     Scores, Trackers ← evaluate_candidates(Candidates, P, R)
 5:     State ← update_state(Scores, Seeds, Trackers, ActiveSizes)
 6:     Prompt ← update_prompt(State)
 7:     if Errors then
 8:         Prompts ← recovery_prompts(Trackers)
 9:     end if
10:     Convergence ← update_budget(ActiveSizes, Budget)
11: end while
12: return Seeds
```

size, trackers monitor the best resource usage and consecutive non-improving iterations to detect convergence. Error tracking enables graceful recovery from invalid LLM outputs, and the seeds retain the best inputs per size for subsequent iterations.

Evaluation. During each iteration, candidate inputs are generated for all active sizes (line 3) and evaluated according to the specified resource metric (line 4). Valid candidates are mapped to their sizes, with per-size scores and errors tracked to enable independent selection and feedback.

Fitness Scoring and Selection. Within each size class, `PathoGen` updates the stored seeds only if a candidate achieves a higher resource usage score (line 5). This size-based competition prevents trivial improvements via larger inputs and encourages the discovery of costly structural patterns. Trackers are updated each iteration, resetting on improvement and incrementing otherwise to monitor convergence.

Prompt Update and Error Handling. After updating the state, prompts are regenerated to incorporate performance feedback (line 6). If candidates fail validation, error-recovery prompts with prior errors as feedback are issued (line 8), guiding the LLM to produce valid inputs in subsequent iterations. This ensures that computation is not wasted on repeated invalid outputs.

Convergence and Termination. Sizes that have converged to optimal resource usage are pruned from the active set, focusing effort on remaining active sizes (line 10). The loop continues until either the budget is exhausted or all sizes have converged. Finally, the algorithm returns the best inputs per size, representing the discovered pathological inputs (line 12).

4 Evaluation

To assess the effectiveness of our approach, we implemented it in a prototype tool called PathoGen. This section outlines the benchmark design and describes our evaluation methodology.

Benchmarks. We evaluate PathoGen on a benchmark suite compiled from prior work on performance fuzzing and complexity analysis, including Revealer [15], Acquirer [14], and WISE [5]. The benchmarks cover domains such as regular expression parsing, sorting algorithms, and graph algorithms. For complexity-bound inference, we selected programs with well-defined worst-case behaviors to provide theoretical bounds as ground truth. We also included programs from real-world software, such as Java's regex parser.

The benchmark suite was curated to evaluate PathoGen's capabilities in two key aspects: first, whether it can generate inputs that achieve the theoretical worst-case complexity for a given implementation; and second, how its performance compares with state-of-the-art pathological input generators in producing slowdowns in real-world applications.

Setups. Experiments were conducted on a Debian 12 system with an AMD Ryzen Threadripper PRO 3995WX 64-core CPU, 125GB RAM, 497GB NVMe SSD, and an NVIDIA GeForce RTX 5090 GPU, using the OpenAI GPT-4-turbo [19] and Ollama gpt-oss:20b [18] models. Each experiment was repeated five times, with median results reported.

4.1 Asymptotic Bound Analysis

We evaluate PathoGen's ability to rediscover known worst-case complexity bounds across a diverse set of classical algorithms, including sorting, data structure operations, and graph algorithms with well-established theoretical asymptotics. The benchmarks are drawn from the WISE suite [5], which has also been used by Acquirer [14] to evaluate complexity bound discovery.

Table 1. Evaluation on textbook algorithms.

Program	Worst	Found
Sorted Linked-List	$O(n^2)$	✓
Heap Insert	$O(n \log n)$	✓
Red-Black Tree	$O(n \log n)$	✓
Quicksort	$O(n^2)$	✓
Binary Search Tree	$O(n^2)$	✓
Merge Sort	$O(n \log n)$	✓
Bellman-Ford	$O(n^3)$	✓
Dijkstra's	$O(n^2)$	✓
Traveling Salesman	$O(n!)$	✓
Insertion Sort	$O(n^2)$	✓

For each algorithm, we run PathoGen and record the maximum instruction count observed per size. For each algorithm, we compare the observed performance against the expected theoretical worst-case performance using linear regression. A bound is considered validated if the observed data aligns with the theoretical complexity class with $R^2 > 0.90$. As summarized in Table 1, PathoGen successfully recovers the correct asymptotic complexity for all benchmarks, demonstrating its ability to discover different complexity classes for programs with diverse input structures.

4.2 Comparison to State-of-the-Art

We evaluate `PathoGen` against state-of-the-art tools spanning both domain-independent and domain-specific categories of pathological input generation. On the domain-independent side, `SlowFuzz` [20] serves as the primary baseline, as few tools are designed to discover algorithmic complexity vulnerabilities without domain knowledge. We also include `Singularity` [28], which is only partially domain-independent: while it generalizes across programs, it relies on manually crafted grammars to ensure valid input generation. In contrast, the domain-specific space is richer, with many approaches tailored to particular formats or vulnerability classes. From this category, we select representative tools: `Acquirer` [14], which uses manually crafted vulnerability patterns to guide search in Java programs, and `Revealer` [15], which targets regex engines through crafted attack strings. Slowdown is measured relative to randomly generated inputs as a baseline, with a thirty-minute timeout per benchmark for all tools.

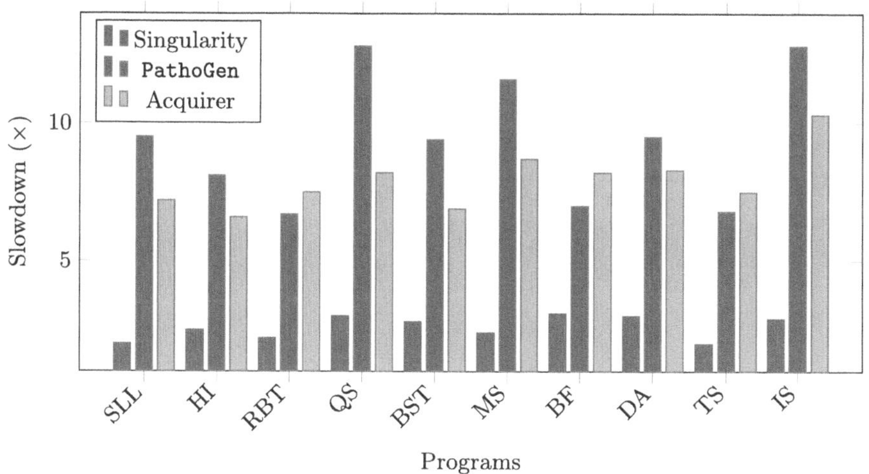

Fig. 2. Slowdown factor comparison of `PathoGen`, `Singularity` and `Acquirer` across textbook algorithms.

Our results highlight the difference between domain-informed approaches and naive exploration. `PathoGen`, `Acquirer`, and `Revealer` achieve significant slowdowns in less than 10 min on average, whereas `SlowFuzz` and `Singularity`, which rely on byte-level or grammar-based mutations without deeper semantic guidance, often require hours to reach comparable results. `Acquirer` leverages statically identified vulnerable code patterns, while Revealer exploits regex-specific models based on nondeterministic finite automata (NFA). In contrast, PathoGen uses LLMs to generate high-quality inputs rapidly, without relying on handcrafted grammars or domain-specific knowledge.

Input validity further differentiates the tools. SlowFuzz produces up to 80% invalid regex inputs, whereas PathoGen maintains at most 15% invalid inputs, depending on the LLM used. OpenAI GPT-4-turbo achieves the highest precision, and the results reported here use OpenAI GPT-4-turbo. Other models, such as Ollama gpt-oss:20b, generate less precise inputs yet still surpass SlowFuzz in both efficiency and input validity, while outperforming Singularity in efficiency.

Program-Level Slowdowns. Figure 2 compares PathoGen, Singularity, and Acquirer across 10 textbook algorithms. PathoGen consistently outperforms Singularity, achieving up to 380% higher slowdowns. Singularity's reliance on handcrafted grammars and naive exploration requires substantially more time to converge, often needing up to three hours to reach slowdowns that PathoGen achieves in just ten minutes. While Acquirer sometimes produces slightly higher slowdowns for certain graph algorithms, PathoGen surpasses it in other cases, particularly sorting, demonstrating competitive performance without relying on static analysis or pre-encoded vulnerability patterns. Moreover, since we do not analyze the Java regex engine source code but instead measure its performance via lightweight API calls, Acquirer's statically detected vulnerability patterns are ineffective in this domain.

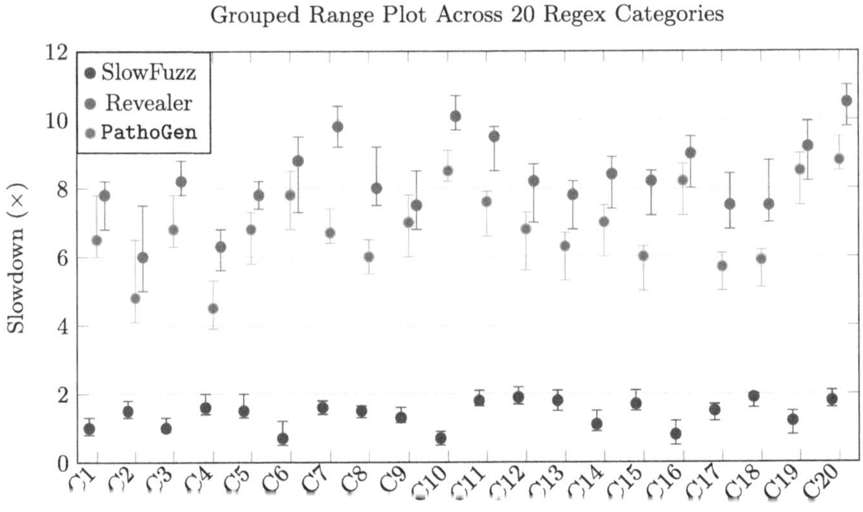

Grouped Range Plot Across 20 Regex Categories

Fig. 3. Grouped range plot showing min, median, and max slowdown for SlowFuzz, PathoGen, and Revealer across 20 regex categories.

Regex-Level Slowdowns. Figure 3 shows performance across 200 regular expression (regex) patterns taken from the benchmark used to evaluate `Revealer`'s algorithmic vulnerability detection. These regexes have also been used to evaluate other tools such as `ReScue` [24]. The full `Revealer` benchmark contains many more regexes across 20 different categories; we randomly selected 10 regexes per category because `PathoGen`'s LLM-guided generation is computationally expensive, making the evaluation of the entire dataset cost-prohibitive. Nonetheless, 200 regexes are sufficient to produce meaningful results. In this experiment, we use the Java 17 built-in regex parser, demonstrating that `PathoGen` can handle practical applications.

`Revealer` consistently achieves higher slowdowns than `PathoGen`, reflecting its domain-specific optimizations based on modeling NFA used in Java's regex parsing engine. In contrast, `SlowFuzz` performs substantially worse due to unguided input mutations and our limited fuzzing budget, requiring up to three hours to generate significant results. Additionally, `SlowFuzz` mutates binary encodings of the regexes to achieve domain independence; however, this approach produces mostly invalid inputs. `PathoGen`'s domain-independent approach achieves performance close to `Revealer` while maintaining broad applicability.

Across all benchmarks, `PathoGen` demonstrates the effectiveness of LLM-guided fuzzing in balancing efficiency, input validity, and generality. It outperforms domain-independent fuzzers and matches or slightly trails domain-specific tools in their targeted areas, illustrating that LLMs can replace handcrafted grammars or vulnerability patterns while still generating competitive pathological inputs.

5 Discussion

`PathoGen` advances domain-independent pathological input fuzzing by producing high-quality, slowdown-inducing inputs without handcrafted grammars, while maintaining strong validity and broad applicability. Key trade-offs remain for practical deployment and future work.

LLM Dependency. Leveraging LLMs offers both benefits and challenges. Large models such as GPT-4 provide high-quality inputs across domains without handcrafted grammars or vulnerability patterns, though they can be costly or access-restricted. Smaller open-source models like Ollama `llama3:7b` are more accessible but less effective for complex inputs. Crucially, as LLM capabilities improve, `PathoGen` automatically benefits from enhanced input generation, whereas domain-specific fuzzers require manual extensions with additional grammars or patterns to achieve similar gains.

Domain Generalization. `PathoGen` relies on LLMs to generate structured inputs, which can lead to lower-quality outputs for uncommon or specialized formats not well represented in the model's training data. However, as companies increasingly adopt LLMs in their production environments, these models are often finetuned on the organization's codebase and typical input formats. When PathoGen uses such a finetuned LLM for performance testing on the same codebase, it can generate increasingly effective pathological inputs, surpassing traditional fuzzers that rely on manually crafted grammars or domain-specific patterns. This approach allows PathoGen to improve automatically with the adoption and refinement of LLMs, while maintaining broad applicability across applications.

6 Related Work

Fuzzers for pathological inputs fall into two categories: domain-independent and domain-specific. SlowFuzz [20] pioneered the domain-independent approach by mutating inputs at the byte level to maximize instruction counts, later extended by PerfFuzz [12] with multi-dimensional feedback to better explore hot paths. These methods generalize across formats but often yield invalid inputs, wasting resources.

In contrast, Singularity [28] adopts a partially domain-independent strategy by relying on manually crafted grammars to produce valid, pathological inputs via program synthesis across different application domains. Acquirer [14] adopts a hybrid analysis that statically identifies vulnerable code patterns and guides evolutionary search towards program paths with such patterns. A prominent line of work within domain-specific fuzzing targets Denial-of-Service (DoS) vulnerabilities, particularly regex engines where crafted inputs cause excessive backtracking. Revealer [15] combines static analysis with dynamic testing, modeling regexes as extended NFA to generate attack strings, while HotFuzz [3] applies micro-fuzzing at the method level, using genetic algorithms to evolve inputs that maximize execution time in Java programs. Though effective, these tools are tailored to domains with well-characterized vulnerability patterns and do not generalize to broader algorithmic complexity issues.

Recent advances have explored leveraging LLMs to enhance fuzzing across a variety of domains. Techniques such as Fuzz4All [30] improve input diversity, TELPA [31] increase coverage, TitanFuzz [8] target deep learning libraries, and BENCIGENS [1] advance combinatorial testing. Other approaches focus on automated unit test generation [11,23]. To our knowledge, PathoGen is the first LLM-based fuzzer explicitly designed for pathological input generation, bridging the gap between domain-independent generality and domain-specific performance optimization.

7 Conclusion

We introduce PathoGen, an LLM-guided evolutionary fuzzing framework for discovering inputs that trigger worst-case performance. PathoGen bridges the gap between domain-specific precision and domain-independent applicability, enabling scalable pathological input generation across languages and input formats.

For future work, we plan to extend PathoGen to support additional user-defined resources such as memory usage and API call patterns, in addition to runtime performance. We also aim to leverage the structural understanding capabilities of LLMs to uncover recurring patterns in discovered pathological inputs. This insight will improve debugging and help developers optimize performance more effectively.

Acknowledgments. We thank the anonymous reviewers for their helpful comments. This material is based in part upon work supported by the National Science Foundation under grant numbers 2422036, 2319131, 2238133, and 2200621, and by an Amazon Research Award.

Disclosure of Interests. The authors have no competing interests to declare that are relevant to the content of this article.

References

1. Arcaini, P., Bombarda, A., Gargantini, A.: A search-based benchmark generator for constrained combinatorial testing models. In: 2025 IEEE International Conference on Software Testing, Verification and Validation Workshops (ICSTW), pp. 278–287. IEEE (2025)
2. Berglund, M., Drewes, F., Van Der Merwe, B.: Analyzing catastrophic backtracking behavior in practical regular expression matching. arXiv preprint arXiv:1405.5599 (2014)
3. Blair, W., Mambretti, A., Arshad, S., Weissbacher, M., Robertson, W., Kirda, E., Egele, M.: Hotfuzz: discovering temporal and spatial denial-of-service vulnerabilities through guided micro-fuzzing. ACM Trans. Priv. Secur. **25**(4), 1–35 (2022)
4. Breck, J., Cyphert, J., Kincaid, Z., Reps, T.: Templates and recurrences: better together. In: Proceedings of the 41st ACM SIGPLAN Conference on Programming Language Design and Implementation, PLDI 2020, pp. 688–702. Association for Computing Machinery, New York, NY, USA (2020)
5. Burnim, J., Juvekar, S., Sen, K.: Wise: automated test generation for worst-case complexity. In: 2009 IEEE 31st International Conference on Software Engineering, pp. 463–473. IEEE (2009)
6. Carter, K., Ho, S.M.G., Larsen, M.M.A., Sundman, M., Kirkeby, M.H.: Energy and time complexity for sorting algorithms in java. arXiv preprint arXiv:2311.07298 (2023)
7. Cormen, T.H., Leiserson, C.E., Rivest, R.L., Stein, C.: Introduction to Algorithms. MIT Press (2009)
8. Deng, Y., Xia, C.S., Peng, H., Yang, C., Zhang, L.: Large language models are zero-shot fuzzers: fuzzing deep-learning libraries via large language models. In: Proceedings of the 32nd ACM SIGSOFT International Symposium on Software Testing and Analysis, pp. 423–435 (2023)
9. Doan, L., Nguyen, T.: AI-assisted autoformalization of combinatorics problems in proof assistants. In: 2025 IEEE/ACM 47th International Conference on Software Engineering: New Ideas and Emerging Results (ICSE-NIER), pp. 1–5. IEEE (2025)
10. Ishimwe, D., Nguyen, K., Nguyen, T.: Dynaplex: analyzing program complexity using dynamically inferred recurrence relations. Proc. ACM Program. Lang. **5**(OOPSLA), 1–23 (2021)

11. Lemieux, C., Inala, J.P., Lahiri, S.K., Sen, S.: Codamosa: escaping coverage plateaus in test generation with pre-trained large language models. In: 2023 IEEE/ACM 45th International Conference on Software Engineering (ICSE), pp. 919–931. IEEE (2023)
12. Lemieux, C., Padhye, R., Sen, K., Song, D.: Perffuzz: automatically generating pathological inputs. In: Proceedings of the 27th ACM SIGSOFT International Symposium on Software Testing and Analysis, pp. 254–265 (2018)
13. Li, Y., et al.: {RegexScalpel}: regular expression denial of service ({{{{{ReDoS}}}}}) defense by {Localize-and-Fix}. In: 31st USENIX Security Symposium (USENIX Security 2022), pp. 4183–4200 (2022)
14. Liu, Y., Meng, W.: Acquirer: a hybrid approach to detecting algorithmic complexity vulnerabilities. In: Proceedings of the 2022 ACM SIGSAC Conference on Computer and Communications Security, pp. 2071–2084 (2022)
15. Liu, Y., Zhang, M., Meng, W.: Revealer: detecting and exploiting regular expression denial-of-service vulnerabilities. In: 2021 IEEE Symposium on Security and Privacy (SP), pp. 1468–1484. IEEE (2021)
16. Nam, D., Macvean, A., Hellendoorn, V., Vasilescu, B., Myers, B.: Using an LLM to help with code understanding. In: Proceedings of the IEEE/ACM 46th International Conference on Software Engineering, pp. 1–13 (2024)
17. Noller, Y., Kersten, R., Păsăreanu, C.S.: Badger: complexity analysis with fuzzing and symbolic execution. In: International Symposium on Software Testing and Analysis, pp. 322–332 (2018)
18. Ollama: Gpt-oss:20b (2025). https://ollama.com/library/gpt-oss%3A20b
19. OpenAI: GPT-4 technical report. CoRR abs/2303.08774 (2023). https://doi.org/10.48550/arXiv.2303.08774
20. Petsios, T., Zhao, J., Keromytis, A.D., Jana, S.: Slowfuzz: automated domain-independent detection of algorithmic complexity vulnerabilities. In: Proceedings of the 2017 ACM SIGSAC Conference on Computer and Communications Security, pp. 2155–2168 (2017)
21. Pornprasit, C., Tantithamthavorn, C.: Fine-tuning and prompt engineering for large language models-based code review automation. Inf. Softw. Technol. **175**, 107523 (2024)
22. Raimondi, F., Chang, B.Y.E.: Calculating the differential cost of code changes (2022). https://www.amazon.science/blog/calculating-the-differential-cost-of-code-changes
23. Schäfer, M., Nadi, S., Eghbali, A., Tip, F.: Adaptive test generation using a large language model. arXiv preprint arXiv:2302.06527 (2023)
24. Shen, Y., Jiang, Y., Xu, C., Yu, P., Ma, X., Lu, J.: Rescue: crafting regular expression DoS attacks. In: Proceedings of the 33rd ACM/IEEE International Conference on Automated Software Engineering, pp. 225–235 (2018)
25. Sobania, D., Briesch, M., Hanna, C., Petke, J.: An analysis of the automatic bug fixing performance of chatgpt. In: 2023 IEEE/ACM International Workshop on Automated Program Repair (APR), pp. 23–30. IEEE (2023)
26. Wang, D., Hoffmann, J.: Type-guided worst-case input generation. Proc. ACM Program. Lang. **3**(POPL), 1–30 (2019)
27. Wang, P., Wang, D., Chlipala, A.: Timl: a functional language for practical complexity analysis with invariants. Proc. ACM Program. Lang. **1**(OOPSLA), 79 (2017)

28. Wei, J., Chen, J., Feng, Y., Ferles, K., Dillig, I.: Singularity: pattern fuzzing for worst case complexity. In: Proceedings of the 2018 26th ACM Joint Meeting on European Software Engineering Conference and Symposium on the Foundations of Software Engineering, pp. 213–223 (2018)
29. Wüstholz, V., Olivo, O., Heule, M.J.H., Dillig, I.: Static detection of DoS vulnerabilities in programs that use regular expressions. In: Legay, A., Margaria, T. (eds.) TACAS 2017. LNCS, vol. 10206, pp. 3–20. Springer, Heidelberg (2017). https://doi.org/10.1007/978-3-662-54580-5_1
30. Xia, C.S., Paltenghi, M., Le Tian, J., Pradel, M., Zhang, L.: Fuzz4all: universal fuzzing with large language models. In: Proceedings of the IEEE/ACM 46th International Conference on Software Engineering, pp. 1–13 (2024)
31. Yang, C., Chen, J., Lin, B., Wang, Z., Zhou, J.: Advancing code coverage: incorporating program analysis with large language models. ACM Trans. Softw. Eng. Methodol. (2025)
32. Žikelić, Đ., Chang, B.Y.E., Bolignano, P., Raimondi, F.: Differential cost analysis with simultaneous potentials and anti-potentials. In: Proceedings of the 43rd ACM SIGPLAN International Conference on Programming Language Design and Implementation, pp. 442–457 (2022)
33. Zlomislić, V., Fertalj, K., Sruk, V.: Denial of service attacks, defences and research challenges. Clust. Comput. **20**(1), 661–671 (2017). https://doi.org/10.1007/s10586-017-0730-x

Optimised Fitness Functions for Automated Improvement of Software's Execution Time

Dimitrios Stamatios Bouras[1], Carol Hanna[2](✉), and Justyna Petke[2]

[1] Peking University, Beijing, China
[2] University College London, London, UK
{carol.hanna.21,j.petke}@ucl.ac.uk

Abstract. Precise measurement of software execution time is challenging due to environmental variability and measurement overheads, an issue critical for search-based software improvement systems that evaluate thousands of variants. While precise measurements offer precise fitness measures, they often introduce a significant time overhead. To understand which measures are most effective as fitness functions in search-based software optimisation, we conducted an empirical study of 21 approximates of execution time. These included hardware-level counters from `perf`, RAPL `energy`, and a custom measure based on weighted instruction cycles. To improve reliability, we evaluated each fitness function up to five times, using medians to reduce noise. We integrated the 13 most promising measures into a search-based software optimisation framework called `MAGPIE`. We evaluated these fitness functions plus `Time`, already present in `MAGPIE`, on 7 benchmarks using both code-level and parameter-level mutations. To assess generalizability, we tested the best performing measures with the parameter tuning tool `ParamILS` and analyzed how tool and search strategy affect outcomes. Our results show that `perf`'s `cycles` measure yields the best overall performance, outperforming `Time` by 5.1%. Sampling three times balances reliability and exploration. Energy and the weight-based measure excel in specific scenarios, with `weights` being the best for parameter optimization on `MAGPIE`, but are better suited to longer searches due to their overhead. We highlight a trade-off: low-overhead measures like `Time` work well for short runs, while robust measures such as `cycles` and `weights` benefit longer ones.

Keywords: Software Performance · Search-Based Software Engineering · Genetic Improvement

1 Introduction

Optimisation of non-functional properties of software, such as runtime or its energy use, have been pursued through a variety of strategies at the code level [7]: static methods compare variants to the original without re-evaluation (e.g., [1]);

M. Wagner and M. Zhang (Eds.): SSBSE 2025, LNCS 16228, pp. 50–65, 2026.
https://doi.org/10.1007/978-3-032-24839-8_4

sampling methods test selected variants via random or systematic sampling (e.g., [13]); exploratory methods iteratively refine variants using Bayesian tuning (e.g., [2]) or fuzzing (e.g., [4]); evolutionary approaches, notably genetic improvement [30], that mutates code, have achieved success in domains like bioinformatics (e.g., [23]), while manual methods remain in use when automation is impractical (e.g., [18]). More recently, large language models have been utilised to find efficiency improvements in code [32]. To be useful, they require a large set of training data with reliable measures of the non-functional property of interest.

A recurring challenge in optimisation of naturally noisy measures is selection of reliable fitness functions. Here, we consider the most common non-functional optimisation objective—program's running time [7]. Execution time as a fitness is common but noisy [10,25]; stable proxies like instruction count or executed lines (e.g., [23]) are more repeatable but may not reflect real runtime impact. Search-based methods employed in sampling (e.g., via random search), exploratory (e.g., genetic improvement), and evolutionary approaches (e.g., genetic algorithms) for runtime improvements [7], require evaluation of even thousands of software variants; even more would have to be evaluated to provide a training set for currently popular LLMs. This motivates exploring measures balancing cost to evaluate software variants, and their correlation with the objective of interest, as well as the ability to guide a given search strategy towards improved code. With this work we aim to close this gap in the literature.

First, we evaluated 21 runtime-approximating measures, from `perf` hardware counters to Intel RAPL `energy` readings and a custom instruction-weighted measure, to assess their stability and correlation with execution time. Although the selected measures are generally widely used, we have not found work that compares them all with respect to proxy for execution time.

Next, we integrated the top-performing measures into `MAGPIE` [6], a search-based improvement framework, and tested on seven benchmarks using genetic improvement and parameter tuning. Moreover, we examined multi-run retry strategies to reduce measurement noise and their trade-offs with search breadth. As far as we know, we are the first to compare these measures with the aim of finding the best trade-off between measurement accuracy and its ability to guide search towards improving software variants. Overall, our experiments cover 70 configurations (14 measures $\times$ 5 retry levels) across 22 scenarios (Sect. 3), totalling 1540 software improvement runs. Results show that the `cycles`, `Time`, `branches`, and `cache_references` measures provide strong search guidance, while retry of 3 balances robustness and efficiency. The `energy` and `weights` measures excel for long-running, repeatedly measured tasks despite higher cost.

Furthermore, we integrated the best measures into a parameter tuning tool called `ParamILS` to explore our findings in a different context. We observed that lightweight fitness measures dominate under short, multi-instance searches, while robust measures remain competitive in cost-tolerant contexts.

To sum up, our contributions are:

1. A comparative study of consistency and runtime correlation of 21 measures.

2. Integration of all measures as fitness functions into the search-based improvement framework `MAGPIE`.
3. Analysis of 70 measure–retry setups for optimal cost–effectiveness trade-offs within genetic improvement and parameter tuning settings with both local search and genetic programming searches in `MAGPIE`.
4. A case study evaluating our best performing measures within a different search-based context, a parameter tuning framework `ParamILS`.

2 Research Questions

In order to assess the trade-offs between accuracy of candidate fitness functions as proxies for runtime vs. effectiveness in leading search towards improved variants in search-based software optimisation frameworks, we pose the following research questions:

RQ1: *Which measures are most consistent and which most closely correlate with execution time, potentially serving as its surrogates?*
Knowing which execution time surrogates are most accurate and at the same time most consistent could save valuable resource time wasted on repetitions. Answer to this question goes beyond applicability in the search-based context.

RQ2: *Which performance measures are most effective as fitness functions, in terms of guiding search towards finding the most time-saving software variants within a constrained time budget?*
Within the search-based context we want to know which measures are lightweight, yet accurate enough, to guide search towards improved software variants.

RQ3: *How many repeated measurements (retries) provide the best trade-off between measurement precision and computational overhead?*
Here we are interested in establishing the needed measurement overhead, per measure. Some proxies for time might require less repetitions to provide enough accuracy to guide search towards improved software variants.

RQ4: *Which performance measures and retry parameters lead to the most consistent search, ensuring stable and progressive optimization?*
Answer to this research question will provide recommendations for best use of each measure of interest.

3 Methodology

Performance Measure Collection. We evaluated 21 execution time surrogates (Table 1). We selected these primarily from `perf` hardware counters (e.g., cycles, cache, branches, instructions) due to their established correlation with execution time: hardware performance counters and energy have long been used as reliable surrogates for runtime prediction across architectures and workloads [11,31]. Energy usage was recorded using Intel's RAPL interface. We also used the `weights` metric [8], which applies throughput-based weights [16] to assembly instructions. This involves first profiling with `perf-record`, computing per-function runtime shares via `perf-report`, then identifying per-command shares within functions using `perf-annotate` and lastly multiplying command throughput by its function share and command share, and aggregating. This yields a weighted sum approximating runtime more accurately than raw instruction counts.

Measure Consistency and Correlation with Execution Time. To answer RQ1, we assessed which measures are both consistent and proportional to execution time. We repeated runs on each benchmark 21 times (based on the calculations in the online Appendix D). For each measure–benchmark pair we computed coefficient of variation $CV = (\sigma/\mu) \times 100\%$, then took the median CV across benchmarks. Lower CVs indicate higher reliability, with measures beating `Time` considered stronger guides. Rather than Pearson's r (insensitive to systematic scaling), we examined proportionality: for each measure(M)–benchmark(b) pair we computed the median ratio $\text{Factor}_{M,b} = \frac{\text{Median}(M,b)}{\text{Median}(T_b)}$, and the CV of these factors across benchmarks. Low Factor CV indicates consistent scaling with execution time.

Search-Based Optimisation Frameworks. We selected two frameworks for our evaluation: `MAGPIE` (to answer RQ2–RQ4) and `ParamILS` to show generalisation potential and explore shorter budgets.

`MAGPIE` [6] is a Python-based, language-agnostic framework for search-based software improvement, representing edits as XML sequences to decouple search from specific modification techniques. This way searches across both parameters and modification directly to code are possible. `MAGPIE` supports multiple local search (LS) and genetic programming (GP) search strategies. We adopt the best variants from [5]: First-Improvement local search and GP with uniform concatenation crossover, both at statement and parameter level—i.e., genetic improvement and parameter tuning settings. For GP we used a population of 10, running as many generations as the time budget allowed for.

We integrated 18 `perf` measures as fitness functions, Intel RAPL `energy`, and the weighted-instruction `weights` measure [8]; standard Unix `Time` was already present. We introduced a *retries* parameter into `MAGPIE`, re-executing each variant 1 to 5 times and taking the median to suppress noise. While this increases runtime, stability markedly improves, but early experiments showed no benefit beyond 5 retries. Recall, we need to balance the measurement accuracy against time for the search process. In that sense repetitions of 20–30 tries commonly recommended in the literature *outside of search-based context*, and confirmed in our experiments on measure consistency (Appendix D), are simply impractical.

To test measure effectiveness in a different search context, we used `ParamILS` (v2.3.8) [20]— a mature, model-free parameter optimizer with features like adaptive capping and anytime behavior. Its proven performance across diverse domains and differing search dynamics from `MAGPIE` make it well-suited for evaluating our measures and retry strategies in alternative search contexts, particularly shorter and more localized searches. We modified `ParamILS`'s evaluation script to capture `perf`, `energy`, and `weights` outputs. Experiments focused on parameter tuning over the same benchmarks as MAGPIE, using eight measures: the six best from experiments with MAGPIE plus weights and energy (see answer to RQ2 in Sect. 4.2 for justification).

Benchmarks. We used benchmarks common in related research [7], selected for popularity, maintainability, and computational intensity.

For **RQ1** we used 8 popular controlled micro-benchmarks from standard suites: bzip2, gzip from SPEC [33]; fftp, lu from SPLASH-2 [34]; blackscholes from PARSEC [28]; and bitcount, sha, jpeg from MiBench [27].

For **RQ2–RQ4** and the ParamILS case study 7 larger, optimization-rich benchmarks were employed: MiniSAT, MiniSAT_hack, SAT4J, Weka, LPG (these were used in the original MAGPIE paper and we thus know that optimizations can be found), plus 2 parameter-heavy real-world tasks (scipy.optimize.minimize, zlib.compress). All were parameter-optimized in both MAGPIE and ParamILS; for MAGPIE, code optimization was also applied to MiniSAT, MiniSAT_hack, SAT4J, and Weka. LPG was limited to parameter tuning (legacy library issues), while scipy and zlib lack meaningful code-level variants. We used both the best local search (LS) and genetic programming (GP) variants with MAGPIE, totalling 22 scenarios (4×2 code optimisation tasks plus 7×2 parameter tuning tasks).

Thus, RQ1 used small, stable workloads for consistency/correlation, while RQ2–RQ4 employed benchmarks with substantial optimization potential, spanning both parameter and code optimization contexts.

Experimental Setup. We ran our experiments on a Rocky Linux 9.4 Desktop with an 8-core Intel(R) Xeon(R) E5-1620 CPU with 16 GBs RAM. For MAGPIE, we recorded the number of variants examined under each measure–retry combination. We selected a 30-minute fixed time budget in order to balance practical resource constraints with established practices in the field. This duration aligns with prior studies in search-based software engineering, where similar time budgets have been effectively employed [3,14]. Each configuration of ParamILS was given 5 min per benchmark; for each benchmark–measure pair. Since ParamILS specializes in parameter tuning, exploratory trials showed that runtime can already find near-optimal solutions within this budget. Allowing longer runs would mainly advantage high-overhead measures, while runtime (the baseline) already converges quickly, so 5 min provides a fair comparison of surrogates against execution time. Three optimization runs were executed (as 3 samples were found sufficient to minimize randomness as a factor), and the median of the best configuration of each of the three runs determined ranking.

4 Results and Discussion

Next, we present our experimental results and answer our research questions. Data in each table that answers RQs 2–4 reflects results from one of two setups: MAGPIE with local search (LS) or genetic programming (GP). To recap, each setup has been run across 7 benchmarks, 4 run in genetic improvement mode, making code-level mutations, and all 7 run in parameter tuning mode, thus data from 11 scenarios is aggregated per LS or GP. The number of runtime surrogates and retries considered for each sceanrio are outlined in each subsection.

4.1 RQ1: Measure Consistency and Correlation with Execution Time

First, we present the results of running our initial experiments on measure consistency and correlation to execution time in Table 1.

Table 1. RQ1 Variability and correlation to execution time for 8 standard benchmarks. MCV: Median Coefficient of Variation across benchmarks; MCVR: Median Ranking for CV across benchmarks; FCV: CV of Factor across benchmarks. Lower is better for all measures.

Measure	MCV	MCVR	FCV	Measure	MCV	MCVR	FCV
major-faults	0.000	1.0	108.49	perf_time	0.852	13.5	0.58
minor-faults	0.046	5.0	231.22	dTLB-loads	0.840	12.0	146.79
total-faults	0.040	4.5	231.21	weights	0.523	11.5	24.82
branches	0.004	3.0	90.88	cache-misses	1.972	17.0	113.60
L1-dcache-loads	0.096	6.0	53.82	L1-dcache-load	1.170	15.5	100.05
instructions	0.001	2.0	43.09	-misses			
cycles	0.221	8.0	0.81	cache-references	0.881	13.0	88.76
branch-misses	0.150	7.0	112.40	Time	0.814	16.5	0.00
energy	0.452	10.0	14.96	dTLB-load-misses	3.920	17.5	243.43
task-clock	0.593	13.5	0.30	cs	30.201	20.0	53.23
cpu-clock	0.754	15.0	0.63	migrations	142.980	21.0	106.42

Among traditional runtime proxies, `branches, cycles, branch_misses, L1_dcache_loads`, and `instructions` showed very low CV (0.0013–0.22%), confirming their stability. Fault-related measures such as `total-faults, minor_faults`, and `major_faults` also had extremely low CV (<0.05%), likely due to their rare occurrence. In contrast, raw `Time` and `perf_time` were less reliable (CV ~0.8–0.85%), sensitive to system load. Clock-based metrics such as `cpu_clock, task_clock` performed slightly better (<0.75%), while `context_switches` and `mitigations` were unusable. `Energy` (0.45% CV) and the custom `weights` metric (0.52%) occupied a mid-range. The `weights` CV could be reduced by higher `perf` sampling rates, but experimentation showed little benefit for benchmark runs over ~1 s, while overhead increased sharply. A sampling rate at ~2000 Hz is a practical trade-off. Correlation analysis (Table 1) showed that time-based measures (`perf_time, cpu_clock, task_clock`) best tracked execution time (FCV <0.63%). `Cycles` performed almost as well (0.81%) but with much lower CV, making it a robust surrogate. Surprisingly, `energy` (14.96%) and `weights` (24.8%) correlated more strongly with execution time than instructions or branches, despite moderate CV, highlighting their promise. This is particularly valuable when direct time measurement is impractical or unreliable, such as in parallel or distributed environments. Other low-CV measures (`branch_misses, branches, L1_dcache_loads, instructions`) showed weaker correlates (FCV 43–112%).

> **Answer to RQ1:** `cycles` is the most reliable surrogate for execution time. `energy` and `weights` also show potential, thus we recommend these especially for contexts where direct time measurement is infeasible.

4.2 RQ2: Execution-Time Surrogates as Fitness Functions

To evaluate performance measures for software optimization, we evaluated the best 14 as fitness functions within the `MAGPIE` framework. Original is the program before optimization. We first discuss results obtained with first-improvement local search (LS), followed by genetic programming (GP).

The 7 measures omitted from Table 2 were excluded from later experiments due to excessive variability (MCV>2) or lack of correlation with execution time(FCV>120). With faults we refer to *major_faults* from now on.

For each benchmark, we used one of the 14 measures as the fitness function to optimize the original program and obtain an improved variant with lower execution time. We then ranked each measure by the execution time of its best variant per benchmark and summarized performance by median execution time (MET), average rank across benchmarks, and the mean number of explored variants (Table 2).

Regarding the LS approach, `cycles` emerged as the most effective fitness function (5.02 s), closely followed by `branches` (5.17 s) and `Time` (5.29 s). Other strong performers included `perf_time`, `cache_references`, and `L1_dcache_loads`, confirming `cycles`, `branches`, and cache-related metrics as robust alternatives to raw execution time. `Energy` ranked well (median rank 6) despite a middling mean MET (6.53 s), excelling in three benchmarks.

The custom `weights` measure, though hindered by high overhead ($\approx$ 40% of variants explored vs. `perf`), achieved leading results in `LPG` (18% faster than the runner-up) and `SAT4J`, especially where execution traces were simple and dominated by few options (it was the best for parameter optimization). `Energy` also incurred overhead ($\approx$ 60% of variants explored) but still showed competitive effectiveness. Most `perf` measures achieved comparable search depth since they rely on `perf-stat`. By contrast, measures like `faults`, `cpu_clock`, and `task_clock` underperformed not due to measurement overhead but because they poorly reflect runtime improvements, failing to accelerate patch discovery.

Regarding the GP approach, `cycles` consistently ranked as a top performer, excelling in three cases despite lower performance in two scenarios, which affected its mean MET. The measure of `cache_references` notably achieved the best mean MET (4.635 s), underscoring the significant impact of cache operations on

Table 2. RQ2 Mean Median Execution Times (MET), Median Ranks (MR), and Number of Variants (Nov) for Each Measure. Columns 2–4: experiments with Local Search. Columns 5–7: experiments with Genetic Programming. Lower is better for MET and Rank, for NoV higher is better.

Measure	Mean MET(s)	Median	NoV	Mean MET(s)	Median Rank	NoV
	local search			genetic programming		
Original	10.28	12	-	9.65	13	-
perf-measures						
L1_dcache_loads	5.42	7	240	5.99	7	397
branch_misses	5.46	8	222	5.75	5	431
branches	5.17	6	252	6.22	7	393
cache_misses	5.63	4	255	7.02	8	419
cache_references	5.40	8	234	4.64	5	451
cpu_clock	10.28	14	157	8.85	14	376
cycles	5.02	4	252	6.15	4	426
faults	8.92	11	176	7.28	12	381
instructions	5.59	7	270	6.48	7	384
task_clock	10.45	13	164	9.87	14	387
perf_time	5.43	6	257	5.66	7	409
other						
energy	6.53	6	156	6.21	11	257
Time	5.29	4	260	5.17	4	414
weights	7.02	10	106	6.96	12	275

execution time. `L1_dcache_loads`, `branch_misses`, `branches`, `instructions`, `Time`, and `perf_time` performed well as they did for local search, with mean METs ranging from 5.17 to 6.48. Intel's RAPL energy consumption measure was a viable surrogate with a mean MET of 6.2 s, indicating its potential for representing execution time. Conversely, `faults`, `task_clock_time`, and `cpu_clock_time` were again the least effective measures. The custom `weights` measure, also underperformed (6.96 s) hindered by the number of variants, but demonstrated high consistency and can be very effective given sufficient exploration time.

Answer to RQ2: `cycles`, `Time`, `branches`, `cache_references`, `perf-time`, and `L1_dcache_loads` achieved the lowest MET (5.02âĂŞ5.43s vs. baseline 10.28s in LS setup). `Energy` ranked above average (median rank 6), while `weights` was the best measure in two benchmarks despite high overhead, but underperformed when used with GP.

4.3 RQ3: Optimal Number of Retries for Measures

We ranked retry counts for each benchmark–measure pair median execution time of the optimized variant, and aggregated these rankings across benchmarks (Table 5 for Local Search). Mean (MaR), median (MR), with standard deviation (STD), and interquartile range (IQR) of ranks show that retry = 3 is optimal: it yields the most consistent improvements while exploring enough variants. Beyond 3, retries reduce the number of variants without notable consistency gains, Conversely, 1 or 2 retries explore more variants but less efficiently.

Table 3 provides measure-specific recommendations. Measures with low MCV (e.g., `instructions`) require fewer retries, reflecting inherent stability. Measures with higher MCVs (e.g., `energy`, `weights`) benefit from larger retry counts to mitigate run to run variability. For all results in Tables 3, 4, 5, 6, lower is better.

Table 3. RQ3 Recommended Retry Numbers for Each Measure from LS experiments. MaRN: Mean Retry Number; MRN: Median Retry Number.

Measure	MaRN	MRN	IQR	STD
energy	3.273	4.000	1.000	1.009
L1_dcache_loads	2.636	2.000	2.500	1.433
branch_misses	2.273	2.000	2.000	1.348
branches	2.636	2.000	2.000	1.502
cache_misses	2.273	2.000	2.500	1.272
cache_references	2.545	2.000	2.500	1.572
cpu_clock	2.636	3.000	2.500	1.567
cycles	2.636	2.000	3.000	1.629
faults	2.909	2.000	3.000	1.700
instructions	3.273	3.000	2.500	1.348
task_clock	3.636	4.000	1.500	1.121
perf_time	2.636	1.000	4.000	1.963
Time	2.273	2.000	2.500	1.272
weights	3.091	3.000	1.000	0.944

Table 4. RQ3 Percentage Decrease in Variants examined by Number of Retries in LS experiments. RN: Retry No.; MaDP: Mean Decrease %; MDP: Median Decrease %.

RN	MaDP	MDP	STD	IQR
1	0.0	0.0	0.0	0.0
2	30.71	30.65	19.25	28.47
3	47.54	48.92	20.63	29.11
4	59.37	60.96	18.58	23.52
5	67.49	68.87	16.24	20.73

Retries directly reduce the number of variants explored: compared to 1, retry = 3 reduces steps by ≈ 48% (Table 4). Despite this cost, retries markedly increase reliability of optimization trajectories, enabling clearer convergence toward improved variants. Thus, retry = 3 offered the best balance between search breadth and stability, though the optimum varies by measure.

For GP, retries ranked from 1 (best) to 5 (worst), showing no benefit from higher values (Table 6). Unlike local search, where consistency is vital to not divert the search, GP's population diversity offsets noise, making a single retry most effective, since it increases the number of variants.

Table 5. **RQ3** Statistical Analysis of Retry Rankings Across All Benchmarks from LS experiments. MaR: Mean Rank; MR: Median Rank.

Retries	MR	MaR	STD	IQR
1	3.143	3.078	0.389	0.429
2	3.000	2.974	0.288	0.250
3	2.929	2.974	0.298	0.464
4	2.989	3.005	0.325	0.357
5	3.071	2.992	0.389	0.500

Table 6. **RQ3** Statistical Analysis of Retry Rankings Across All Benchmarks from GP experiments. MaR: Mean Rank; MR: Median Rank.

Retries	MR	MaR	STD	IQR
1	2.36	2.47	0.27	0.39
2	2.93	2.95	0.40	0.50
3	3.00	3.07	0.46	0.71
4	3.29	3.18	0.41	0.39
5	3.36	3.33	0.41	0.32

Regarding recommendations, we observed no significant difference in results between GP and LS experiments, thus to save space, we report on the LS experiments only, and provide results for GP in the available online Appendix B.

Answer to RQ3: Retry = 3 balances exploration and reliability, achieving the best overall ranks despite halving the number of explored variants. The precise optimum varies with the stability of the measure (as indicated by MCV). For GP retry of 1 is often surprisingly sufficient.

4.4 RQ4: Consistency Analysis Across Measures and Retries

When looking at the data to answer RQ4, we observed no significant difference in results between experiments with LS and GP. Given that local search variants proved very effective both in GI [5] and parameter tuning work [20], we report on results from experiments with LS only. We provide result tables obtained from GP runs in the online Appendix B.

Consistency Through MAD. We assessed consistency via Mean Absolute Deviation (MAD) from a best-fit line across retry–measure combinations, a standard robustness metric [21,35]. Table 7 shows median and mean MAD grouped by measure and by retry count. The measure `faults` (3% MAD) was by far the most stable, while `branch_misses`, `cycles`, `cache_misses`, and `Time` also ranked highly consistent. Even `energy` and `weights` maintained relatively low variance (< 19%). Higher retry values systematically reduced MAD, confirming that retries dampen stochastic noise.

Consistency Through Decreases. We further analyzed the search trajectory by: (i) total decreases (TD) in fitness, (ii) average decrease percentage per step (ADPS), and (iii) proportion of decreases (POD). While retries sharply cut the number of evaluated variants (Table 4), the number of decreases fell only mildly, so POD actually rose. ADPS also improved slightly with retries. Thus, retries trade off exploration depth for efficiency: fewer steps, but each more likely and impactful. A retry value of 3 offered the best balance, aligning with Table 5.

Table 7. RQ4: Median and Mean MAD, STD, IQR (lower is better), and Search Performance (TD, ADPS, POD) (higher is better) for Each Measure and Retry Number. TD: Total decreases; ADPS: Percentage of decrease that are achieved per step on average; POD: Percentage of Steps that are overall decreases.

Measure	Med. MAD	Mean MAD	STD	IQR	TD	ADPS	POD
energy	0.157	0.155	0.267	0.266	6.0	0.047	0.098
L1_dcache_loads	0.174	0.166	0.198	0.200	7.0	0.040	0.074
branch_misses	0.145	0.143	0.301	0.324	9.0	0.041	0.079
branches	0.188	0.198	0.307	0.329	8.0	0.040	0.081
cache_misses	0.165	0.167	0.270	0.261	8.0	0.043	0.068
cache_refs	0.163	0.166	0.220	0.219	8.0	0.048	0.077
cpu_clock	0.390	0.329	0.134	0.124	4.0	0.171	0.053
cycles	0.155	0.147	0.288	0.271	10.0	0.043	0.085
faults	0.030	0.031	0.055	0.042	9.0	0.011	0.090
instructions	0.199	0.211	0.306	0.318	9.0	0.038	0.093
task_clock	0.415	0.314	0.175	0.155	4.0	0.200	0.051
perf_time	0.194	0.203	0.320	0.314	8.0	0.045	0.077
Time	0.164	0.166	0.311	0.341	9.0	0.047	0.087
weights	0.187	0.174	0.297	0.276	5.0	0.089	0.077

Retries	Med. MAD	Mean MAD	STD	IQR	TD	ADPS	POD
1	0.245	0.179	0.278	0.291	9.0	0.047	0.040
2	0.214	0.186	0.265	0.266	7.5	0.046	0.062
3	0.177	0.167	0.235	0.265	8.0	0.047	0.079
4	0.180	0.170	0.239	0.258	7.0	0.050	0.095
5	0.157	0.156	0.215	0.233	7.0	0.051	0.110

Measure-Specific Effects. Across measures (irrespective of retries), `energy`, `faults`, `instructions`, `Time`, and `cycles` achieved high POD (> 8.5%), reinforcing their role as reliable guides. Notably, `cycles` combined middle-range ADPS (4.3%) with the highest TD (10), showing how steady, incremental progress can accumulate. In contrast, `weights` produced the largest ADPS (8.9%), but low TD (5) due to fewer opportunities, illustrating the cost of sparse sampling despite steep improvements. For `Time`, high variance meant some "decreases" were likely noise, particularly with low retries.

Example Search Space Comparisons. Figure 1 in the onlineAppendix A compares `task_clock` (retry = 1) vs. `weights` (retry = 3) on `LPG`. The former yields chaotic, untargeted exploration with near-baseline variants and only one late cluster of modest improvements. In contrast, `weights` exhibits better guidance with clear "staircase" of optimization phases producing distinct improved groups.

Answer to RQ4: Larger retries consistently stabilize search (lower MAD), reduce steps but increase per-step efficiency (higher POD and ADPS). Stable measures like `branch_misses`, `cycles`, `cache_misses`, and especially `faults` guided the search reliably. `weights` demonstrated the steepest per-step improvements, though constrained by limited sampling opportunities.

4.5 Cross-Tool Validation with Short Search Budgets

Table 8 reports the results of our `ParamILS` experiments, where each run was limited to 5 min. To ensure stability under this shorter budget, each benchmark configuration was executed 21 times per run, with medians averaged across three searches. We report both the average Median Execution Time (MET) and the average rank of each measure across benchmarks.

`ParamILS` uses adaptive instance-level evaluation, sampling, and racing strategies that preclude meaningful tracking of intermediate variants. Consequently, we focused on the final best configuration as the primary performance indicator. Comparing `MAGPIE`'s interpretable variant counts against `ParamILS`'s end results, offers insights into the trade-offs between search depth, consistency, and efficiency across different search-based optimization paradigms.

Results show a clear trade-off between overhead and guidance. The lightweight metric `time` consistently ranked best, confirming that minimal-overhead measures are most effective when thousands of fast evaluations are required. In contrast, `weights`, which incurs sampling overhead, performed worst. We note that the sampling rate for `weights` was selected after experimentation, as higher rates offered limited benefit for benchmarks exceeding one second per run, while adding substantial cost. Intermediate hardware measures (`L1_dcache_loads`, `branches`, `cycles`) performed competitively with only modest overhead, while `perf_time` showed high variability across benchmarks. The `energy` measure also underperformed, ranking second worst.

These findings suggest that short-budget optimization favors measures that minimize overhead, while more detailed or resource-intensive measures become valuable primarily in longer searches or when exploring fewer variants.

Case Study Insight: Under limited search time, lightweight metrics such as `time` clearly dominate by balancing low overhead with sufficient guidance. Hardware-based counters remain competitive but add cost, while complex or high overhead measures provide little advantage in this setting.

Table 8. ParamILS Experimental Results Across Measures.

Metric	Average MET (s)	Average Rank
time	3.894	3.000
L1_dcache_loads	3.976	3.714
branches	3.983	3.857
cycles	4.148	4.714
cache_references	4.215	4.857
perf_time	4.649	3.714
energy	4.787	6.000
weights	6.200	6.143

5 Threats to Validity

The generalizability of our findings may be limited due to the use of 22 benchmark-search type combinations in this study. While the benchmarks cover a variety of tasks and the search type includes both parameter tuning and source code optimization to broaden applicability, they may not fully represent all potential use cases. In our experiments we selected real-world benchmarks commonly used in the literature to ensure relevance. Our study was conducted on a single computer system due to the need for uniform platform for all measures. This means that certain measures might be influenced by the underlying architecture. However, we are interested in finding measures that could serve as *fitness functions*, thus consistently differentiating between two software variants. Therefore, we believe that our results will generalise, although future studies could enhance the robustness of our findings by replicating the experiments on other hardware configurations. We employed a consistent seed across all runs to ensure a fair starting point and designated a substantial time budget (30 min) to explore hundreds of variants, randomness may still influence outcomes. However, considering the extensive number of combinations (1540 in total) tested in this study, we expect that randomness would average out, mitigating its impact on the overall results. To further address generalisability concerns, we have established an infrastructure that allows for easy inclusion of additional benchmarks, which future researchers can leverage to expand our work. All code, documentation, and results are available at: https://anonymous.4open.science/r/Optimised-fitness-functions-ssbse/README.md.

6 Related Work

Bloat and Petke in their survey of benchmarks for automated improvement of software's non-functional properties [7] conclude that the most targeted non-functional property is execution time, with energy usage and software size being the 2nd and 3rd most improved property in the literature. Various strategies have been adopted to improve code performance at the software level. The most common are compiler optimizations, algorithm configurations, and source code modifications. Among these techniques, the application of metaheuristics for software improvement have emerged as particularly potent methods due to their ability to explore complex search spaces efficiently [7]. Most search-based empirical studies that focus on runtime improvements at the code level use the Unix `Time` command or the `perf-time` commands as the main part of the fitness function, e.g., [20] and [9]. Liou et al. employed GPU kernel runtime [24]. Langdon et al. based their fitness function on the number of task units performed in a specific time window [22], while Garciarena and Santana, [17] used both compilation and execution time. Other works, such as the Cole framework [19], try to achieve multi-objective optimization, which include the execution time as one of their primary objectives, alongside other criteria of memory usage, power consumption, and code size. However, the reliance of all those tools on accurate and consistent time measurements is fundamentally flawed since research has shown the limitations of simple runtime measurements due to their susceptibility to external variations such as background CPU processes, varying CPU loads, and multi-core contention. Carothers and Fujimoto [10] and Meyer et al. [26] have shown that execution time is a very volatile measure that is affected by background processes and CPU load, Mazous et al. [25] studied how time is affected by multi-core or parallel executions. These studies underscore the necessity for incorporating a broader set of performance indicators that can more accurately reflect the true efficiency of software under various conditions. Another potential measure is the weighted sum of the assembly commands in the binary program, based on the commands' CPU cycle throughput. Patterson's and Hennessy's book on computer organization and design [29], proves that execution time and CPU cycles for each command are deeply connected. However, the use of pipelining in modern CPUs makes the two measures no longer analogous. Despite these challenges, the work by Bouras et al. [8], along with additional research on the correlation between cycles-per-instruction and total execution cycles with runtime [15], supports the reasonable assumption of such a correlation.

7 Conclusion

Precision of execution time measurement strongly affects the efficiency of search-based software optimisation. Our study showed that multiple hardware-level measures, notably `cycles`, `branches`, and RAPL's `energy`, can serve as reliable surrogates for execution time, often providing more consistency under noisy conditions. Recomputing fitness values three times and taking the median further improved stability, albeit at the cost of exploring fewer variants. These findings highlight practical trade-offs between precision, overhead, and search efficiency, and point to broader applications where robust performance proxies are valuable. The insights gained from exploring new performance measures as fitness functions underscore the potential for broader applications, inspiring further research to refine these techniques and extend their use in more diverse computational environments. It would be interesting to explore the potential of our weighted measure in the context of recent advances such as Google's AlphaDev [12]. The `weight` measure could provide a more precise measure and thus enhance the robustness of such systems. Furthermore, such measures could be used to efficiently evaluate large corpora of data to provide training bed for LLMs.

References

1. Abdulsalam, S., Lakomski, D., Gu, Q., Jin, T., Zong, Z.: Program energy efficiency: the impact of language, compiler and implementation choices. In: International Green Computing Conference, pp. 1–6 (2014)
2. Ashouri, A.H., Mariani, G., Palermo, G., Park, E., Cavazos, J., Silvano, C.: Cobayn: compiler autotuning framework using Bayesian networks. ACM Trans. Archit. Code Optim. **13**(2) (2016)
3. Ayerdi, J., Terragni, V., Jahangirova, G., Arrieta, A., Tonella, P.: Genmorph: automatically generating metamorphic relations via genetic programming. IEEE Trans. Software Eng. **50**(7), 1888–1900 (2024)
4. Biswas, P., Burow, N., Payer, M.: Code specialization through dynamic feature observation. In: Proceedings of CODASPY, pp. 257–268. CODASPY, Association for Computing Machinery, New York, NY, USA (2021)
5. Blot, A., Petke, J.: Empirical comparison of search heuristics for genetic improvement of software. IEEE Trans. Evol. Comput. **25**(5), 1001–1011 (2021)
6. Blot, A., Petke, J.: Magpie: machine automated general performance improvement via evolution of software (2022)
7. Blot, A., Petke, J.: A comprehensive survey of benchmarks for improvement of software's non-functional properties. ACM Comput. Surv. **57**(7) (2025)
8. Bouras, D.S., Lamprakos, C.P., Catthoor, F., Soudris, D.: Reliable basic block energy accounting. In: Embedded Computer Systems: Architectures, Modeling, and Simulation: 23rd International Conference, SAMOS 2023, Samos, Greece, 2–6 July 2023, Proceedings, pp. 193–208. Springer, Heidelberg (2023)
9. Brownlee, A.E.I., Petke, J., Alexander, B., Barr, E.T., Wagner, M., White, D.R.: Gin: genetic improvement research made easy. In: Proceedings of the Genetic and Evolutionary Computation Conference, GECCO 2019, pp. 985–993. Association for Computing Machinery, New York, NY, USA (2019)
10. Carothers, C., Fujimoto, R.: Background execution of time warp programs. In: Proceedings of Symposium on Parallel and Distributed Tools, pp. 12–19 (1996)
11. Conte, T.M., Menezes, K.N., Mills, P.M., Patel, B.A.: Optimization of instruction fetch mechanisms for high issue rates. In: Proceedings of the 22nd Annual International Symposium on Computer Architecture (ISCA), pp. 333–344 (1996)
12. Mankowitz, D.J., et al.: Faster sorting algorithms discovered using deep reinforcement learning. Nature **618**(7964), 257–263 (2023)
13. Daud, S., Ahmad, R.B., Murthy, N.S.: The effects of compiler optimisations on embedded system power consumption. Int. J. Inf. Com. Tech. **2**(1/2), 73–82 (2009)
14. Eriksson, C., Wiidh, F.: The impact on time efficiency of varying mutation rate and population size in jgenprog (2024)
15. Eyerman, S., Eeckhout, L.: Per-thread cycle accounting. IEEE Micro **30**(1), 71–80 (2010)
16. Fog, A.: Lists of instruction latencies, throughputs and micro-operation breakdowns for intel, AMD, and via CPUs. Technical report, Technical University of Denmark (2022)

17. Garciarena, U., Santana, R.: Evolutionary optimization of compiler flag selection by learning and exploiting flags interactions. In: Proceedings of the 2016 on Genetic and Evolutionary Computation Conference Companion, pp. 1159–1166. GECCO 2016 Companion, Association for Computing Machinery, New York, NY, USA (2016)
18. Hamza, H., Counsell, S.: Exploiting slicing and patterns for RTSJ immortal memory optimization. In: Proceedings of the 2013 International Conference on Principles and Practices of Programming on the Java Platform: Virtual Machines, Languages, and Tools, PPPJ 2013, pp. 159–164. Association for Computing Machinery (2013)
19. Hoste, K., Eeckhout, L.: Cole: compiler optimization level exploration. In: Proceedings of the 6th Annual IEEE/ACM International Symposium on Code Generation and Optimization, CGO 2008, pp. 165–174. Association for Computing Machinery, New York, NY, USA (2008)
20. Hutter, F., Hoos, H.H., Leyton-Brown, K., Stuetzle, T.: Paramils: an automatic algorithm configuration framework. J. Artif. Intell. Res. **36**, 267–306 (2009)
21. King, A.P., Eckersley, R.J.: Chapter 2 - Descriptive statistics ii: bivariate and multivariate statistics. In: King, A.P., Eckersley, R.J. (eds.) Statistics for Biomedical Engineers and Scientists, pp. 23–56. Academic Press (2019)
22. Langdon, W.B.: Performance of genetic programming optimised bowtie2 on genome comparison and analytic testing (GCAT) benchmarks. BioData Mining **8**(1), 1 (2015)
23. Langdon, W.B., Harman, M.: Optimizing existing software with genetic programming. IEEE Trans. Evol. Comput. **19**(1), 118–135 (2015)
24. Liou, J.Y., Forrest, S., Wu, C.J.: Genetic improvement of GPU code. In: GI Workshop, pp. 20–27 (2019)
25. Mazouz, A., Touati, S., Barthou, D.: Study of variations of native program execution times on multi-core architectures. In: 2010 International Conference on Complex, Intelligent and Software Intensive Systems, pp. 919–924 (2010)
26. Meyer, T., Davis, J., Davidson, J.: Analysis of load average and its relationship to program run time on networks of workstations. J. Parallel Distrib. Comput. **44**, 141–146 (1997)
27. MiBench: MiBench performance benchmark (2024). https://github.com/embecosm/mibench. Accessed 09 Sept 2024
28. PARSEC: PARSEC performance benchmark (2024). https://github.com/bamos/parsec-benchmark. Accessed 09 Sept 2024
29. Patterson, D.A., Hennessy, J.L.: Computer Organization and Design: The Hardware/Software Interface, 5th edn. Morgan Kaufmann (2013)
30. Petke, J., Haraldsson, S., Harman, M., Langdon, W., White, D., Woodward, J.: Genetic improvement of software: a comprehensive survey. IEEE Trans. Evol. Comput. (2017)
31. Shao, Y., Brooks, D.: Energy characterization and instruction-level energy model of intel's xeon phi processor. In: Proceedings of the International Symposium on Low Power Electronics and Design (ISLPED), pp. 389–394 (2013)
32. Shypula, A., et al.: Learning performance-improving code edits. In: The Twelfth International Conference on Learning Representations, ICLR 2024, Vienna, Austria, 7–11 May 2024. OpenReview.net (2024)
33. SPEC: SPEC performance benchmark (2024). Accessed 09 Sept 2024
34. SPLASH-2: SPLASH-2 performance benchmark (2024). https://www.capsl.udel.edu/splash/index.html. Accessed 09 Sept 2024
35. Mean Absolute Deviation, pp. 336–337. Springer, New York (2008)

Search-based Hyperparameter Tuning for Python Unit Test Generation

Stephan Lukasczyk[1,2(✉)] and Gordon Fraser[2]

[1] JetBrains Research, Munich, Germany
[2] University of Passau, Passau, Germany

Abstract. Search-based test-generation algorithms have countless configuration options. Users rarely adjust these options and usually stick to the default values, which may not lead to the best possible results. Tuning an algorithm's hyperparameters is a method to find better hyperparameter values, but it typically comes with a high demand of resources. Meta-heuristic search algorithms—that effectively solve the test-generation problem—have been proposed as a solution to also efficiently tune parameters. In this work we explore the use of differential evolution as a means for tuning the hyperparameters of the DynaMOSA and MIO many-objective search algorithms as implemented in the Pynguin framework. Our results show that significant improvement of the resulting test suite's coverage is possible with the tuned DynaMOSA algorithm and that differential evolution is more efficient than basic grid search.

Keywords: Differential Evolution · Grid Search · Hyperparameter Tuning · Search-based Software Testing · Pynguin

1 Introduction

Many algorithms allow adjusting their behaviour by providing parameters, so-called *hyperparameters*, to the user. The more complex an algorithm is or the more hyperparameters it exposes, the harder it is to find values that imply optimal behaviour of the algorithm. Tuning of the hyperparameters is one way to find optimal values, but it is usually time-consuming [31]. Studies show that about 80% of the literature in Software Engineering, Data Mining, and Defect Prediction—fields that heavily use complex algorithms—do not mention tuning at all, although an improvement of up to 60% is possible [18]. In many cases the cost of tuning does not seem to be worth the effort [41].

One category of such complex and heavily configurable algorithms are *evolutionary algorithms* (EAs). They are popular for many optimisation problems, e.g., search-based test generation [30]. Various algorithms, such as DynaMOSA [35] or MIO [2], implemented in mature tools, such as EvoSuite [15] for Java or Pynguin [26] for Python, are representative for this technique. EAs consist of various operators, each with numerous hyperparameters

M. Wagner and M. Zhang (Eds.): SSBSE 2025, LNCS 16228, pp. 66–81, 2026.
https://doi.org/10.1007/978-3-032-24839-8_5

with significant influence [22]. While tools typically come with default hyperparameter values that allow their off-the-shelf usage, it is an open question whether these default values are actually suitable for a problem at hand.

Among many existing tuning approaches and techniques [21], the *differential evolution* [39] search algorithm has been extensively studied and is reported to provide very good tuning results in short time [17–19]. In this paper we therefore explore how well differential evolution can tune a set of hyperparameters of the DynaMOSA and MIO algorithms as implemented in the Pynguin test-generation framework for Python. To assess the improvements and computational costs, we compare against a baseline of *grid search* [9]. In detail, the contributions of this paper are the following:

1. We conduct a large scale hyperparameter tuning experiment for the DynaMOSA and MIO algorithms in the Pynguin test-generation framework.
2. We tune each algorithm's hyperparameters with two tuning algorithms, differential evolution and grid search.

The results confirm that hyperparameter tuning is a time-consuming task, with our experiments consuming almost 72 years of runtime. For both tuned test-generation algorithms the tuning with differential evolution was faster than with grid search. However, only for the DynaMOSA algorithm our tuning lead to a significantly better performance in terms of coverage of the resulting test suites. While this improvement can justify the effort, this depends on the use case: The tuning of MIO confirms that default values can still lead to reasonable results [5].

2 Background

2.1 Grid Search

Exhaustive tuning strategies explicitly and systematically check all possible combinations of hyperparameter values, whether a combination satisfies the desired properties. This approach is also known as *brute force*. A standard technique to exhaustively explore the space of combinations is *grid search* [9], which considers every possible combination of a given set of hyperparameters [9]. The number of joint values in the grid grows exponentially with the number of hyperparameters to tune (*curse of dimensionality* [7,8]). While this can cause enormous runtime requirements, the algorithm is inherently parallel [20] because all individual tuning runs are independent of each other. The computation of the grid requires discrete values for each hyperparameter. For hyperparameters with real values this requires the user to decide on a discretisation, which may cause that one misses the optimal value for a hyperparameter.

2.2 Differential Evolution

Differential evolution attempts to find the global optimum of non-linear, non-convex, multi-modal, and non-differentiable functions defined in the continuous parameter space [39]. Its structure is similar to an EA, however, it generates an offspring $\boldsymbol{x}_0'$ (an n-dimensional vector in the parameter space) by randomly choosing three distinct individuals $\boldsymbol{x}_r$, $\boldsymbol{x}_s$, and $\boldsymbol{x}_t$ from the population and combining them with a scale factor F, such that $\boldsymbol{x}_0' = \boldsymbol{x}_t + F(\boldsymbol{x}_r - \boldsymbol{x}_s)$ [33]. Given an objective function f, differential evolution aims to find the global minimum of $f(\boldsymbol{x})$ in the decision space [33]. The simplicity of differential evolution and its robustness and versatility allow engineers, practitioners, and researchers to apply and adapt it in countless ways. Various literature surveys, e.g. [12,33], present the large flexibility of the algorithm and its applications.

2.3 DynaMOSA and MIO Algorithms

DynaMOSA [35] is a state-of-the-art EA that aims to optimise many objectives at the same time. In the context of test generation, with branch coverage as an optimisation goal, each branch is an objective to the algorithm. By incorporating the hierarchical structure of the program under test, DynaMOSA is able to optimise for only those goals that are reachable at a given time. The algorithm uses an archive as a second population, which stores those individuals that successfully covered an optimisation goal.

MIO [2] explicitly targets subjects with thousands of (independent) optimisation goals. It combines the simplicity of a (1+1)EA with feedback-directed target selection, a dynamic population, a dynamic exploration/exploitation switch, and archives to store populations for each goal. The idea of the phase switch is that in the beginning exploration helps discovering large parts of the search space, whereas later in the process, exploitation allows to focus on better results.

2.4 Pynguin

Pynguin [26] is a state-of-the-art unit test generation tool for the Python programming language. It implements various standard test-generation algorithms, such as, Whole Suite [16], DynaMOSA [35], or MIO [2]. Pynguin aims to generate Python unit tests that reach high branch coverage for given subject systems.

3 Search-Based Hyperparameter Tuning for SBST

The DynaMOSA [35] implementation in Pynguin showed the best performance in previous work [28] compared to the other test-generation algorithms implemented in the framework, including Pynguin's implementation of MIO [2]. The implementation of these algorithms in Pynguin uses parameter values taken from EvoSuite [15], a state-of-the-art unit-test generation tool for Java.

3.1 General Hyperparameters

While both DynaMOSA and MIO are EAs, they are considerably different in how they are built and what operators they use. Both algorithms share that they use *test cases* as their chromosomes, in the form of sequences of statements. Because shorter test cases are considered more readable and understandable for developers [11], tuning the maximum *chromosome length*, i.e., the number of statements in a chromosome, is a natural choice. Both algorithms handle their chromosome population differently, thus, we decided to use different size ranges for them. Additionally, while differential evolution works on continuous intervals of floating-point numbers, grid search requires a discretisation of the values. We use the differential-evolution implementation from the Python library scipy for this study, which also supports intervals over integers.

- *DynaMOSA:* We constrain the chromosome length to the interval $[5, 100] \subset \mathbb{N}$ for differential evolution; for grid search, we use $\{5, 10, 25, 50, 100\}$.
- *MIO:* We bind the chromosome length to the interval $[10, 50] \subset \mathbb{N}$ for differential evolution; we use $\{10, 25, 50\}$ for grid search.

Mutation is one of the three standard operators of an EA. Usually, it is only applied once in every iteration of the algorithm and due to its stochastic nature there is only a certain probability for a change. MIO, however, allows applying mutation more than once to an individual before sampling a new one. We transfer the idea of applying mutation more than once to DynaMOSA, thus allowing to tune the *number of mutations* with the following value ranges and discretisations:

- *DynaMOSA:* We constrain the number of mutations to the interval $[0, 25] \subset \mathbb{N}$ for differential evolution; for grid search, we use $\{0, 1, 5, 10, 25\}$.
- *MIO:* Since MIO does not use crossover at all, we do not want to disable mutation. Thus, we constrain the number of mutations for differential evolution to $[1, 25] \subset \mathbb{N}$; for grid search, we use $\{1, 10, 25\}$. Note that these intervals apply to both phases of MIO; we tune the number of mutations for both independently.

Since we cannot assume that an EA will find an optimal solution, it is necessary to define a *search budget*. This often is the only parameter a user of a tool will adjust, because it is directly understandable to them [5]. While different budget types, e.g., algorithm iterations, are possible, we decided to use a timeout of 180 s because a user usually wants to control the execution time of a tool.

3.2 DynaMOSA-Specific Parameters

A DynaMOSA-specific parameter is the *population size*, i.e., the number of individuals in the EA's population. A large size allows for more diversity in the population, which can escape local optima in the fitness landscape easier. However, a large size can also slow down convergence towards the global optimum [5]. For differential evolution, we constrain the population size to $[4, 200] \subset \mathbb{N}$, for grid search to $\{4, 10, 50, 100, 200\}$, same as in previous work [5].

The *crossover rate* specifies the probability that two selected individuals are crossed over. For grid search, we use $\{0, 0.25, 0.5, 0.75, 1\}$, for differential evolution $[0, 1]$. For the selection of individuals, we choose between rank and tournament selection; for grid search, we set the rank bias to $\{1.2, 1.7\}$ and for differential evolution to $[1.01, 1.99]$. The tournament size is bound to $\{2, 7\}$ for grid search and $[1, 20] \subset \mathbb{N}$ for differential evolution.

3.3 MIO-Specific Parameters

Characteristic to MIO is its switch between exploration and exploitation phases. The former shall explore large parts of the fitness landscape whereas the latter shall fine-tune the individuals in the population. We allow degenerating MIO to only use either exploration or exploitation by using $[0, 1]$ for differential evolution and $\{0, 0.25, 0.5, 0.75, 1\}$ for grid search.

Number of tests per target is similar to the population size. For each optimisation goal, MIO holds one population in its archive. During exploration we allow numbers from $[1, 25] \subset \mathbb{N}$ for differential evolution and $\{1, 10, 25\}$ for grid search, respectively. MIO only keeps one test per target in the exploitation phase [2].

Similarly, during exploration MIO can either select a test from the archive or sample a new one. The probability of this sampling is set to $[0, 1]$ for differential evolution and $\{0, 1/3, 2/3, 1\}$ for grid search. In the exploitation phase, the probability is always 0 because the algorithm shall only refine existing test cases.

3.4 Fitness Function for the Tuner

Since PYNGUIN aims to generate test suites with high coverage, the coverage of the final test suite provides an obvious choice for selecting the best set of hyperparameters. However, it may also be desirable to achieve coverage as quickly as possible, which might not be reflected by the final coverage. The area under the curve of the coverage achieved over time therefore provides an alternative metric. This lets us define five different fitness functions for the tuning algorithms: solely coverage (denoted as DE 1+0), only area under curve (DE 0+1), the sum of coverage and area under curve (DE 1+1), and two weighted sums: ten times coverage plus area under curve (DE 10+1) and vice versa (DE 1+10). Note that the aforementioned notation refers to the respective objective function used for differential evolution. Grid search also requires a metric to choose the best configuration after all configurations from the grid have been explored successfully. We decided to use the same metrics as for differential evolution's objective function. We use GS $\alpha + \beta$ to denote these functions, respectively.

4 Empirical Evaluation

To evaluate differential evolution as a tuning algorithm for DynaMOSA and MIO in PYNGUIN with grid search as a baseline tuning algorithm, we investigate the following research questions:

- **RQ1:** How much do the tuning algorithms improve the performance?
- **RQ2:** How do the algorithms compare in terms of computational costs?

4.1 Experimental Setup

We conducted an empirical evaluation using a set of modules as evaluation subjects from previous work on PYNGUIN [28]. In line with previous work on tuning [5] and recent work on search-based unit test generation (e.g., [24]), we incorporate only those modules into our evaluation subjects where PYNGUIN uses up the entire search budget and achieves between 80 % and 100 % branch coverage, since the choice of parameter values will have no influence on code that is either trivial or impossible to cover for PYNGUIN. This leads to 101 modules, which we split into a training and test set using an 80 % split.

We use PYNGUIN in git revision `fd9a6e96` for the evaluation and execute it inside Docker containers for process isolation. We limit the search budget of PYNGUIN to 180 s and disable its assertion generation and test-code export. To minimise the influence of randomness, we execute PYNGUIN on each subject 15 times. Both values are in line with previous research [5]. All runs were executed on dedicated compute servers equipped with an AMD EPYC 7443P CPU and 256 GB RAM. We assign one CPU core and 4 GB RAM to each execution. All measured values are rounded to three significant digits. We use the Vargha-Delaney effect size $\hat{A}_{12}$ [40] and the Mann-Whitney-U test [29] at $\alpha = 0.05$ to compare two result sets, as recommended by the literature [3].

4.2 Threats to Validity

Threats to its *internal validity* may result from bugs in PYNGUIN or our experiment framework, although both have been tested carefully. The stochastic nature of the test-generation algorithms and differential evolution can cause results by chance. We repeat each PYNGUIN experiment 15 times with different random seeds and follow rigorous statistical procedures to evaluate the results. However, we do not repeat executions of differential execution due to the already huge resource effort. The study's *external validity* is influenced by the small size of 101 modules for the study, which may not allow to generalise the results. In general, the results from tuning are inherently tied to the used subjects. Another set of subjects might result in different optimal configurations. The fact that our evaluation only relies on branch coverage implies a threat to *construct validity*: practitioners might be interested in other metrics, too, such as test-suite size or readability of test cases. We consider these factors negligible for this study but admit that one might need to consider them in other use cases.

4.3 RQ1: Performance Improvement Due to Tuning

Figure 1 shows the development of the coverage over *DynaMOSA*'s generation time of 180 s for the configurations produced by the different tuning algorithms and objectives. All differential evolution configurations achieve similar coverage values in the end; for grid search, applying the different tuning fitness functions always yielded the same configuration, which we denote as *GS*. However, all configurations show a higher final coverage than with the algorithm's default

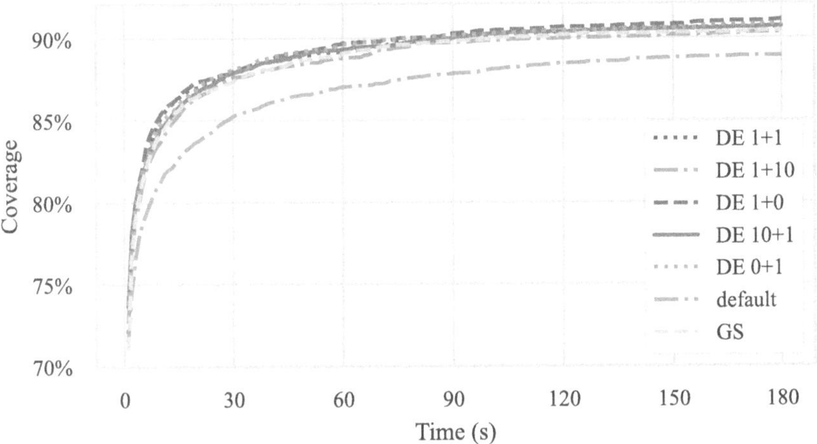

Fig. 1. Development of the mean branch coverage over time for the best DynaMOSA configurations.

settings. The similarities between the tuned algorithm variants and the difference to the default can also be seen from the coverage distributions (Fig. 2). While all tuned algorithm variants perform similar, DE 1+0 is the best in this experiment.

Table 1 shows the best hyperparameter settings for each tuning method for DynaMOSA. All configurations use rank selection, in contrast to the default configuration. Note that while the tournament size (column $\mathfrak{S}$) changes due to how differential evolution applies its changes, it does not affect the result because it is never used by rank selection. For all configurations, except DE 1+10, a larger chromosome length is preferable, whereas the crossover probability can be smaller and more mutations are beneficial. Furthermore, a smaller rank bias is also preferable as is a smaller population size.

For *MIO*, we see different results than for DynaMOSA. While the coverage over time (Fig. 3) evolves differently for the different configurations in the first 30 s to 60 s, one can barely distinguish them after 180 s. We note that there are now two grid-search configurations: GS 114, which is best for GS 1+0 and GS 10+1, and GS 325, which is best for the other grid-search configurations. The coverage distributions only differ slightly (Fig. 4). Table 2 shows the corresponding hyperparameter settings. Note that the number of tests per target $|T_k|$ and the probability to randomly sample a new test case P_r are fixed to $|T_k| = 1$ and $P_r = 0$ as a characteristic property of the exploitation [2]. Outstanding is GS 114, which has no exploration phase at all; other configurations also have the phase switch after less than 10 %; they all favour exploitation over exploration.

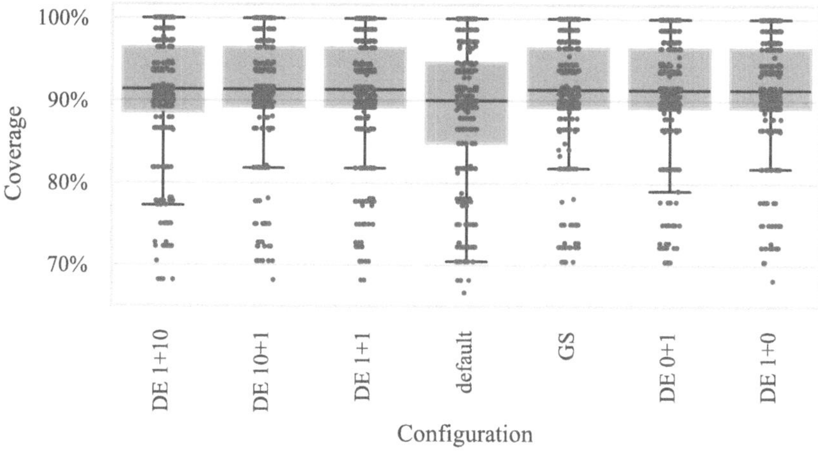

Fig. 2. Coverage distributions for the best DynaMOSA configurations.

Table 1. Best hyperparameter settings for DynaMOSA per tuning fitness function.

Configuration	l_c	P_c	n_m	N	$\mathfrak{B}$	Selection	$\mathfrak{S}$
DE 1+1	53	0.737	3	18	1.39	rank	4
DE 1+10	39	0.676	2	18	1.34	rank	12
DE 1+0	48	0.648	3	10	1.68	rank	4
DE 10+1	45	0.573	4	8	1.44	rank	12
DE 0+1	46	0.549	3	10	1.34	rank	3
default	40	0.750	1	50	1.70	tournament	5
GS	100	0.750	1	4	1.20	rank	5

chromosome length l_c, crossover rate P_c, number of mutations n_m, population size N, rank bias $\mathfrak{B}$, tournament size $\mathfrak{S}$

RQ1 Summary

All tuned DynaMOSA configurations improve over the default configuration, but there is no improvement for MIO. Differential evolution achieves better results than grid search.

Discussion: All tuned variants of DynaMOSA show an improvement in coverage over the default configuration, which indicates that the default hyperparameter values are not optimal. Table 3 reports the mean branch and relative [5] coverages for the tuned configurations and compares them to the default settings. All tuned configurations yield significantly higher mean coverage.

Comparing the DynaMOSA configurations reveals that a larger maximum chromosome length and a significantly smaller population size are beneficial. Usually, one would expect a larger population size, which allows for higher diver-

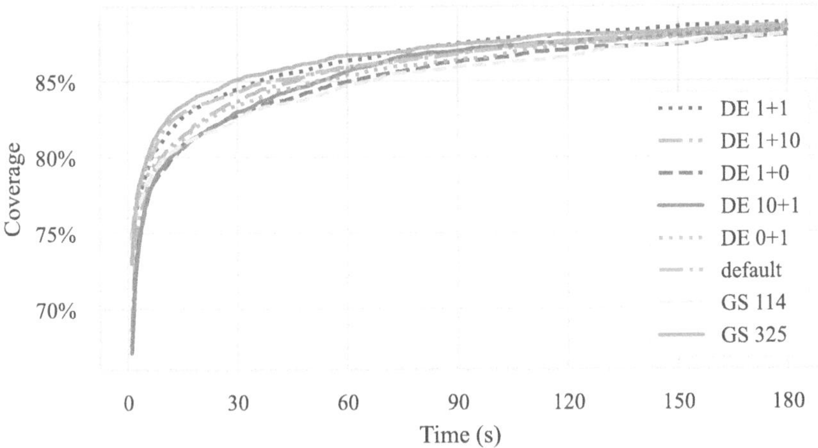

Fig. 3. Development of the mean branch coverage over time for the best MIO configurations.

sity in the population. Still, for grid search, a population of only four individuals is sufficient to outperform the default configuration with 50 individuals. However, in this case, the diversity might come from the larger chromosome length: the test cases have not been minimised after generation, thus, it is possible that individual test cases actually cover more than one focal method. Additionally, other work that applied tuning to the population-size parameter of DynaMOSA reports that a smaller-than-default size is better [10]. Furthermore, introducing the possibility to run more than one mutation per evolution step seems to be beneficial. This, together with the smaller crossover rates indicates that mutation is actually more important for DynaMOSA's performance than one might expect.

None of the tuned variants of MIO show an improvement over the default configuration. Worse, if one compares the $\hat{A}_{12}$ effect sizes of the variants and the default configuration, this effect is slightly in favour of the default when measuring it on mean branch coverage; for relative coverage, two configurations have a slightly positive, although not significant, effect towards the tuned configurations.

No tuned configuration shows improvement over the default for MIO. The choice of hyperparameters and their value ranges might limit the results; selecting them differently could change the result. However, the chosen hyperparameters are those that are directly related to the MIO algorithm, and that are also similar to the hyperparameters chosen for the DynaMOSA tuning, to also allow for some inter-algorithm reasoning. The wide range of values for the different hyperparameters, see Table 2, however, does not directly allow the conclusion that the selection of the value ranges imposes this result. The MIO algorithm performs very similar, independently of its settings.

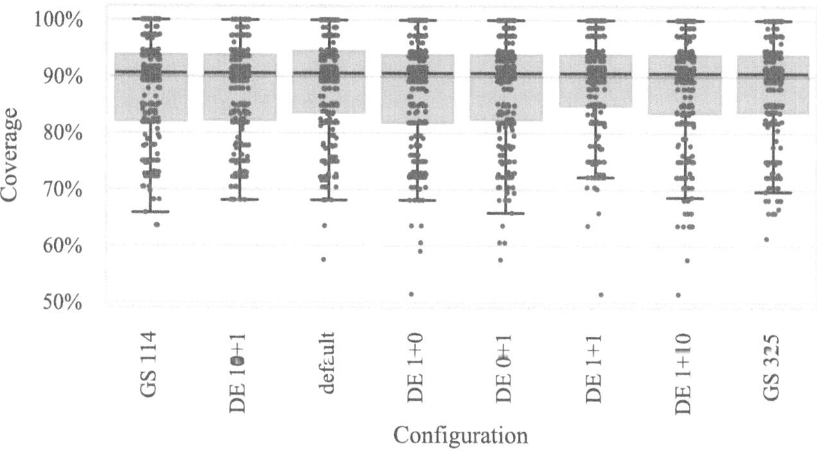

Fig. 4. Coverage distributions for the best MIO configurations.

The results of both algorithms, DynaMOSA performing better than MIO, are in line with previous research [10,28]. However, there also exists research that states the opposite [2]. We hypothesise that the choice of subjects plays a large role in this: the subjects we chose are from libraries. Since the test generation works on module level the number of goals per individual subject is not huge. MIO was designed for subjects with many *independent* goals, e.g., to generate system tests. Its computationally cheap evolution step allows it to explore much larger parts of the fitness landscape in the same time than the computationally costly DynaMOSA. Important to this hypothesis is probably the term *independent*: DynaMOSA's optimisation over its predecessor, MOSA [34], was that it used a structural property of the subject, the nesting of branches: nested branches are only relevant as goals for the search if the surrounding branch was covered, i.e., there exists a test case in the population that evaluates the branch's condition to true. MIO's underlying assumption is the independence of the goals, which is obviously not given for nested branches. MIO always takes all goals into account, although the nested ones might not even be reachable and thus irrelevant. This can cause a considerable waste of computational resources. However, future research is necessary to test this hypothesis.

4.4 RQ2: Tuning Costs

Hyperparameter tuning is a time-consuming task [13]. Thus, if one wants to invest the resources, it is advisable to choose a tuning method that ekes the resources and yields high-quality results. We study the amount of resources consumed in order to provide recommendations for the best tuning method. We report PYNGUIN's total runtime here, which does not include, e.g., the overhead for running Docker. While we admit that the overhead is considerable, we assume it as almost constant and not influencing the tuning itself.

Table 2. Best hyperparameter settings for MIO per tuning fitness function.

Configuration	l_c	F	Exploration			Exploitation		
			$\|T_k\|$	P_r	n_m	$\|T_k\|$	P_r	n_m
DE 1+1	48	0.762	24	0.673	1	1	0	5
DE 1+10	12	0.092 6	16	0.728	6	1	0	1
DE 1+0	28	0.092 9	1	0.023 2	6	1	0	2
DE 10+1	17	0.295	24	0.312	7	1	0	4
DE 0+1	35	0.078 4	16	0.333	1	1	0	13
default	40	0.500	10	0.500	1	1	0	10
GS 114	10	0.0	10	0.667	1	1	0	10
GS 325	10	0.250	1	0.333	1	1	0	1

chromosome length l_c, phase switch F, number of tests per target $|T_k|$, probability of random sampling a new test case P_r, number of mutations n_m.

Table 3. Branch and relative coverage for DynaMOSA compared to the default configuration, together with their respective effect sizes and $p-$value

Configuration	Branch Coverage			Relative Coverage		
	mean %	$\hat{A}_{12}$	$p-$value	mean %	$\hat{A}_{12}$	$p-$value
default	88.9	—	—	71.3	—	—
DE 1+1	90.6	0.557	0.013 5	83.7	0.578	4.78×10^{-5}
DE 1+10	90.3	0.548	0.036 4	82.1	0.570	0.000 274
DE 1+0	91.1	0.567	0.003 40	85.8	0.591	1.54×10^{-6}
DE 10+1	90.7	0.557	0.012 8	82.3	0.571	0.000 213
DE 0+1	90.8	0.564	0.005 38	84.7	0.583	1.25×10^{-5}
GS	90.4	0.546	0.043 5	81.9	0.562	0.001 44

For the *MIO* tuning, grid search consumed a total amount of 9 440 d. Because of the five different fitness functions for the differential evolution tuning, it was necessary to execute differential evolution five times, each time with another fitness function. This is not required for grid search, because the selection of the best can be done after all raw data has been computed. For DE 1+1, running the tuning lasted for 766 d; DE 1+0 consumed 576 d, DE 0+1 consumed 384 d, DE 10+1 consumed 385 d, and DE 1+10 consumed 1 150 d. Still, the time required for grid search is almost thrice the time required to run *all* differential evolution.

For the *DynaMOSA* tuning, grid search ran for 4 800 d. Differential evolution consumed 1 780 d for DE 1+1, 1 550 d for DE 1+0, 2 350 d for DE 0+1, 1 110 d for DE 10+1, and 1 990 d for DE 1+10. Due to the shorter runtime of grid search and the higher runtime of differential evolution, compared to MIO, executing all five variants of differential evolution takes longer than grid search; however, an

Table 4. Branch and relative coverage for MIO compared to the default configuration, together with their respective effect sizes and $p-$values.

Configuration	Branch Coverage			Relative Coverage		
	mean %	$\hat{A}_{12}$	$p-$value	mean %	$\hat{A}_{12}$	$p-$value
default	88.7	—	—	77.4	—	—
DE 1+1	88.8	0.498	0.921	78.3	0.509	0.676
DE 1+10	88.3	0.494	0.790	76.3	0.502	0.924
DE 1+0	88.0	0.487	0.564	72.7	0.475	0.239
DE 10+1	88.2	0.486	0.549	74.7	0.483	0.424
DE 0+1	88.4	0.496	0.875	75.3	0.489	0.586
GS 114	88.1	0.481	0.405	74.0	0.477	0.285
GS 325	88.6	0.498	0.936	76.9	0.497	0.872

individual run of differential evolution only consumes between 23.1 % and 49.0 % of the time required for grid search.

RQ2 Summary

Differential evolution consumes significantly less time than grid search, while, at least for DynaMOSA, yielding better results.

Discussion: The experiments show—in line with previous research—that hyperparameter tuning is very resource intensive. The full experiment required a total runtime of Pynguin of 26 300 d, i.e., almost 72 years, which is only achievable with highly parallel computation. For a cost estimation, if we had executed the experiments on AWS-EC2 cloud services, where a comparable machine costs US-$ 0.038 4 per hour, it would have resulted in a total cost of US-$ 24 220.57. Consequently, tuning might not pay off if the test-generation algorithms only seldom run, but for frequently running algorithms, even small improvements can make a large difference over time. We believe that this is individual to the concrete use case and cannot be decided in a study like this.

5 Related Work

Many studies indicate the necessity of hyperparameter tuning in various fields and also its effectiveness [17,18,41]. Some authors use random search to tune hyperparameters [9,41,42], while we decided to use an exhaustive technique, grid search, and a non-exhaustive technique, differential evolution. Hyperparameter tuning of EAs is a well-studied problem. Aspects, such as the methods to control and set their parameters [14] or various methods to tune the parameter of a standard genetic algorithm for continuous function optimisation [31] have been explored. While these works target different aspects than ours, they also show that tuning the algorithm is a necessary task because its performance is impacted by many factors, such as parallel programming, genetic encoding, goal selection, or termination characteristics [32]. These factors even indicate the future work for test-generation shall incorporate more factors.

Closest to our work are the studies by Arcuri and Fraser [4] and Kotelyanskii and Kapfhammer [23]: the former apply parameter tuning to EvoSuite and their results indicate that the default parameter values in the literature perform reasonably well for test generation, however, tuning is acceptable for researchers and can lead to improved performance [4,5]. The latter use the sequential parameter optimisation toolbox (SPOT) [6] to tune EvoSuite with similar results as Arcuri and Fraser [23]. Previous studies on Pynguin [27,28] used default parameters, but our study suggests that better parameter-value choices exist.

Parameter control is complementary approach to improve an algorithm's performance: while tuning is applied before running the algorithm, parameter control adjusts the parameter values during the algorithm's runtime [13]. Parameter control has also been applied in search-based software testing [1,36,38]. Since tuning is extremely time-consuming, parameter control may be a more practical solution [13,37]. An alternative to reduce the costs of tuning lies in predicting the possible performance gain before applying tuning [43].

6 Conclusions

We applied hyperparameter tuning to the DynaMOSA and MIO test-generation algorithms in the Pynguin framework. Our results show that tuning MIO did not result in an improvement in terms of coverage, independently of the tuning method used. However, for tuning DynaMOSA, we were able to achieve significant improvements in terms of coverage over the default hyperparameter settings in Pynguin. Differential evolution yielded the best results overall while requiring significantly fewer computational resources, compared to grid search. Future work will include comparing these findings with other tuning techniques and popular tuning frameworks such as SPOT [6], ParamILS [22], or irace [25].

References

1. Almulla, H.K., Gay, G.: Learning how to search: generating effective test cases through adaptive fitness function selection. Empir. Softw. Eng. **27**(2), 38 (2022). https://doi.org/10.1007/s10664-021-10048-8
2. Arcuri, A.: Test suite generation with the many independent objective (MIO) algorithm. Inf. Softw. Technol. **104**, 195–206 (2018). https://doi.org/10.1016/j.infsof.2018.05.003
3. Arcuri, A., Briand, L.C.: A hitchhiker's guide to statistical tests for assessing randomized algorithms in software engineering. Softw. Test. Verification Reliab. **24**(3), 219–250 (2014). https://doi.org/10.1002/stvr.1486
4. Arcuri, A., Fraser, G.: On parameter tuning in search based software engineering. In: Proceedings of the SSBSE 2011. LNCS, vol. 6956, pp. 33–47. Springer, Heidelberg (2011). https://doi.org/10.1007/978-3-642-23716-4_6

5. Arcuri, A., Fraser, G.: Parameter tuning or default values? An empirical investigation in search-based software engineering. Empir. Softw. Eng. **18**(3), 594–623 (2013). https://doi.org/10.1007/s10664-013-9249-9
6. Bartz-Beielstein, T.: SPOT: an R package for automatic and interactive tuning of optimization algorithms by sequential parameter optimization. CoRR abs/1006.4645 (2010)
7. Bellman, R.E.: Dynamic Programming. Princeton University Press (1957)
8. Bellman, R.E.: Adaptive Control Processes: A Guided Tour. Princeton University Press (1961)
9. Bergstra, J., Bengio, Y.: Random search for hyper-parameter optimization. J. Mach. Learn. Res. **13**, 281–305 (2012). https://doi.org/10.5555/2503308.2188395
10. Campos, J., Ge, Y., Albunian, N., Fraser, G., Eler, M., Arcuri, A.: An empirical evaluation of evolutionary algorithms for unit test suite generation. Inf. Softw. Technol. **104**, 207–235 (2018). https://doi.org/10.1016/j.infsof.2018.08.010
11. Daka, E., Campos, J., Fraser, G., Dorn, J., Weimer, W.: Modeling readability to improve unit tests. In: Proceedings ESEC/FSE, pp. 107–118. ACM (2015). https://doi.org/10.1145/2786805.2786838
12. Das, S., Mullick, S.S., Suganthan, P.N.: Recent advances in differential evolution - an updated survey. Swarm Evol. Comput. **27**, 1–30 (2016). https://doi.org/10.1016/J.SWEVO.2016.01.004
13. Eiben, A.E., Hinterding, R., Michalewicz, B.: Parameter control in evolutionary algorithms. IEEE Trans. Evol. Comput. **3**(2), 124–141 (1999). https://doi.org/10.1109/4235.771166
14. Eiben, A.E., Michalewicz, Z., Schoenauer, M., Smith, J.E.: Parameter control in evolutionary algorithms. In: Parameter Settings in Evolutionary Algorithms, Studies in Computational Intelligence, vol. 54, pp. 19–46. Springer (2007). https://doi.org/10.1007/978-3-540-69432-8_2
15. Fraser, G., Arcuri, A.: Evosuite: automatic test suite generation for object-oriented software. In: Proceedings ESEC/FSE, pp. 416–419. ACM (2011). https://doi.org/10.1145/2025113.2025179
16. Fraser, G., Arcuri, A.: Whole test suite generation. IEEE Trans. Software Eng. **39**(2), 276–291 (2013). https://doi.org/10.1109/TSE.2012.14
17. Fu, W., Menzies, T.: Easy over hard: a case study on deep learning. In: Proceedings ESEC/FSE, pp. 49–60. ACM (2017). https://doi.org/10.1145/3106237.3106256
18. Fu, W., Menzies, T., Shen, X.: Tuning for software analytics: is it really necessary? Inf. Softw. Technol. **76**, 135–146 (2016). https://doi.org/10.1016/j.infsof.2016.04.017
19. Fu, W., Nair, V., Menzies, T.: Why is differential evolution better than grid search for tuning defect predictors? CoRR abs/1609.02613 (2016)
20. Herlihy, M., Shavit, N.: The Art of Multiprocessor Programming. Elsevier (2012)
21. Huang, C., Yao, X., Li, Y.: A survey of automatic parameter tuning methods for metaheuristics. IEEE Trans. Evol. Comput. **24**(2), 201–216 (2020). https://doi.org/10.1109/TEVC.2019.2921598
22. Hutter, F., Hoos, H.H., Leyton-Brown, K., Stützle, T.: ParamILS: an automatic algorithm configuration framework. J. Artif. Intell. Res. **36**, 267–306 (2009). https://doi.org/10.1613/JAIR.2861
23. Kotelyanskii, A., Kapfhammer, G.M.: Parameter tuning for search-based test-data generation revisited: support for previous results. In: Proceedings QSIC, pp. 79–84. IEEE (2014). https://doi.org/10.1109/QSIC.2014.43

24. Lemieux, C., Inala, J.P., Lahiri, S.K., Sen, S.: CodaMOSA: escaping coverage plateaus in test generation with pre-trained large language models. In: Proceedings ICSE, pp. 919–931. IEEE (2023). https://doi.org/10.1109/ICSE48619.2023.00085
25. López-Ibáñez, M., Dubois-Lacoste, J., Cáceres, L.P., Birattari, M., Stützle, T.: The irace package: iterated racing for automatic algorithm configuration. Oper. Res. Perspect. **3**, 43–58 (2016). https://doi.org/10.1016/j.orp.2016.09.002
26. Lukasczyk, S., Fraser, G.: Pynguin: automated unit test generation for Python. In: Proceedings ICSE Companion, pp. 168–172. IEEE/ACM (2022). https://doi.org/10.1145/3510454.3516829
27. Lukasczyk, S., Kroiß, F., Fraser, G.: Automated unit test generation for Python. In: Proceedings of the SSBSE 2020. LNCS, vol. 12420, pp. 9–24. Springer, Cham (2020). https://doi.org/10.1007/978-3-030-59762-7_2
28. Lukasczyk, S., Kroiß, F., Fraser, G.: An empirical study of automated unit test generation for Python. Empir. Softw. Eng. **28**(2), 36:1–36:46 (2023). https://doi.org/10.1007/s10664-022-10248-w
29. Mann, H.B., Whitney, D.R.: On a test of whether one of two random variables is stochastically larger than the other. Ann. Math. Stat. **18**(1), 50–60 (1947). https://doi.org/10.1214/aoms/1177730491
30. McMinn, P.: Search-based software test data generation: a survey. Softw. Test. Verification Reliab. **14**(2), 105–156 (2004). https://doi.org/10.1002/stvr.294
31. Montero, E., Riff, M., Neveu, B.: A beginner's guide to tuning methods. Appl. Soft Comput. **17**, 39–51 (2014). https://doi.org/10.1016/J.ASOC.2013.12.017
32. Mosayebi, M., Sodhi, M.: Tuning genetic algorithm parameters using design of experiments. In: Proceedings GECCO, pp. 1937–1944. ACM (2020). https://doi.org/10.1145/3377929.3398136
33. Neri, F., Tirronen, V.: Recent advances in differential evolution: a survey and experimental analysis. Artif. Intelli. Rev. **33**(1–2), 61–106 (2010). https://doi.org/10.1007/S10462-009-9137-2
34. Panichella, A., Kifetew, F.M., Tonella, P.: Reformulating branch coverage as a many-objective optimization problem. In: Proceedings ICST, pp. 1–10. IEEE Computer Society (2015). https://doi.org/10.1109/ICST.2015.7102604
35. Panichella, A., Kifetew, F.M., Tonella, P.: Automated test case generation as a many-objective optimisation problem with dynamic selection of the targets. IEEE Trans. Software Eng. **44**(2), 122–158 (2018). https://doi.org/10.1109/TSE.2017.2663435
36. Poulding, S.M., Clark, J.A., Waeselynck, H.: A principled evaluation of the effect of directed mutation on search-based statistical testing. In: Proceedings ICST Workshops, pp. 184–193. IEEE Computer Society (2011). https://doi.org/10.1109/ICSTW.2011.36
37. Preuss, M., Rudolph, G., Wessing, S.: Tuning optimization algorithms for real-world problems by means of surrogate modeling. In: Proceedings GECCO, pp. 401–408. ACM (2010). https://doi.org/10.1145/1830483.1830558
38. Ribeiro, J.C.B., Zenha-Rela, M., de Vega, F.F.: Adaptive evolutionary testing: an adaptive approach to search-based test case generation for object-oriented software. In: Proceedings NICSO. SCI, vol. 284, pp. 185–197. Springer (2010). https://doi.org/10.1007/978-3-642-12538-6_16
39. Storn, R., Price, K.V.: Differential evolution - a simple and efficient heuristic for global optimization over continuous spaces. J. Glob. Optim. **11**(4), 341–359 (1997). https://doi.org/10.1023/A:1008202821328

40. Vargha, A., Delaney, H.D.: A critique and improvement of the CL common language effect size statistics of McGraw and Wong. J. Educ. Behav. Stat. **25**(2), 101–132 (2000). https://doi.org/10.3102/10769986025002101
41. Villalobos-Arias, L., Quesada-López, C.: Comparative study of random search hyper-parameter tuning for software effort estimation. In: Proceedings PROMISE, pp. 21–29. ACM (2021). https://doi.org/10.1145/3475960.3475986
42. Villalobos-Arias, L., Quesada-López, C., Guevara-Coto, J., Martínez, A., Jenkins, M.: Evaluating hyper-parameter tuning using random search in support vector machines for software effort estimation. In: Proceedings PROMISE, pp. 31–40. ACM (2020). https://doi.org/10.1145/3416508.3417121
43. Zamani, S., Hemmati, H.: A pragmatic approach for hyper-parameter tuning in search-based test case generation. Empir. Softw. Eng. **26**(6), 1–35 (2021). https://doi.org/10.1007/s10664-021-10024-2

Search-Based Inference of Class Invariants: How Far Can Simulated Annealing Take Us?

Juan Manuel Copia[1,2], Facundo Molina[1(✉)], Alessandra Gorla[1], Nazareno Aguirre[3,4,5], and Pablo Ponzio[3,4]

[1] IMDEA Software Institute, Madrid, Spain
facundo.molina@imdea.org
[2] Universidad Politécnica de Madrid, Madrid, Spain
[3] Universidad Nacional de Río Cuarto, Río Cuarto, Argentina
[4] CONICET, Buenos Aires, Argentina
[5] Guangdong Technion-Israel Institute of Technology, Shantou, China

Abstract. Many formal verification and software testing techniques rely on repOK routines to verify the consistency and validity of software components with complex data representations. For a given class under analysis, a repOK encodes its so-called *class invariant*, i.e., the state properties required on an instance for it to be considered a valid object of the class. While repOK routines can enable early error detection and simplify debugging, writing correct and complete repOKs can be challenging, even for advanced Large Language Models (LLMs). This paper explores the effectiveness of search-based techniques to automatically generate class invariants in the form of imperative repOKs.

We perform an evaluation using Express, a recent simulated annealing-based framework that automatically generates repOKs, on a set of 7 Java classes from widely-used libraries, and show that the framework can generate *correct repOKs for all cases*, ensuring no valid instances are erroneously discarded. Furthermore, Express produces *complete* repOKs in 3 out of 7 cases. Combining Express with an LLM further enhances effectiveness, generating *correct* and *complete* repOK routines for 5 out of 7 subjects. In addition, Express yields more complete invariants (i.e., it generates stronger properties) than the best related approach in 5 out of 7 cases. These results highlight the potential of search-based techniques for automating consistency checks in software systems, bridging gaps in current manual and automated software analyses.

1 Introduction

Software reliability is a core aspect of software quality, and a primary concern in software engineering [19]. Advances in automated program analysis have enabled the efficient creation of extensive program input sets as well as the examination

M. Wagner and M. Zhang (Eds.): SSBSE 2025, LNCS 16228, pp. 82–96, 2026.
https://doi.org/10.1007/978-3-032-24839-8_6

of large-scale program executions [7,15,33,35], facilitating automated reliability analyses. However, determining whether automatically generated executions exhibit correct behavior or uncover defects requires a formal specification of the program's intended behavior. This challenge, commonly referred to as the oracle problem [5], remains a significant problem in software testing.

In object-oriented design, where the software is organized into classes, intended behavior can be specified through constructs such as preconditions, postconditions, and class invariants [22,25]. *Class invariants* are particularly important because they define constraints on the state of a class's objects that must hold true throughout the object's lifecycle. For instance, a class invariant might specify that a list-based object representation does not contain duplicate elements, or that a queue's maximum capacity must not be exceeded. Class invariants can be captured by so-called *repOK routines*, methods that check whether receiver objects satisfy their corresponding class invariants [22]. These routines can be used to check the internal consistency of objects during testing, debugging and run-time monitoring, and have proved to be very valuable for test generation [3,7,11,23], bug detection [21,33], and verification [12,16,17,21], among other tasks. Despite their usefulness and effectiveness for automated analysis, formal class invariant specification is complex, and thus class invariants are often only informally specified as ambiguous natural language comments, limiting practical utility for automated analysis.

To address this gap, various techniques have been proposed to automatically infer specifications, including class invariants [4,6,9,13,14,18,24,26–28,30,38,40]. Most of these are symbolic approaches, in the sense that they infer the invariants using a pre-defined set of rules and patterns. Daikon [14], the most prominent tool for dynamic invariant detection, leverages program executions to infer invariants from predefined templates. However, Daikon's template-based approach limits expressiveness, prompting the development of more sophisticated tools such as SpecFuzzer [27], Daryaft [24] and Express [9]. While these tools represent significant progress, the inferred invariants often fall short in practical applicability. For instance, Daikon [14] and SpecFuzzer [27] output invariants as assertion expressions, that are either limited in expressiveness or require some effort to make them executable and integrated into the codebase. Deryaft [24] generates executable repOK routines directly, but their invariants are often incomplete, lacking the expressiveness needed for real-world applications. These limitations motivated the development of EXPRESS [9], a novel framework that leverages simulated annealing to automatically generate class invariants in the form of imperative repOK routines. Given a target class and its accompanying test suite, the main goal of EXPRESS is to infer a repOK that is *correct* with respect to the test suite, meaning it does not discard any valid instance created during test execution, and that is *complete*, discarding as many invalid instances as possible. Despite its promising direction, EXPRESS has not been evaluated on real-world subjects, and its performance compared to existing techniques remains unknown.

At the same time, neural approaches, based on deep learning methods, have been less explored to infer class invariants, with only machine learning techniques being used to train binary classifiers to behave as class invariants [28,39], but not to produce executable code. Recently, more advanced neural techniques, based on state-of-the-art Large Language Models (LLMs) have been successfully applied to derive other kind of specifications [13,29,31,36]. For instance, nlp2postcondition [13] generates postcondition assertions by using a zero-shot prompt template to instruct chat-based LLMs (such as GPT-4 [32]). Tratto [31] implements a neuro-symbolic approach to derive axiomatic test oracles, leveraging large code models (such as Code Llama [37]), to produce oracles in a token-by-token fashion. These advances suggest that LLM-based neural techniques, including neuro-symbolic approaches that combine LLMs with symbolic reasoning, can be effective in inferring class invariants as well. To the best of our knowledge, no such techniques have been proposed yet.

In this paper, we aim to study the effectiveness of search-based methods to automatically infer class invariants in the form of imperative repOK routines, and how it compares with other symbolic and neural approaches. Concretely, we evaluate EXPRESS, a simulated annealing-based framework that automatically generates repOK methods, on a set of 7 Java classes from widely-used libraries, to understand how correct and complete the generated repOK routines are. More precisely, we compare EXPRESS with Daikon, a well-known symbolic invariant inference tool, and with GPT-4, a state-of-the art neural approach.

Our results show that EXPRESS can generate correct repOK routines for all the analyzed subjects, while producing complete repOK routines for 3 subjects, outperforming related techniques. Moreover, we show that invariants produced by LLM-based neural approaches can complement invariants generated by EXPRESS, producing correct and complete repOK routines for 5 subjects. This provides initial evidence that hybrid approaches combining search-based symbolic techniques and neural methods can improve class invariant inference.

2 Background

2.1 Class Invariants and RepOK Routines

Class invariants are formal conditions that must hold true for an object for it to be considered valid, serving as a foundation for reasoning about the correctness of a class's implementation and playing a critical role in automated analyses such as testing, debugging, and verification.

As an example, consider the `LinkedList` class in Fig. 1, a simplified version of the implementation in the `java.util` package. This class represents sequences of elements using a doubly-linked list, with two primary fields: `header`, pointing to the first element, and `size`, storing the number of elements. Each list element is represented by an `Entry` object, containing the fields `element`, `next`, and `previous`. From the fields alone, the developer's intent regarding the data structure's constraints may not be immediately clear. However, such intent can often be inferred from the behavior of the class's methods. If the programmer

```
public class Entry {
    private Entry next, previous;
    private Object element;
    ...
}

public class LinkedList {
    private Entry header;
    private int size;

    public boolean repOK() { return isCircular() && isSizeOk(); }

    public boolean isCircular() {
        Set<Entry> visited = new HashSet<Entry>();
        if (header == null) return false;
        visited.add(header);
        Entry current = header;
        while (true) {
            Entry next = current.next;
            if (next == null) return false;
            if (next.previous != current) return false;
            current = next;
            if (!visited.add(next)) break;
        }
        if (current != header) return false;
        return true;
    }
    ...
```

Fig. 1. LinkedList class declaration and its class invariant.

intended the list to be cyclic, the class invariant must ensure that the list forms a closed loop (the `next` and `previous` pointers are consistent). Figure 1 demonstrates how such a circularity check can be implemented as a `repOK`.

In this paper, we study the challenge of automatically generating class invariants for Java classes, expressed as imperative routines. We study the generation of *correct* and *complete*, executable invariants, which can enhance automated analyses, and enable robust and scalable reliability assessments.

2.2 Simulated Annealing

EXPRESS, the search-based tool we consider in this paper, is based on simulated annealing [20]. Simulated annealing is a probabilistic optimization algorithm that explores a search space by iteratively mutating candidate solutions and evaluating them based on an objective function. The algorithm begins with a random feasible solution and generates new candidates by applying small modifications. A candidate solution is accepted based on the following criteria:

- **Improvement in the objective function:** If the new solution improves the objective function value, it is always accepted.
- **Acceptance of worse solutions:** To escape local minima, worse solutions are also accepted, with the acceptance probability given by:

$$P(\text{accept}) = \exp\left(-\Delta f / T\right),$$

where $\Delta f = f_{\text{candidate}} - f_{\text{current}}$ represents the change in the objective function value, and T is the *temperature*, a control parameter that determines the likelihood of accepting worse solutions.

The temperature follows a predefined cooling schedule (e.g., linear decay), gradually reducing T over time. As T decreases, the algorithm shifts from exploration to refinement, focusing on optimizing the best solutions found so far.

3 Evaluating Simulated Annealing for Class Invariant Inference

To assess search-based inference of class invariants, and compare it with other approaches, we perform an empirical evaluation using EXPRESS as a representative search-based technique for class invariant inference. We conduct a series of experiments focused on the following research questions:

RQ1 *How effective is search-based class invariant inference?*
RQ2 *How does search-based class invariant inference compare with related approaches?*

RQ1 analyzes the effectiveness of a search-based technique – EXPRESS – to generate class invariants for a set of Java classes, while RQ2 compares search-based class invariant inference with two related approaches: Daikon [14], a well-established and widely used dynamic invariant detection tool, and OpenAI's GPT-4 [32], a state-of-the-art LLM. A replication package for all the experiments in the paper and additional experimental data can be found in [2].

3.1 Experimental Setup

Subjects. We analyze seven Java classes with diverse class invariants for which ground truth invariants are already known [8]. These classes are: `LinkedList`, `HashMap`, and `TreeMap` from the `java.util` package of the Java Standard Library; `NodeCachingLinkedList` (NCLL), a specialized linked list implementation from Apache Commons Collections; and classes `AvlTree`, `BinomialHeap`, and `Schedule`, used in prior research on automated verification [8,10].

Approaches. We consider three approaches for class invariant inference:

- EXPRESS: The simulated annealing based approach, representative of search-based inference. To run EXPRESS, we first generate a diverse set of valid instances, using EvoSuite [15], a state-of-the-art test generation tool that produces test suites optimized for code coverage. Since EvoSuite generates minimal test suites, we manually added an average of 12 additional test cases per class to increase instance diversity. EXPRESS executes these tests and collects the generated instances as the set of valid states, which are then mutated to produce invalid instances. EXPRESS then runs its search process

to generate a `repOK` that classifies the instances. The parameter values for EXPRESS, including the initial temperature, cooling schedule, and number of mutations for generating invalid instances, were selected by experimenting with different configurations, and selecting the best-performing one: 15.0 as initial temperature, an exponential cooling schedule with a cooling rate of 0.005, and 9 mutations per valid instance to generate invalid ones.
- Daikon: A well-known dynamic invariant detection tool that infers invariants from a set of test cases. To ensure a fair comparison, we execute Daikon from exactly the same test suite used for EXPRESS. Since Daikon expresses invariants in a textual format, we manually converted them into imperative repOKs for direct evaluation.
- GPT-4: A state-of-the-art LLM, used as a representative of neural approaches for class invariant inference. We use GPT-4 through ChatGPT [1], OpenAI's web interface, using a zero-shot prompting approach, and providing the model with the complete implementation of the target class, including comments. We query the model once per subject and use its output without further modifications, as it consistently produces repOK routines. While more sophisticated prompting techniques could be explored, this is beyond the scope of this work. The prompt we use is available on the paper's website [2].

Metrics. To evaluate the approaches, we compare the inferred invariants against ground truth invariants using Korat [7], a bounded exhaustive input generation tool. Given a class and its ground truth invariant, we collect all valid and invalid instances explored by Korat within a scope of 9, except for HashMap, where we use a scope of 3 due to the large number of generated instances.

We assess each inferred `repOK` using standard classification metrics, based on the following cases. *True Positive (TP)*: A valid instance correctly classified as valid (`repOK` returns `true`). *False Positive (FP)*: An invalid instance incorrectly classified as valid. *True Negative (TN)*: An invalid instance correctly classified as invalid (`repOK` returns `false`). *False Negative (FN)*: A valid instance incorrectly classified as invalid. From these values, we compute Precision, Recall and Accuracy as follows: Precision, computed as $Precision = TP/(TP{+}FP)$, measures the proportion of all instances predicted as valid that are actually valid. That is, the higher the precision of the inferred invariants, the more *complete* they are (fewer FPs). Recall, computed as $Recall = TP/(TP{+}FN)$, measures the proportion of all valid instances that were correctly predicted as valid. That is, the higher the recall of the inferred invariants, the more *correct* they are (less FNs). Finally, accuracy, computed as $Accuracy = (TP{+}TN)/(TP{+}TN{+}FP{+}FN)$, measures the proportion of all instances that are correctly classified.

3.2 Effectiveness of Search-Based Class Invariant Inference (RQ1)

Table 1 summarizes the results of the effectiveness of the search-based class invariant inference performed by EXPRESS. For each subject, we report the number of valid and invalid instances generated from the ground truth (using Korat). We also report the number of true positives (TP), true negatives (TN), false positives (FP), and false negatives (FN), and the precision, recall, and accuracy of

Table 1. Effectiveness of EXPRESS to generate class invariants.

Subject	Input Instances		Effectiveness						
	#Valid	#Invalid	TP	TN	FP	FN	Prec.(%)	Rec.(%)	Acc.(%)
TreeMap	4880	1655572	4880	1651219	4353	0	52.9	100	99.7
Schedule	89958	333585	89958	333249	336	0	99.6	100	99.9
HashMap	22136	177371936	22136	174083876	3288060	0	0.7	100	98.1
LinkedList	9	231	9	231	0	0	100	100	100
AvlTree	2698	616347	2698	613236	3111	0	46.4	100	99.5
BinomialHeap	1749224	920023	1749224	717737	202286	0	89.6	100	92.4
NCLL	660	1309	660	1309	0	0	100	100	100

the inferred invariants. Remarkably, EXPRESS produces no false negatives for all subjects, indicating that the inferred class invariants never reject valid instances. Hence, EXPRESS achieves perfect recall in all subjects. In other words, all properties included in the repOKs generated by EXPRESS are correct. This is an important feature of the approach, since it means that the user does not have to debug and manually fix incorrect properties in the inferred repOKs. Notice that, this can be attributed to the design of EXPRESS's simulated annealing algorithm, which aims to prioritize the avoidance of false negatives.

Precision, however, is affected by false positives: invalid instances that are incorrectly accepted by the inferred invariants. Less than 100% precision indicates that some properties of the class's representation invariant remain unlearned. This is expected, as the search space for invariants is vast, and certain properties are difficult to discover without improving EXPRESS's search process.

EXPRESS achieves over 89% precision in 4 out of 7 classes, with perfect precision in the `LinkedList` and `NCLL` subjects. The low precision observed for `HashMap` is not a reflection of poor performance by EXPRESS; instead, it is due to the significant imbalance between valid instances and invalid instances, in the space of instances generated by Korat for `HashMap`. However, as we show in the next section, where we analyze the properties of the ground truth invariants that each tool learns in our case studies, EXPRESS learns most of the expected properties, even for the `HashMap` subject.

To conclude, it is important to mention that the average runtime for generating invariants using EXPRESS was 13 min. In the worst case, EXPRESS took 25 min. We believe the running times are reasonable for the task of learning high quality (i.e., sound and reasonably complete) representation invariants. The running times for all case studies are reported in the paper's website [2].

3.3 Search-based Class Invariant Inference Compared with Related Techniques (RQ2)

The results of the comparison between EXPRESS, Daikon and ChatGPT are summarized in Table 2. Among the three approaches, Daikon produces the most imprecise class invariants. While it achieves perfect recall for four subjects, it

Table 2. Comparison of EXPRESS with Daikon and ChatGPT.

Subject	Approach	Performance Precision (%)	Recall (%)	Accuracy (%)
		LinkedList		
LinkedList	Daikon	10.0	100	66.2
	ChatGPT	90.0	100	99.6
	EXPRESS	100	100	100
	EXPRESS+ChatGPT	100	100	100
		NodeCachingLinkedList		
NCLL	Daikon	39.4	100	48.5
	ChatGPT	-	-	-
	EXPRESS	100	100	100
	EXPRESS+ChatGPT	100	100	100
		AvlTree		
AvlTree	Daikon	1.2	100	63.3
	ChatGPT	100	100	100
	EXPRESS	46.4	100	99.5
	EXPRESS+ChatGPT	100	100	100
		Schedule		
Schedule	Daikon	23.4	73.0	43.6
	ChatGPT	23.7	100	31.6
	EXPRESS	99.6	100	99.9
	EXPRESS+ChatGPT	100	100	100
		TreeMap		
TreeMap	Daikon	0.9	100	65.8
	ChatGPT	100	100	100
	EXPRESS	52.9	100	99.7
	EXPRESS+ChatGPT	100	100	100
		HashMap		
HashMap	Daikon	0.5	80.9	98.0
	ChatGPT	0.4	100	96.5
	EXPRESS	0.7	100	98.1
	EXPRESS+ChatGPT	0.7	100	98.1
		BinomialHeap		
BinomialHeap	Daikon	74.9	99.8	77.9
	ChatGPT	-	-	-
	EXPRESS	89.6	100	92.4
	EXPRESS+ChatGPT	89.6	100	92.4

has a very low precision, ranging from 0.5% to 39.4% in 6 out of 7 cases. In other words, Daikon is not capable of learning most of the properties of the repOKs in our ground truth, making it the least effective approach. Moreover, there was no class for which Daikon inferred a correct and complete class invariant.

GPT-4 achieves good results, generating sound and complete invariants in 2 subjects, `AvlTree` and `TreeMap`. It produces class invariants with a perfect recall in 5 out of 7 subjects. However, as expected, GPT-4 generates repOK methods with errors, in particular issues that cause the execution of repOK to get stuck in infinite loops while traversing the object state. This happened for two classes, `BinomialHeap` and `NCLL`. In these cases, the invariants are not useful without manual fixes from the developer, or further processing to remove the errors. In summary, EXPRESS outperforms GPT-4, as it generates better invariants in 5 out of 7 cases (including two cases where GPT-4 generates completely unsound invariants), whereas GPT-4 generates better invariants in 2 cases.

Express+GPT-4. This technique combines the invariants generated by GPT-4 and EXPRESS. It operates by first invoking the `repOK` of EXPRESS to check if the structure is valid. If EXPRESS identifies a violation of the invariant, `false` is returned. Otherwise, the result of the `repOK` generated by GPT-4 is returned. This approach leads to improvements in three subjects, `AvlTree`, `Schedule`, and `TreeMap`, where the precision of the combined invariants reaches 100%. This suggests that the invariants generated by GPT-4 can in fact complement the ones inferred by EXPRESS, and represents a promising direction for future research, where hybrid approaches can be developed to combine the strengths of search-based techniques and LLMs.

Analysis of the Inferred Invariants. To better assess invariant quality, we manually analyzed the inferred invariants in terms of the properties they express with respect to the properties in the ground truth (i.e., the *expected* properties in the real representation invariant). Table 3 summarizes the results. For each class, we manually analyzed the ground truth to extract the expected properties (Expected Property column), and analyzed whether the inferred invariants expressed such properties. We identified a total of 48 expected properties.

Daikon infers about one expected property for most of the classes, and these are properties typically related to checking for null values. This explains the very low precision exhibited by Daikon, and indicates that the predefined set of templates used by Daikon is not rich enough for it to find many important properties of complex representation invariants.

GPT-4 is able to infer many of the expected properties, inferring all of them for `AvlTree` and `TreeMap`. In the remaining subjects, GPT-4 misses some of the properties, which is also consistent with the precision results in Table 3. In total, GPT-4 infers 30 out of the 48 expected properties. It is important to recall that GPT-4 yields invariants with errors for `BinomialHeap` and `NCLL`, hence we cannot consider that it learns any useful property in those cases.

Surprisingly, EXPRESS is able to infer a larger number of expected properties compared to Daikon and GPT-4. It generates *all* the properties in two cases, and most of the properties in the remaining ones. In total, EXPRESS generates 40 out of the 48 expected properties, which is a significant improvement over the other approaches. Furthermore, the combined technique EXPRESS+GPT-4 is able to capture 46 out of the 48 expected properties. Some examples of the properties that EXPRESS cannot infer are balance properties of tree structures (`TreeMap`, `AvlTree` and `BinomialHeap`), and that the keys of `TreeMap`, `AvlTree` must be stored in sorted order. These are complex properties that would require the addition of more sophisticated mutators (and traversals) to EXPRESS's algo-

Table 3. Properties inferred by each approach.

Subject	Expected Property	Daikon	ChatGPT	Express	Express+GPT
Treemap	Is acyclic binary tree	✗	✓	✓	✓
	Parent of root is null	✓	✓	✓	✓
	Parent references match	✗	✓	✓	✓
	Size is consistent	✗	✓	✓	✓
	Balanced tree	✗	✓	✗	✓
	Sorted keys	✗	✓	∼	✓
AvlTree	Is acyclic binary tree	✗	✓	✓	✓
	Size is consistent	✗	✓	✓	✓
	Sorted keys	✗	✓	∼	✓
	Balanced tree	✗	✓	✗	✓
	Height fields are correct	✗	✓	∼	✓
LinkedList	Header $\neq$ null	✓	✓	✓	✓
	Previous and next match	✗	∼	✓	✓
	List is circular DLL.	✗	✓	✓	✓
	Size is consistent	✗	✓	✓	✓
NCLL	Header $\neq$ null	✓	✓	✓	✓
	Header is circular DLL.	✗	✗	✓	✓
	Size is consistent	✗	✓	✓	✓
	Cache is acyclic	✗	✗	✓	✓
	Size of cache is consistent	✗	✓	✓	✓
	No node sharing	✗	✗	✓	✓
HashMap	Buckets are acyclic	✗	✓	✓	✓
	Buckets don't share nodes	✗	∼	✓	✓
	Size is consistent	✗	✓	✓	✓
	Size $\leq$ threshold	✗	✓	✓	✓
	Keys and hashes match	∼	✓	✓	✓
	Keys are in correct bucket	✗	✗	✗	✗
	No repeated keys	✗	✓	✓	✓
Schedule	P0 = null	✓	✗	✓	✓
	P1, p2, p3, blockqueue $\neq$ null	✗	✗	✓	✓
	Queues do not share jobs	✗	✓	✓	✓
	Queues have no aliasing	✗	✗	✓	✓
	Queues are acyclic DLL	✗	✓	✓	✓
	Job.priority matches queue	✗	✓	✗	✓
	Job.val are unique	✗	✗	✓	✓
	Job.val $\geq$ 0	✗	✗	✓	✓
	CurProc is in queues	✗	✓	✓	✓
	Job.priority $\geq$ 0	✗	∼	✓	✓
	Job.priority $\leq$ MAXPRIO	✗	∼	✓	✓
	NumProc is consistent	✗	✗	✓	✓
	List.mem_count is consistent	✗	✓	✓	✓
	NumProc $\leq$ allocProcNum	✗	✓	✓	✓
BinomialHeap	Is acyclic binary tree	✗	∼	✓	✓
	Parent of root points to null	✓	✗	✓	✓
	Parent references match	✗	✓	✓	✓
	Size is consistent	✗	✓	✓	✓
	Sorted keys	✗	✗	✓	✓
	Is Binomial Heap	✗	∼	∼	∼

rithm, and better mutation approaches for primitive-typed fields. These are all interesting lines of research for future work.

Overall, these results show that EXPRESS outperforms the related approaches Daikon and GPT-4 in terms of the number of (expected) properties inferred. Taken together with the precision numbers from Table 3 we can conclude that EXPRESS is the approach that learns the more complete invariants in this evaluation. In addition, combining the invariants inferred by EXPRESS with GPT-4's invariants can lead to more complete sets of properties.

4 Threats to Validity

Threats to external validity may arise from our experimental evaluation, which is focused on a limited number of classes, selected from previous work. Nevertheless, we believe that these classes include invariants that are representative of various types of properties, of varying complexity. As future work, we plan to extend the evaluation to classes from open-source projects, to assess the effectiveness of search-based techniques in more realistic settings. This will imply abandoning the effectiveness assessments with respect to ground truths, due to the effort and expertise that would involve expressing target invariants for arbitrary open-source projects.

5 Related Work

Several approaches have been proposed for inferring class invariants. Deryaft infers representation invariants as imperative Java methods [24], similar to EXPRESS. Like Daikon, Deryaft relies on a fixed set of predefined templates to infer properties. However, this template-based approach limits its expressiveness, making it less practical for real-world applications. Additionally, since no replication package is publicly available, we could not include it in our evaluation.

Molina et al. [28] propose a machine learning approach based on training neural networks to classify valid and invalid instances based on test executions. While effective, neural networks introduce interpretability challenges, making debugging difficult. In our experiments, we use a state-of-the-art LLM as a representative of neural approaches.

Rather than focusing on class invariants, other approaches focus on inferring other properties, such as method postconditions. SpecFuzzer [27] uses grammar-based fuzzing to generate postconditions. Similarly, EvoSpex [30] defines a classic genetic algorithm for the same task. These approaches employ a declarative language for expressing the assertions, namely a first order logic based language extended with reachability operators. Though these search-based techniques could be adapted to learn representation invariants, they are not designed for this purpose, and thus we did not include them in our evaluation. GAssert [38] is another evolutionary approach for learning assertions, which focuses on relatively simple logical and arithmetic constraints. It does not allow for quantified expressions and reachability operators, which are required to express many of the properties of representation invariants. Precis [34] infers contracts (pre and postconditions) for methods. Its target language consists of basic logical and arithmetic operators (without quantification/reachability). Finally, Natural language processing (NLP) has also been used to infer specifications from comments. Jdoctor [6] extracts executable specifications for methods from Javadoc comments. nlp2postcondition [13] use LLMs for this task. To the best of our knowledge, LLMs have not been used to generate representation invariants.

6 Conclusion

We performed a comprehensive evaluation of EXPRESS, a recent search-based approach for automatically inferring class invariants in the form of `repOK` methods. We compare EXPRESS with Daikon, a well-known approach for invariant inference, and with GPT-4, a state-of-the-art large language model (LLM).

Our evaluation, based on a set of seven classes with known class invariants, shows that EXPRESS is able to infer very precise invariants, achieving perfect recall across all studied subjects, meaning that all valid instances are correctly accepted. EXPRESS outperforms related techniques in most of our subjects in terms of precision and recall, being able to infer a larger number of properties that are expected for the target classes, and that related techniques are not able to infer. Finally, we show that combining EXPRESS's invariants with LLM-generated ones can lead to more robust and complete invariants, highlighting the potential of hybrid approaches that integrate search-based techniques with LLM-generated code. Overall, our results provide initial but strong evidence that search-based techniques can produce highly reliable class invariants.

Acknowledgments. This work is supported by the Ramón y Cajal fellowship RYC2020-030800-I, by the Spanish Government through grants TED2021-132464B-I00 (PRODIGY), PID2022-142290OB-I00 (ESPADA), and CEX2024-001471-M/funded by MICIU/AEI/10.13039/501100011033 and by the Comunidad de Madrid as part of the ASCEND project co-funded by FEDER Funds of the European Union.

References

1. OpenAI's ChatGPT (2025). https://openai.com/index/chatgpt
2. Replication package of this paper (2025). https://zenodo.org/records/17300555
3. Abad, P., et al.: Improving test generation under rich contracts by tight bounds and incremental SAT solving. In: Sixth IEEE International Conference on Software Testing, Verification and Validation, ICST 2013, 18–22 March 2013, Luxembourg, Luxembourg, pp. 21–30. IEEE Computer Society (2013). https://doi.org/10.1109/ICST.2013.46
4. Astorga, A., Saha, S., Dinkins, A., Wang, F., Madhusudan, P., Xie, T.: Synthesizing contracts correct modulo a test generator. Proc. ACM Program. Lang. **5**(OOPSLA), 1–27 (2021). https://doi.org/10.1145/3485481

5. Barr, E.T., Harman, M., McMinn, P., Shahbaz, M., Yoo, S.: The oracle problem in software testing: a survey. IEEE Trans. Software Eng. **41**(5), 507–525 (2015). https://doi.org/10.1109/TSE.2014.2372785
6. Blasi, A., et al.: Translating code comments to procedure specifications. In: Tip, F., Bodden, E. (eds.) Proceedings of the 27th ACM SIGSOFT International Symposium on Software Testing and Analysis, ISSTA 2018, 16–21 July 2018, Amsterdam, The Netherlands, pp. 242–253. ACM (2018). https://doi.org/10.1145/3213846.3213872
7. Boyapati, C., Khurshid, S., Marinov, D.: Korat: automated testing based on java predicates. In: Frankl, P.G. (ed.) Proceedings of the International Symposium on Software Testing and Analysis, ISSTA 2002, 22–24 July 2002, Roma, Italy, pp. 123–133. ACM (2002). https://doi.org/10.1145/566172.566191
8. Copia, J.M., Molina, F., Aguirre, N., Frias, M.F., Gorla, A., Ponzio, P.: Precise lazy initialization for programs with complex heap inputs. In: 34th IEEE International Symposium on Software Reliability Engineering, ISSRE 2023, 9–2 October 2023, Florence, Italy, pp. 752–762. IEEE (2023). https://doi.org/10.1109/ISSRE59848.2023.00080
9. Copia, J.M., Molina, F., Gorla, A., Ponzio, P., Aguirre, N.: Search-based inference of class invariants. In: Proceedings of the Genetic and Evolutionary Computation Conference Companion, GECCO, 14–18 July 2025, Málaga, Spain. ACM (2025)
10. Copia, J.M., Ponzio, P., Aguirre, N., Gorla, A., Frias, M.F.: LISSA: lazy initialization with specialized solver aid. In: 37th IEEE/ACM International Conference on Automated Software Engineering, ASE 2022, 10–14 October 2022, Rochester, MI, USA, pp. 1–12. ACM (2022). https://doi.org/10.1145/3551349.3556965
11. d'Amorim, M., Pacheco, C., Xie, T., Marinov, D., Ernst, M.D.: An empirical comparison of automated generation and classification techniques for object-oriented unit testing. In: 21st IEEE/ACM International Conference on Automated Software Engineering (ASE 2006), 18–22 September 2006, Tokyo, Japan, pp. 59–68. IEEE Computer Society (2006). https://doi.org/10.1109/ASE.2006.13
12. Dennis, G., Chang, F.S., Jackson, D.: Modular verification of code with SAT. In: Proceedings of the ACM/SIGSOFT International Symposium on Software Testing and Analysis, ISSTA 2006,17–20 July 2006, Portland, Maine, USA, pp. 109–120. ACM (2006). https://doi.org/10.1145/1146238.1146251
13. Endres, M., Fakhoury, S., Chakraborty, S., Lahiri, S.K.: Can large language models transform natural language intent into formal method postconditions? Proc. ACM Softw. Eng. **1**(FSE), 1889–1912 (2024). https://doi.org/10.1145/3660791
14. Ernst, M.D., et al.: The daikon system for dynamic detection of likely invariants. Sci. Comput. Program. **69**(1–3), 35–45 (2007). https://doi.org/10.1016/j.scico.2007.01.015
15. Fraser, G., Arcuri, A.: EvoSuite: automatic test suite generation for object-oriented software. In: SIGSOFT FSE, pp. 416–419. ACM (2011)
16. Furia, C.A., Nordio, M., Polikarpova, N., Tschannen, J.: AutoProof: auto-active functional verification of object-oriented programs. Int. J. Softw. Tools Technol. Transf. **19**(6), 697–716 (2017). https://doi.org/10.1007/s10009-016-0419-0
17. Galeotti, J.P., Rosner, N., Pombo, C.L., Frias, M.F.: Analysis of invariants for efficient bounded verification. In: Proceedings of the Nineteenth International Symposium on Software Testing and Analysis, ISSTA 2010, 12–16 July 2010, Trento, Italy, pp. 25–36. ACM (2010). https://doi.org/10.1145/1831708.1831712
18. Garg, A., Degiovanni, R., Molina, F., Cordy, M., Aguirre, N., Papadakis, M., Traon, Y.L.: Enabling efficient assertion inference. In: 34th IEEE International Sympo-

sium on Software Reliability Engineering, ISSRE 2023, 9–12 October 2023, Florence, Italy, pp. 623–634. IEEE (2023). https://doi.org/10.1109/ISSRE59848.2023.00039
19. Ghezzi, C., Jazayeri, M., Mandrioli, D.: Fundamentals of Software Engineering, 2nd edn. Prentice Hall PTR, Upper Saddle River (2002)
20. Kirkpatrick, S., Jr., D.G., Vecchi, M.P.: Optimization by simmulated annealing. Sci. **220**(4598), 671–680 (1983). https://doi.org/10.1126/SCIENCE.220.4598.671
21. Leavens, G.T., Cheon, Y., Clifton, C., Ruby, C., Cok, D.R.: How the design of JML accommodates both runtime assertion checking and formal verification. Sci. Comput. Program. **55**(1–3), 185–208 (2005). https://doi.org/10.1016/j.scico.2004.05.015
22. Liskov, B., Guttag, J.V.: Program Development in Java - Abstraction, Specification, and Object-Oriented Design. Addison-Wesley (2001)
23. Liu, L.L., Meyer, B., Schoeller, B.: Using contracts and Boolean queries to improve the quality of automatic test generation. In: Gurevich, Y., Meyer, B. (eds.) Tests and Proofs - 1st International Conference, TAP 2007, 12–13 February 2007, Zurich, Switzerland. Revised Papers. Lecture Notes in Computer Science, vol. 4454, pp. 114–130. Springer (2007). https://doi.org/10.1007/978-3-540-73770-4_7
24. Malik, M.Z., Pervaiz, A., Uzuncaova, E., Khurshid, S.: Deryaft: a tool for generating representation invariants of structurally complex data. In: Schäfer, W., Dwyer, M.B., Gruhn, V. (eds.) 30th International Conference on Software Engineering (ICSE 2008), 10–18 May 2008, Leipzig, Germany, pp. 859–862. ACM (2008). https://doi.org/10.1145/1368088.1368223
25. Meyer, B.: Object-Oriented Software Construction, 2nd ed. Prentice-Hall (1997)
26. Molina, F., et al.: An evolutionary approach to translating operational specifications into declarative specifications. Sci. Comput. Program. **181**, 47–63 (2019). https://doi.org/10.1016/J.SCICO.2019.05.006
27. Molina, F., d'Amorim, M., Aguirre, N.: Fuzzing class specifications. In: 44th IEEE/ACM 44th International Conference on Software Engineering, ICSE 2022, 25–27 May 2022, Pittsburgh, PA, USA, pp. 1008–1020. ACM (2022). https://doi.org/10.1145/3510003.3510120
28. Molina, F., Degiovanni, R., Ponzio, P., Regis, G., Aguirre, N., Frias, M.F.: Training binary classifiers as data structure invariants. In: Atlee, J.M., Bultan, T., Whittle, J. (eds.) Proceedings of the 41st International Conference on Software Engineering, ICSE 2019, 25–31 May 2019, Montreal, QC, Canada, pp. 759–770. IEEE/ACM (2019). https://doi.org/10.1109/ICSE.2019.00084
29. Molina, F., Gorla, A., d'Amorim, M.: Test oracle automation in the era of LLMs. ACM Trans. Softw. Eng. Methodol. (2025). https://doi.org/10.1145/3715107. just Accepted
30. Molina, F., Ponzio, P., Aguirre, N., Frias, M.F.: EvoSpex: an evolutionary algorithm for learning postconditions. In: 43rd IEEE/ACM International Conference on Software Engineering, ICSE 2021, 22–30 May 2021, Madrid, Spain, pp. 1223–1235. IEEE (2021). https://doi.org/10.1109/ICSE43902.2021.00112
31. Molinelli, D., Martin-Lopez, A., Zackrone, E., Eken, B., Ernst, M.D., Pezzè, M.: Tratto: a neuro-symbolic approach to deriving axiomatic test oracles. In: Proceedings of the 2025 International Symposium on Software Testing and Analysis, ISSTA 2025, 25–28 June 2025, Trondheim, Norway. ACM (2025)
32. OpenAI: GPT-4 technical report (2024). https://arxiv.org/abs/2303.08774
33. Pacheco, C., Lahiri, S.K., Ernst, M.D., Ball, T.: Feedback-directed random test generation. In: 29th International Conference on Software Engineering (ICSE

2007), 20–26 May 2007, Minneapolis, MN, USA, pp. 75–84. IEEE Computer Society (2007). https://doi.org/10.1109/ICSE.2007.37
34. Pasareanu, C.S.: Symbolic Execution and Quantitative Reasoning: Applications to Software Safety and Security. Synthesis Lectures on Software Engineering, Morgan & Claypool Publishers (2020). https://doi.org/10.2200/S01010ED2V01Y202005SWE006
35. Pasareanu, C.S., Visser, W., Bushnell, D.H., Geldenhuys, J., Mehlitz, P.C., Rungta, N.: Symbolic pathfinder: integrating symbolic execution with model checking for java bytecode analysis. Autom. Softw. Eng. **20**(3), 391–425 (2013). https://doi.org/10.1007/S10515-013-0122-2
36. Pei, K., Bieber, D., Shi, K., Sutton, C., Yin, P.: Can large language models reason about program invariants? In: Krause, A., Brunskill, E., Cho, K., Engelhardt, B., Sabato, S., Scarlett, J. (eds.) International Conference on Machine Learning, ICML 2023, 23–29 July 2023, Honolulu, Hawaii, USA. Proceedings of Machine Learning Research, vol. 202, pp. 27496–27520. PMLR (2023). https://proceedings.mlr.press/v202/pei23a.html
37. Rozière, B., et al.: Code Llama: open foundation models for code (2024). https://arxiv.org/abs/2308.12950
38. Terragni, V., Jahangirova, G., Tonella, P., Pezzè, M.: Evolutionary improvement of assertion oracles. In: Proceedings of the 28th ACM Joint Meeting on European Software Engineering Conference and Symposium on the Foundations of Software Engineering, ESEC/FSE 2020, pp. 1178–1189. Association for Computing Machinery, New York (2020). https://doi.org/10.1145/3368089.3409758
39. Usman, M., Wang, W., Vasic, M., Wang, K., Vikalo, H., Khurshid, S.: A study of the learnability of relational properties: model counting meets machine learning (MCML). In: Donaldson, A.F., Torlak, E. (eds.) Proceedings of the 41st ACM SIGPLAN International Conference on Programming Language Design and Implementation, PLDI 2020, 15–20 June 2020, London, UK, pp. 1098–1111. ACM (2020). https://doi.org/10.1145/3385412.3386015
40. Wei, Y., Furia, C.A., Kazmin, N., Meyer, B.: Inferring better contracts. In: Taylor, R.N., Gall, H.C., Medvidovic, N. (eds.) Proceedings of the 33rd International Conference on Software Engineering, ICSE 2011, 21–28 May 2011, Waikiki, Honolulu , HI, USA, pp. 191–200. ACM (2011). https://doi.org/10.1145/1985793.1985820

The Pursuit of Diversity: Multi-objective Testing of Deep Reinforcement Learning Agents

Antony Bartlett(✉), Cynthia Liem, and Annibale Panichella

Delft University of Technology, Delft, The Netherlands
{a.j.bartlett,c.c.s.liem,a.panichella}@tudelft.nl

Abstract. Testing deep reinforcement learning (DRL) agents in safety-critical domains requires discovering diverse failure scenarios. Existing tools such as INDAGO rely on single-objective optimization focused solely on maximizing failure counts, but this does not ensure discovered scenarios are diverse or reveal distinct error types. We introduce INDAGO-Nexus, a multi-objective search approach that jointly optimizes for failure likelihood and test scenario diversity using multi-objective evolutionary algorithms with multiple diversity metrics and Pareto front selection strategies. We evaluated INDAGO-Nexus on three DRL agents: humanoid walker, self-driving car, and parking agent. On average, INDAGO-Nexus discovers up to 83% and 40% more unique failures (test effectiveness) than INDAGO in the SDC and Parking scenarios, respectively, while reducing time-to-failure by up to 67% across all agents.

Keywords: Multi-objective search · deep reinforcement learning · surrogate models

1 Introduction

Reinforcement Learning (RL) [27], and more recently Deep Reinforcement Learning (DRL) [21], have emerged as powerful tools for automating complex tasks in dynamic and uncertain environments [22,26]. DRL agents learn through trial-and-error interactions with their environment and are increasingly deployed in Cyber-Physical Systems (CPS), such as self-driving cars (SDCs) and humanoid robots [4], where safety, reliability, and adaptability are critical.

Ensuring the reliability of DRL-based systems remains a significant challenge [2,29]. Unlike conventional software, DRL agents are opaque, stochastic, and highly sensitive to reward signals. Their behavior depends not only on a learned policy but also on vast environment and action spaces. As a result, edge-case scenarios—those most likely to trigger failures—are difficult to identify, and traditional testing approaches often fall short [29]. Real-world incidents involving autonomous agents [9,12,18] underscore the consequences of failing to detect such rare conditions during testing.

M. Wagner and M. Zhang (Eds.): SSBSE 2025, LNCS 16228, pp. 97–112, 2026.
https://doi.org/10.1007/978-3-032-24839-8_7

Simulation-based testing is a widely adopted technique for evaluating DRL agents, especially in safety-critical domains such as autonomous agents. It allows developers to generate and execute test scenarios in a controlled and reproducible setting, substantially reducing the time, cost, and safety risks of real-world testing [10,16]. A test scenario refers to a specific configuration of the environment—including initial agent state, obstacle placement, and task-specific parameters—that defines the context in which the agent is evaluated. Despite its advantages, simulation-based testing still remains resource-intensive, and exhaustive exploration of the test input space is often infeasible due to its combinatorial complexity.

To address these challenges, Biagiola and Tonella [2] proposed the use of surrogate models to guide test generation for DRL agents. Their framework, `INDAGO`, builds a surrogate model from training logs to predict whether a given test scenario is likely to cause agent failure—without executing it in simulation. `INDAGO` combines this model with two search strategies: Hill Climbing (HC) and a single-objective Genetic Algorithm (GA). Their empirical evaluation across multiple DRL tasks showed that (1) surrogate models substantially reduced simulation time, and (2) both HC and GA outperformed earlier random-search-based methods [29] in identifying more failure-inducing scenarios.

While `INDAGO` effectively increases the number of failing scenarios, it focuses solely on failure likelihood, overlooking diversity. This is a key limitation—generating more failures does not guarantee that they are distinct. Diversity is crucial in testing as it promotes broader coverage of the agent's operational space and improves the chances of uncovering unique faults, helping to address the *curse of rarity* problem [20].

In this paper, we propose `INDAGO-Nexus`, a multi-objective search framework for DRL testing that jointly optimizes for failure probability and scenario diversity. We investigate:

RQ1: *How does multi-objective search perform in finding diverse failures?*
RQ2: *How effective is* `INDAGO-Nexus` *compared to state-of-the-art* `INDAGO`*?*

To tackle this inherently multi-objective problem, we employed multi-objective evolutionary algorithms (MOEAs). MOEAs are well-suited for this task as they efficiently explore trade-offs and produce a set of Pareto-optimal solutions [6,14,15]. We experimented with two diversity metrics (Euclidean distance and PCA-based clustering), two MOEAs (NSGA-II [7] and AGE-MOEA [23]), and two Pareto-front selection strategies (highest failure likelihood and knee point [31]). We benchmarked `INDAGO-Nexus` on three DRL agents: self-driving car, humanoid walker, and parking agent.

Our results indicate `INDAGO-Nexus` discovers up to 83% and 40% more unique failures than `INDAGO` in the SDC and Parking scenarios, respectively, while reducing time-to-failure by up to 67%. Knee-point selection consistently produces the best results across most configurations, while different diversity metrics show varying effectiveness depending on the scenario.

Therefore, our contributions are:

- We propose `INDAGO-Nexus`, a multi-objective approach to generate diverse test environments for DRL agents.
- We demonstrate `INDAGO-Nexus` discovers up to 83% more unique failures than `INDAGO` while reducing time-to-failure by up to 67%.
- We provide a complete replication package with implementation and experimental data[1].

2 Background and Related Work

This section describes the key background concepts used in this work and summarizes the related work.

2.1 Deep Reinforcement Learning

Deep Reinforcement Learning (DRL) extends Reinforcement Learning (RL) by using deep neural networks as function approximators to handle high-dimensional inputs (e.g., images) and continuous action spaces (e.g., steering angles in autonomous driving) [22]. Instead of explicitly representing policies or value functions, DRL learns them directly from raw observations and rewards using deep learning architectures.

This capability makes DRL particularly suitable for complex tasks in cyber-physical systems such as self-driving cars (SDCs), where the environment is dynamic and the decision space is large. In this work, we focus on *model-free* DRL algorithms, where agents learn directly from interactions without an explicit model of the environment. For example, the DRL agent for the parking scenario we consider in our case study (see Sect. 4) was trained with *Proximal Policy Optimization (PPO)* [24], a widely adopted policy-gradient method known for its stability and sample efficiency.

> *The agent's goal is to maximize the cumulative reward it receives in the long run* [27].

2.2 Black-Box Testing

In black-box testing, diversity is a common strategy for exposing faults by varying inputs and observing outputs [13]. For DRL agents, we focus on input diversity—variations in environment configurations—to guide test generation without costly simulations, combined with a surrogate to estimate failure likelihood.

Related work on diversity-based testing for deep neural networks includes approaches that optimize for input diversity to improve fault detection. Aghababaeyan et al. [1] proposed black-box testing techniques that use test case diversity to generate diverse test inputs for deep neural networks. While

[1] 10.6084/m9.figshare.29204687.

their work demonstrates the effectiveness of diversity-based approaches, their diversity metrics are primarily designed for image inputs rather than the tabular data that characterizes our MLP-based surrogate models. Our work adapts the concept of diversity-driven testing to the specific context of DRL environment configurations, which are typically represented as structured tabular data with both continuous and categorical features.

2.3 Surrogates


```
"env_config": {
    "goal_lane_idx": 0,
    "heading_ego": 0.96,
    "parked_vehicles_lane_indices": [
        1, 3, 6, 8, 9,
        10, 11, 12, 14, 18
    ],
    "position_ego": [
        1.83, -4.96
    ]
}
```


(a) Environment configuration

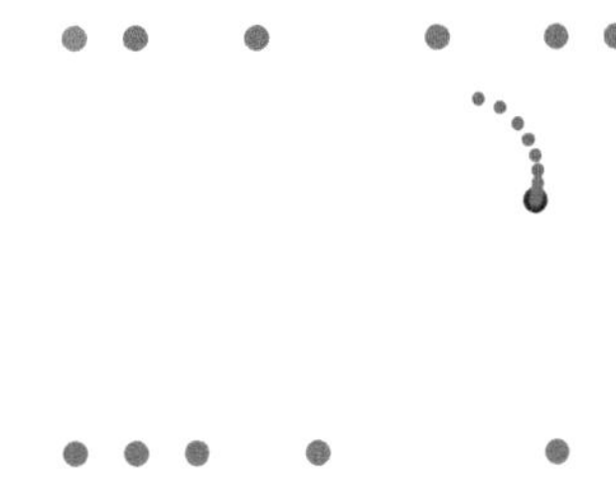

(b) Agent behavior visualization

Fig. 1. Parking scenario showing (a) environment configuration details used by DRL as a starting point, and (b) the DRL agent behavior. In (b), the red dot indicates the target parking spot, green dots represent parked cars, the black dot marks the agent's starting position, and the blue dots trace its trajectory (Color figure online).

Surrogate models are lightweight machine learning approximations that learn to predict the behavior or outcomes of computationally expensive processes based on historical data. In the context of DRL testing, these models have proven particularly effective at reducing evaluation costs [2]. Specifically, given an environment configuration (Fig. 1a), a surrogate model can predict the failure probability in the range $[0, 1]$, thereby enabling efficient test generation without requiring costly simulation executions.

2.4 Testing DRL Agents

The most directly related work is by Biagiola and Tonella [2], who introduced `INDAGO`, a test generation framework that leverages surrogate models trained on DRL logs to predict whether a given test environment is likely to cause failure. These surrogates return a continuous score in $[0, 1]$, representing the estimated failure probability of an environment. `INDAGO` combines this prediction with search-based strategies, namely Hill Climbing [25] and Genetic Algorithms [11], to efficiently explore the input space.

Our work builds on `INDAGO` by introducing a second optimization objective: input diversity. This extension aims to increase the diversity of the discovered failures, thereby improving coverage of the agent's operational space.

3 Approach

The goal of our approach is to *generate test scenarios that are both failure-inducing and diverse*, increasing the likelihood of uncovering unique faults in DRL agents. We build upon the `INDAGO` framework [2], which uses a surrogate model trained on DRL training logs to predict whether a given environment is likely to cause a failure. While `INDAGO` focuses solely on failure likelihood, we extend it to a *multi-objective test generation framework* that also accounts for scenario diversity—crucial for uncovering unique faults. Hence, we formulate the problem of generative diverse failure-inducing test scenarios as follows:

Problem Definition 1 *Given a DRL agent A, a set of test scenarios E, and a surrogate model $s : E \to [0, 1]$ that estimates the likelihood of failure for a given e, the goal is to generate a set of test scenarios $E_{sel} \subseteq E$ that maximize the likelihood of A to fail while maximizing diversity among the selected scenarios. More formally, the goal is to find a set of environments E_{sel} that optimizes the following objectives:*

$$\begin{cases} \max O_1 = s(e) & \textit{(Failure Likelihood)} \\ \max O_2 = Div(e, E_{sel}) & \textit{(Input Diversity)} \end{cases} \tag{1}$$

where O_1 (Failure Likelihood) is the predicted likelihood of failure for a given environment e; and O_2 (Input Diversity) is a measure of how diverse the selected environments are compared to the other test scenarios in E_{sel}.

In the following, we describe the surrogate model, diversity metrics, and the multi-objective optimization framework.

3.1 Surrogate Models

Following the prior work by Biagiola and Tonella [2], we adopt a lightweight surrogate model to estimate the failure likelihood of a test scenario without executing it. Specifically, we utilize a multi-layer perceptron (MLP) classifier trained on data collected during the DRL agent's training episodes. The MLP architecture is well-suited for this task due to the relatively small training dataset (up to 10k labeled environments) and the low-dimensional nature of environment feature vectors (e.g., 24-dimensional in the parking scenario). The surrogate outputs $s(e) \in [0, 1]$, representing failure probability for environment e.

3.2 Diversity Metrics

We explore two diversity methods: **Euclidean distance** computes the mean distance between a new scenario and previously selected ones, and **PCA-based**

Algorithm 1. Multi-Objective Test Generation for DRL Agents

```
Require: s, classifier (surrogate model);
Require: TR, test runs;
Require: G, generations;
Require: PS, population size;
Require: CR, crossover rate;
Require: E_train, set of environment configurations where the DRL agent failed during training;
Ensure: E_sel, the archive storing a diverse set of likely-failing test scenarios.
1: currentTestRun ← 0;
2: while currentTestRun ≤ TR do
3:     population ← GENERATE-POPULATION(PS, E_train);
4:     COMPUTE-OBJECTIVES(population, s, E_sel);
5:     currentGeneration ← 0;
6:     while currentGeneration ≤ G do
7:         newPop ← ∅ ;
8:         while |newPop| < PS do
9:             p_1 ← SELECTION(population)
10:            p_2 ← SELECTION(population)
11:            if getRandomFloat() < CR then
12:                o_1, o_2 ← crossover(p_1, p_2)
13:            end if
14:            o_1 ← MUTATE(o_1)
15:            o_2 ← MUTATE(o_2)
16:            newPop ← newPop ∪{o_1, o_2}
17:        end while
18:        population ← ELITISM(← newPop ∪ population);
19:        if stagnation detected or currentGeneration ≥ G then
20:            E_sel ← E_sel∪ GET-BEST-INDIVIDUAL(population)
21:        end if
22:    end while
23: end while
24: return E_sel
```

clustering [8] measures distance to the nearest cluster centroid in reduced dimensionality space. Both methods handle variable-length features through one-hot encoding and zero-padding.

3.3 Multi-objective Evolutionary Testing

To generate a diverse set of failure-inducing test scenarios, `INDAGO-Nexus` employs MOEAs that evolve environment configurations to simultaneously maximize (1) the likelihood of failure, as predicted by a surrogate model, and (2) diversity with respect to a growing archive of previously selected tests. We use two MOEAs: NSGA-II [7] and AGE-MOEA [23] to optimize both failure likelihood and diversity.

Algorithm 1 outlines this process. The search begins with a population of size PS. Each individual is evaluated without test execution using heuristics described in Sects. 3.1 and 2.2. The algorithm proceeds for G generations. In each generation, two parents are selected (Lines 9–10), the crossover is applied with probability CR (Line 11), and both offspring are mutated (Lines 14–15). Offspring are added to the new population (Line 16), and elitism selects the best individuals for the next generation (Line 18).

To avoid stagnation, `INDAGO-Nexus` monitors hypervolume changes across generations. If improvement falls below a threshold, or we have reached the maximum number of generations G, the best individual is archived (Line 20).

To explore new regions of space, the process continues until the total test runs TR is met. The resulting archive E_{sel} contains diverse, likely-failing scenarios, which are then executed on the DRL agent for validation.

While `INDAGO-Nexus` builds on established MOEAs like NSGA-II [7] and AGE-MOEA [23], it introduces several domain-specific adaptations: failure-based population seeding, surrogate-based fitness estimation, diversity measured against an evolving archive, and a stagnation-aware reset strategy for enhanced exploration. We describe these customizations in the following paragraphs.

Population Initialization. We seed the initial population with environments where the DRL agent failed during training (E_{train}), biasing the search towards failure-prone regions [2].

Selection. Selection determines which individuals are chosen for reproduction. `INDAGO-Nexus` uses binary tournament selection based on Pareto dominance [7], and the non-dominated sorting in particular.

Objective Calculation. Each individual is evaluated without test execution. The surrogate model s estimates failure likelihood, while diversity is computed with respect to the archive E_{sel} using either Euclidean distance or PCA-based clustering metrics as described in Sect. 3.2.

Crossover and Mutation. `INDAGO-Nexus` applies single-point crossover (Line 12) probabilistically based on the crossover rate CR, randomly selecting a crossover point in the feature vector and swapping segments between parents.

Mutation (Lines 14–15) is *always* applied to both offspring and uses *saliency-based feature selection* [26], which computes the gradient of the surrogate model's output with respect to each input feature. The saliency determines which features impact the surrogate's prediction, guiding mutation decisions. For *fixed-length features* (position, heading), we apply polynomial mutation [6] with type-specific handling (real-valued, integer, binary, categorical). For *variable-length features* (parked vehicle lists), we randomly apply removal, addition, or modification operations. A repair operator ensures validity after mutations.

Elitism. We retain the best individuals using NSGA-II's fast non-dominated sorting with crowding distance [7] or AGE-MOEA's adaptive survival score [23].

Stagnation and Archive Update. `INDAGO-Nexus` maintains an archive E_{sel} of selected scenarios. Stagnation is detected by monitoring the change in hypervolume of the Pareto front P_g at generation g relative to a reference point $\mathbf{r}$ (Eq. 2). The hypervolume metric reflects both diversity and convergence by measuring the volume dominated by P_g with respect to $\mathbf{r}$:

$$|HV(P_g, \mathbf{r}) - HV(P_{g-n_{\text{last}}}, \mathbf{r})| < \text{tol} \tag{2}$$

When stagnation is detected, `INDAGO-Nexus` selects a representative individual from the Pareto front using two strategies: *Maximum Failure Likelihood* (highest predicted failure probability) or *Knee Point* (best trade-off between failure likelihood and diversity) [31].

4 Empirical Evaluation

Our empirical evaluation aims to answer the following research questions:

RQ1: *How does multi-objective search perform in finding diverse failures?*
RQ2: *How effective is* `INDAGO-Nexus` *compared to state-of-the-art* `INDAGO`*?*

4.1 Case Studies

We evaluate `INDAGO-Nexus` on three diverse DRL agents from Biagiola and Tonella [2], each representing different application domains and complexity:

Parking. The first environment we consider is the `parking` environment [19]. In this scenario, the DRL agent begins at a specific location with a defined heading direction. The agent must park in a designated goal lane while avoiding collisions with any of the already parked vehicles. An example of this environment is illustrated in Fig. 1a. The environment consists of 24 elements, including goal lane, heading, 20 parking slots, and the x, y coordinates of the starting position.

Humanoid. Next, we examine the `Humanoid` environment, one of the more challenging environments from the MuJoCo simulator [28]. In this scenario, the agent must control a bipedal robot to walk on a smooth surface within a 3D space. The environment configuration of the Humanoid robot consists of two arrays: joint position and joint velocity. The joint position array contains 24 elements representing the positions and rotations of the robot's joints, while the joint velocity array contains the linear and angular velocities of the joints.

Self-Driving Car. The final environment we consider is the Self-Driving Car (SDC), developed using the DonkeyCar simulator [17]. In this environment, the DRL agent must navigate a car from the starting point of a track to the end without leaving track boundaries. The environment configuration consists of a list with 12 pairs, where each pair comprises a command and a value. For example, a command could be a left or right turn, with the value specifying the turn length.

4.2 Baseline

To ensure fair comparison of all approaches, we utilize the original models from the `INDAGO` paper. For our baseline, we employed the GA from the original `INDAGO` tool. This approach uses the predictive value of the surrogate model as a fitness value to gradually mutate environments in the search for failures. We executed this with the `saliency_failure` test policy, which ensures the initial population is created from previously failing environments sourced from the training data, incorporating saliency (as discussed in Sect. 3) during crossover and mutation. We selected this method as it demonstrated the highest rate of failure in the original study [2] against other approaches (`random search` and `hill climbing`). Due to the stochastic nature of evolutionary search, we executed the baseline 50 times, applying the process across all three agent scenarios.

4.3 Implementation and Parameter Settings

We implemented AGE-MOEA and NSGA-II using Pymoo v0.6.1 [3]. Experiments used 50 generations, population size 50, crossover rate 0.75, with stagnation-based termination ($tol = 5 \times 10^{-6}$, $n_{\text{last}} = 10$). The reference point for hypervolume calculation is set to $r = [1.2, 20.2]$, representing the upper bounds for the objectives. Experiments were conducted within Docker containers on a machine equipped with an AMD EPYC 7713 64-Core CPU (2.6 GHz), 256 threads, and an NVIDIA A40 GPU (48GB GDDR6) for tensor-based computation.

4.4 Evaluation Criteria

We measure: (1) *unique failures* via PCA+K-means clustering of execution traces, (2) *input/output diversity* using entropy across clusters, and (3) *time-to-failure (TTF)* efficiency. Statistical significance is assessed using Wilcoxon rank-sum test ($\alpha = 0.05$) and VarghaâĂŞDelaney effect size.

4.5 Failure Detection and Diversity Assessment

To assess the effectiveness of our multi-objective search strategies (**RQ1**), we executed both NSGA-II and AGE-MOEA across all combinations of diversity metrics and Pareto front selection strategies.

We focused on three aspects: the number of unique failures discovered, the diversity of these failures, and the efficiency in detecting them. We define a failure as a test scenario in which the DRL agent violates its task specification (e.g., crashing, falling, or missing the goal). To measure *unique failures*, we cluster the execution traces (i.e., output trajectories) of failing tests using Principal Component Analysis (PCA) followed by K-means. Each resulting cluster corresponds to a distinct failure type, providing a behavior-grounded notion of uniqueness. Since trajectory lengths vary, we normalize them via zero-padding. For the Parking and SDC scenarios, we track the agent's position over time, while in the Humanoid scenario, we monitor the robot's vertical movement to detect falls.

To determine the optimal number of clusters K^*, we apply silhouette analysis and increase K only if the silhouette score improves by at least 20%, reducing the effect of noisy improvements. This clustering method is used both to compute output diversity and to count unique failures. It is important to distinguish this post hoc clustering from the PCA-based metric used within the search itself (Sect. 3.2). The former relies on test execution results while the latter (our objective) relies on the input features (i.e., without running the tests).

We also evaluate the diversity of failures from both input and output perspectives. *Output diversity* is measured using the same clustering of output trajectories used to identify unique failures. For *input diversity*, we cluster the failing environment configurations using PCA and K-means, providing insight into the structural variety of the input scenarios, regardless of the agent's behavior.

In both cases, we calculate two diversity metrics: *unique failures*, which reflects how many clusters are populated, and *entropy*, which quantifies how evenly failures are distributed across clusters. We follow the definitions provided in the INDAGO framework [2].

To assess *test efficiency*, we compute the average time required to find the first failing test case. This metric reflects how quickly each approach exposes failures. The same metrics are then used in the comparison between INDAGO-Nexus and the baseline INDAGO (**RQ2**). To assess statistical significance, we apply the Wilcoxon rank-sum test [5] with a confidence level of $\alpha = 0.05$, and we report the VarghaâĂŞDelaney $\hat{A}_{12}$ statistics for the effect size [30].

5 Results

This section presents the results of our study, addressing in turn each research question introduced earlier.

5.1 Configuration Comparison (RQ1)

Table 1 outlines the performance of each INDAGO-Nexus configuration across the three case studies:

Choice of MOEA: AGE-MOEA generally outperforms NSGA-II in unique failures discovered. In Parking, AGE-MOEA achieves 4–7 unique failures compared to NSGA-II's 3–7. Both perform similarly in SDC, while Humanoid proves challenging for both algorithms. AGE-MOEA's adaptive survival score mechanism appears better suited for the multi-objective DRL testing problem compared to NSGA-II's crowding distance approach.

Diversity Metrics: PCA-based diversity consistently outperforms Euclidean distance across all scenarios. In Parking, PCA configurations achieve substantially higher input entropy (24.79–69.05) compared to Euclidean (11.72–63.95), demonstrating PCA's superior ability to capture meaningful relationships in high-dimensional feature spaces. The Euclidean approach occasionally achieves slightly higher total failure counts, revealing an important trade-off between failure quantity and diversity quality. This suggests that while Euclidean distance may find failures faster in certain regions, PCA-based diversity better explores the full failure space.

Pareto Selection Strategy: Knee-point selection consistently yields superior diversity compared to the extreme O_1 point across all scenarios. The knee point represents a balanced trade-off between objectives, achieving higher unique failures and entropy scores.

Table 1. Performance metrics across different configurations for all three agents, displaying median and Interquartile Range (IQR) across 50 runs. (Gray cells indicate top values for each agent and approach.)

(a) Parking Agent

	Failures		Entropy		
Configuration	**#Total**	**#Unique**	**Input**	**Output**	**TTF**
AGE-MOEA					
PCA/Knee	10 (3.75)	7 (1.00)	69.05 (19.19)	62.34 (15.62)	106.12 (26.89)
PCA/O_1	7 (3.00)	4 (2.00)	24.79 (41.62)	39.28 (18.25)	108.13 (26.74)
Euclidean/Knee	10 (3.75)	7 (2.75)	63.95 (18.20)	61.98 (16.33)	123.27 (27.51)
Euclidean/O_1	7 (2.00)	4 (1.00)	11.72 (37.64)	39.85 (14.35)	123.73 (26.27)
NSGA-II					
PCA/Knee	10 (3.00)	7 (2.00)	73.00 (20.13)	63.64 (9.77)	109.19 (23.00)
PCA/O_1	7 (2.75)	4 (1.75)	10.26 (42.01)	41.05 (14.81)	108.12 (25.46)
Euclidean/Knee	11 (3.00)	6 (1.00)	64.12 (14.18)	60.59 (10.26)	120.34 (25.98)
Euclidean/O_1	7 (2.00)	3 (1.00)	0.00 (39.71)	36.12 (15.04)	120.70 (27.56)

(b) Humanoid Agent

	Failures		Entropy		
Configuration	**#Total**	**#Unique**	**Input**	**Output**	**TTF**
AGE-MOEA					
PCA/Knee	-	-	-	-	-
PCA/O_1	2 (1.75)	1 (0.75)	10.65 (34.60)	0.00 (0.00)	78.94 (27.12)
Euclidean/Knee	1 (2.00)	1 (1.00)	0.00 (38.69)	0.00 (0.00)	96.06 (29.95)
Euclidean/O_1	2 (2.00)	1 (1.00)	0.00 (35.59)	0.00 (0.00)	102.53 (27.58)
NSGA-II					
PCA/Knee	-	-	-	-	-
PCA/O_1	2 (1.75)	1 (1.00)	0.00 (32.88)	0.00 (0.00)	79.32 (28.42)
Euclidean/Knee	2 (2.00)	1 (1.00)	0.00 (40.90)	0.00 (0.00)	90.94 (27.65)
Euclidean/O_1	2 (2.00)	1 (0.75)	0.00 (28.95)	0.00 (0.00)	95.70 (23.58)

(c) Self-Driving Car (SDC)Agent

	Failures		Entropy		
Configuration	**#Total**	**#Unique**	**Input**	**Output**	**TTF**
AGE-MOEA					
PCA/Knee	31 (5.75)	5 (6.00)	56.97 (12.51)	63.03 (75.90)	1578.16 (130.69)
PCA/O_1	36 (3.75)	6 (6.00)	71.96 (12.36)	77.34 (86.13)	1092.10 (49.04)
Euclidean/Knee	31 (5.00)	5.5 (6.00)	57.06 (18.83)	71.90 (79.67)	1072.26 (43.36)
Euclidean/O_1	50 (1.00)	6 (6.00)	74.70 (5.84)	64.99 (75.69)	2435.78 (274.89)
NSGA-II					
PCA/Knee	30 (4.00)	5 (6.00)	54.50 (18.05)	62.75 (74.53)	1521.15 (102.29)
PCA/O_1	34 (5.75)	6 (6.75)	70.97 (13.84)	77.00 (85.31)	1087.94 (59.30)
Euclidean/Knee	30 (4.75)	5 (6.00)	56.12 (9.07)	71.07 (80.27)	1073.21 (45.60)
Euclidean/O_1	50 (1.00)	6 (6.00)	72.19 (6.10)	66.78 (74.89)	2588.43 (270.45)

Different configurations perform best in different scenarios. Overall, AGE-MOEA tends to produce more unique and diverse failures than NSGA-II. Pareto knee-point selection consistently yields better results than the extreme O_1 point. However, the choice of configuration can significantly impact performance, highlighting the need for adaptive strategies that consider the specific context and objectives.

5.2 Comparison with INDAGO (RQ2)

Table 2 presents a direct comparison between INDAGO-Nexus (AGE-MOEA *Euclidean/Knee* configuration) and the state-of-the-art INDAGO approach. The results demonstrate significant improvements across multiple metrics:

Unique Failure Discovery: INDAGO-Nexus consistently finds more unique failures than INDAGO. In the Parking scenario, INDAGO-Nexus discovers 7 unique failures compared to INDAGO's 5 (+40% improvement). For the SDC scenario, INDAGO-Nexus finds 5.5 unique failures versus INDAGO's 3 (+83% improvement). The Humanoid scenario shows comparable performance between both approaches, which aligns with our observation that this scenario is inherently challenging for all testing methods.

Diversity Enhancement: The multi-objective approach significantly improves both input and output diversity. In the Parking case, INDAGO-Nexus achieves 63.95 input entropy compared to INDAGO's 0.00, and 61.98 output entropy versus 49.37. This demonstrates that explicitly optimizing for diversity as an objective leads to more varied test scenarios and failure modes. The diversity improvements are particularly important for comprehensive testing, as they increase the likelihood of discovering edge cases and systematic weaknesses.

Efficiency Gains: INDAGO-Nexus demonstrates superior efficiency in finding failures across all scenarios. Time-to-failure improvements range from 18% (Parking: 123.27 vs 150.53) to 67% (SDC: 1072.26 vs 3251.97), with Humanoid showing 36% improvement (96.06 vs 150.50). These efficiency gains suggest that the multi-objective approach not only finds more diverse failures but does so more quickly than single-objective methods. The efficiency improvements are statistically significant (Wilcoxon test, $p < 0.001$) with large effect sizes across all scenarios (Vargha-Delaney $\hat{A}_{12} > 0.9$) for TTF.

Statistical Significance: All reported improvements show statistical significance at $\alpha = 0.05$ level using the Wilcoxon rank-sum test. Effect sizes calculated using Vargha-Delaney $\hat{A}_{12}$ statistics indicate substantial practical differences, particularly for efficiency metrics where INDAGO-Nexus consistently achieves large effect sizes ($\hat{A}_{12} > 0.7$), indicating that INDAGO-Nexus significantly outperforms INDAGO in key performance areas.

Table 2. Comparison between INDAGO-Nexus and INDAGO across different agents, displaying median and Interquartile Range (IQR) across 50 runs. Statistical significance markers for the Wilcoxon rank-sum test: * p-value<0.05, ** p-value<0.01, *** p-value<0.001.

(a) Parking Agent

	Failures		**Entropy**		
Approach	**#Total**	**#Unique**	**Input**	**Output**	**TTF**
INDAGO-Nexus	10 (3.75)	7 (2.75)**	63.95 (18.20)***	61.98 (16.33)***	123.27 (27.51)***
INDAGO	14.5 (4.00)	5 (2.00)	0.00 (35.72)	49.37 (12.56)	150.53 (0.03)

(b) Humanoid Agent

	Failures		**Entropy**		
Approach	**#Total**	**#Unique**	**Input**	**Output**	**TTF**
INDAGO-Nexus	1 (2.00)	1 (1.00)	0.00 (38.69)	0.00 (0.00)	96.06 (29.95)***
INDAGO	2 (2.75)	1 (1.00)	28.90 (39.31)	0.00 (50.89)	150.50 (0.01)

(c) Self-Driving Car (SDC) Agent

	Failures		**Entropy**		
Approach	**#Total**	**#Unique**	**Input**	**Output**	**TTF**
INDAGO-Nexus	31 (5.00)***	5.50 (6.00)**	57.06 (18.83)	71.90 (79.67)***	1072.26 (43.36)***
INDAGO	17.00 (5.75)	3.00 (3.00)	61.72 (21.59)	34.36 (48.71)	3251.97 (0.35)

INDAGO-Nexus finds more unique failures and higher input/output diversity in Parking and SDC. Instead, it matches INDAGO in the challenging Humanoid scenario. Finally, INDAGO-Nexus finds unique failures faster across all DRL agents.

6 Threats To Validity

Internal Validity: Our experimental design addresses several potential threats through careful control of variables and statistical rigor. We ensure fair comparison by running all algorithms under identical conditions with the same hardware and time constraints. Each experiment is repeated 50 times to account for the stochastic nature of evolutionary algorithms, and we apply appropriate statistical tests (Wilcoxon rank-sum) with effect size measurements (Vargha-Delaney $\hat{A}_{12}$) to assess practical significance. The clustering approach for measuring unique failures uses established silhouette analysis with conservative thresholds (20% improvement requirement) to avoid over-segmentation due to noise.

External Validity: Our evaluation covers three diverse DRL domains with different state/action spaces and failure modes. However, generalizability to other

DRL applications, training algorithms beyond PPO, or different architectures requires further investigation.

Construct Validity: The choice of evaluation metrics reflects established practices in the DRL testing literature, particularly building on the INDAGO framework. Our clustering-based approach to measuring unique failures provides a behavior-grounded assessment of diversity that captures meaningful differences in agent behavior rather than superficial input variations. The entropy-based diversity measures provide quantitative assessments that complement the qualitative notion of test case variety.

Conclusion Validity: The statistical methods employed (non-parametric tests, effect size calculations) are appropriate for the experimental design and address the non-normal distribution of performance metrics commonly observed in evolutionary computation experiments. The large number of experimental repetitions (50 per configuration) provides sufficient statistical power to detect meaningful differences between approaches. Furthermore, a small number of SDC configurations were executed on a smaller hardware setup (AMD Ryzen Threadripper 3970X 32-Core Processor, 64GB memory, NVIDIA GeForce RTX 3080 10GB). Although less powerful then the main setup, the results were considerably faster. However, other validation metrics remain consistent.

7 Conclusion and Future Work

This paper introduced INDAGO-Nexus, a multi-objective search approach for generating diverse failures in DRL environments. Unlike prior methods that focus solely on inducing agent failures, INDAGO-Nexus simultaneously optimizes for failure likelihood and scenario diversity, leading to a more comprehensive exploration of failure modes. Our empirical evaluation across three DRL environments—Parking, Humanoid, and Self-Driving Car (SDC)—shows that the multi-objective INDAGO-Nexus consistently outperforms the single-objective baseline INDAGO in terms of unique failures discovered, diversity (measured via input and output entropy), and search efficiency.

We found that the effectiveness of INDAGO-Nexus varies across scenarios, with AGE-MOEA generally achieving more unique and diverse failures than NSGA-II. Both the choice of diversity metric (Euclidean vs. PCA) and the Pareto selection strategy (knee point vs. extreme O_1) significantly influence the outcomes. In particular, knee-point selection consistently led to better results across most configurations. Nonetheless, the Humanoid scenario remains particularly challenging, exposing limitations in current diversity metrics and search robustness.

Future Work: Several research directions emerge from this work. First, exploring many-objective optimization with additional objectives such as test case complexity, execution cost, or coverage metrics could further improve testing effectiveness. Second, investigating adaptive diversity metrics that automatically adjust based on the characteristics of discovered failures could enhance the approach's generalizability. Third, extending the framework to other DRL training algorithms (beyond PPO) and neural network architectures would broaden its applicability. Finally, developing theoretical foundations for understanding when and why multi-objective approaches outperform single-objective methods in testing contexts would provide valuable insights for the testing community.

`INDAGO-Nexus` introduces multi-objective search for generating diverse DRL failures, consistently outperforming `INDAGO` in unique failures and efficiency. AGE-MOEA with knee-point selection proves most effective, though Humanoid scenarios remain challenging. Future work includes many-objective extensions, improved surrogate models, and broader domain evaluation.

References

1. Aghababaeyan, Z., et al.: Black-box testing of deep neural networks through test case diversity. IEEE Trans. Softw. Eng. **49**(5), 3182–3204 (2023). https://doi.org/10.1109/tse.2023.3243522
2. Biagiola, M., Tonella, P.: Testing of deep reinforcement learning agents with surrogate models. ACM Trans. Softw. Eng. Methodol. **33**(3) (2024). https://doi.org/10.1145/3631970
3. Blank, J., Deb, K.: PYMOO: multi-objective optimization in python. IEEE Access **8**, 89497–89509 (2020)
4. Bloom, J., et al.: Decentralized multi-agent reinforcement learning with global state prediction (2023). https://arxiv.org/abs/2306.12926
5. Conover, W.J.: Practical Nonparametric Statistics, vol. 350. John Wiley & Sons (1998)
6. Deb, K.: Multi-objective optimisation using evolutionary algorithms: an introduction, pp. 3–34. Springer (2011)
7. Deb, K., et al.: A fast and elitist multiobjective genetic algorithm: NSGA-II. IEEE Trans. Evol. Comput. **6**(2), 182–197 (2002)
8. Ding, C., He, X.: K-means Clustering Via Principal Component Analysis, p. 29. ICML '04, Association for Computing Machinery, New York (2004). https://doi.org/10.1145/1015330.1015408
9. Ghoshal, A.: Why did this humanoid robot go nuts and nearly injure its handlers? New Atlus (2025). https://newatlas.com/ai-humanoids/humanoid-robot-nearly-injures-handlers-unitree/
10. Giubilato, R., et al.: Simulation framework for mobile robots in planetary-like environments (2020). https://arxiv.org/abs/2006.00057
11. Goldberg, D.E., Holland, J.H.: Genetic algorithms and machine learning. Mach. Learn. **3**(2), 95–99 (1988). https://doi.org/10.1023/A:1022602019183
12. Guardian, T.: Us investigates 2.4m tesla self driving vehicles after reported collisions. The Guardian (2024). https://www.theguardian.com/technology/2024/oct/18/tesla-self-driving-car-investigation
13. Guidotti, R., et al.: A survey of methods for explaining black box models. ACM Comput. Surv. (CSUR) **51**(5), 1–42 (2018)
14. Haq, F.U., et al.: Efficient online testing for DNN-enabled systems using surrogate-assisted and many-objective optimization, pp. 811–822 (2022)
15. Ishibuchi, H., et al.: Evolutionary many-objective optimization: a short review, pp. 2419–2426. IEEE (2008)
16. Kaur, P., et al.: A survey on simulators for testing self-driving cars (2021). https://arxiv.org/abs/2101.05337

17. Kramer, T., contributors: Self driving car sandbox. https://github.com/tawnkramer/sdsandbox (2021). gitHub repository
18. Lambert, F.: Tesla full self-driving veers off road, flips car in scary crash driver couldn't prevent. Electrek (2025). https://electrek.co/2025/05/23/tesla-full-self-driving-veers-off-road-flips-car-scary-crash-driver-couldnt-prevent/
19. Leurent, E.: An environment for autonomous driving decision-making. https://github.com/eleurent/highway-env (2018)
20. Liu, H.X., Feng, S.: "curse of rarity" for autonomous vehicles (2022). https://arxiv.org/abs/2207.02749
21. Mnih, V., et al.: Playing atari with deep reinforcement learning (2013). https://arxiv.org/abs/1312.5602
22. Mnih, V., et al.: Human-level control through deep reinforcement learning. Nature **518**(7540), 529–533 (2015)
23. Panichella, A.: An Adaptive Evolutionary Algorithm Based on Non-euclidean Geometry for Many-objective Optimization, pp. 595–603. GECCO '19, Association for Computing Machinery, New York (2019). https://doi.org/10.1145/3321707.3321839
24. Schulman, J., Wolski, F., Dhariwal, P., Radford, A., Klimov, O.: Proximal policy optimization algorithms. CoRR **abs/1707.06347** (2017). http://arxiv.org/abs/1707.06347
25. Selman, B., Gomes, C.P.: Hill-climbing Search. John Wiley & Sons, Ltd (2006). https://doi.org/10.1002/0470018860.s00015, https://onlinelibrary.wiley.com/doi/abs/10.1002/0470018860.s00015
26. Simonyan, K., et al.: Deep inside convolutional networks: visualising image classification models and saliency maps (2014). https://arxiv.org/abs/1312.6034
27. Sutton, R.S., Barto, A.G.: Reinforcement Learning: An Introduction. The MIT Press, 2nd edn. (2018). http://incompleteideas.net/book/the-book-2nd.html
28. Todorov, E., et al.: Mujoco: a physics engine for model-based control. In: 2012 IEEE/RSJ International Conference on Intelligent Robots and Systems, pp. 5026–5033 (2012). https://api.semanticscholar.org/CorpusID:5230692
29. Uesato, J., et al.: Rigorous agent evaluation: an adversarial approach to uncover catastrophic failures (2018). https://arxiv.org/abs/1812.01647
30. Vargha, A., Delaney, H.D.: A critique and improvement of the CL common language effect size statistics of McGraw and Wong. J. Educ. Behav. Stat. **25**(2), 101–132 (2000)
31. Zhang, X., et al.: A knee point-driven evolutionary algorithm for many-objective optimization. IEEE Trans. Evol. Comput. **19**(6), 761–776 (2014)

RENE/NIER Track

Test Case Generation for Simulink Models: An Experience from the E-Bike Domain

Michael Marzella[1(✉)], Andrea Bombarda[1], Marcello Minervini[1], Nunzio Marco Bisceglia[1], Angelo Gargantini[1], and Claudio Menghi[1,2]

[1] University of Bergamo, Bergamo, Italy
{m.marzella,n.bisceglia1}@studenti.unibg.it, {andrea.bombarda,marcello.minervini,angelo.gargantini, claudio.menghi}@unibg.it

[2] McMaster University, Hamilton, Canada

Abstract. Building reliable Cyber-physical systems often requires engineers to search for software defects. Search-based software testing (SBST) is a standard technology that supports this activity. To increase practical adoption, industries need empirical evidence of the usefulness of SBST techniques on different benchmarks. To address this need, this replication study reports on our experience assessing the usefulness of SBST in generating failure-revealing test cases. Our study subject is within the electric bike (e-Bike) domain and concerns the software controller of an e-Bike motor. We assessed the effectiveness and efficiency of HECATE, an SBST framework for Simulink® models. HECATE successfully identified failure-revealing test cases in practical time. We present the lessons learned, the relevance of our results for industrial applications, and the improvement in the state of practice.

Keywords: Motor Control · E-Bikes · Model Development · Simulink® · Search-based Software Testing

1 Introduction

Simulink® [19] is a modeling and simulation language widely used by the Cyber-physical system (CPS) industry [27]. It is used by more than 60% of engineers for CPS design and in many domains, such as automotive [29]. Simulink® appeals to engineers, due to its graphical language. It enables engineers to model their systems by specifying their components and connections [19] and offers many add-ons with components targeting different problems.

Search-based software testing (SBST) is widely applied during the development of CPSs to check for software defects. It is used in many domains, including real-time, embedded, and safety-critical systems [1]. SBST tools automatically generate test cases to check for violations of requirements [18].

To increase the *industrial applicability* of SBST, it is paramount to empirically evaluate its effectiveness and provide practitioners with guidelines and

M. Wagner and M. Zhang (Eds.): SSBSE 2025, LNCS 16228, pp. 115–130, 2026.
https://doi.org/10.1007/978-3-032-24839-8_8

lessons learned that can help them choose the appropriate tools and assess their level of maturity [1]. It is also necessary to assess whether SBST techniques scale to realistic development artifacts [1]. Indeed, despite being widely recognized as useful tools, the effectiveness of SBST test generators strongly depend on the application domain [17]. Different domains may require different properties from the SBST frameworks. The research and industrial communities widely recognize the need for replicable experiments and empirical data assessing the benefits of software engineering approaches in practice [1,11,26,30,32,36]. The need for replicating experiments is of particular importance for Simulink® models [6,8,39], as Simulink® projects and models are typically created and maintained in an industrial context and are usually not publicly available due to confidentiality agreements or license restrictions [5]. Therefore, access to these models is limited, making results hard (if not impossible) to replicate [7].

Several *SBST tools for* Simulink® are available in the literature (e.g., [13,14,31]). Many of the tools are compared by the falsification category [25] of the ARCH competition, an international competition of verification tools for CPSs. In this paper, we consider HECATE [14]. Unlike other existing tools, HECATE generates test cases specified as Test Sequences [22], which are automatically adapted to search for requirement violations, and Test Assessments [21], representing the requirements of interest. Since HECATE directly works with Test Sequences and Test Assessments, which are built-in components within Simulink Test™ [20], it does not require engineers to learn new frameworks to specify their test oracles and generate their test cases. This makes HECATE particularly suitable for industrial applications. For example, HECATE has been successfully applied to support the development of a cruise controller for an industrial simulator [15]. Nevertheless, HECATE is still primarily an academic tool. Replicating the experiments to assess HECATE on a different study subject provides insightful results to industrial practitioners [24,38]. Therefore, they are pivotal for technology transfer and support the industrial adoption of HECATE.

This work focuses on the e-Bikes domain. The global e-Bike market size was USD 27.15 billion in 2022 and is projected to grow to USD 82.84 billion by 2030 [23]. We focus on the (software) controller of the electrical motor of the e-Bike. The software runs on 100% of e-Bikes [41] and is often designed in Simulink® [40]. It governs the motor's responsiveness to the speed demand and regulates the battery management. Ensuring software reliability and performance is essential: It affects user experience, safety, and battery life. Software testing is necessary to check for software failures. This activity is normally performed by physically testing the e-Bikes within different scenarios [34].

In this paper, we replicate previous experiments (from the automotive domain [15]) assessing the effectiveness of SBST with HECATE in generating failure-revealing test cases by considering our e-Bike study subject. We considered a complex model of an e-Bike and two controllers: the Buck hardware controller and the PWM software controller. These controllers must satisfy three requirements (functional, regulatory, and safety). We also considered six different testing scenarios obtained from different Parameterized Test Sequences. We considered two search algorithms: Uniform Random (UR) and Simulated Annealing (SA). Therefore, we conducted 72 experiments (2 models × 3 requirements × 6 Parameterized Test Sequences × 2 search algorithms). For each experiment, we ran HECATE and checked whether it could generate a failure-revealing test case. Our results show that HECATE could effectively generate failure-revealing test cases for ≈ 83% (60 out of 72) of our experiments. We confirmed the failures we found by discussing them with the engineer who developed the models. HECATE required on average $5'\,51''$ ($min = 59''$, $max = 2h\,0'\,18''$, $StdDev = 8'\,54''$). We critically analyze our results, present the lessons learned, and discuss the relevance of our results for industrial applications. We also compare our results with those previously obtained in the automotive domain [15].

This paper is organized as follows. Section 2 presents our study subject. Section 3 describes HECATE. Section 4 presents our results, and Sect. 5 discusses them. Section 6 outlines the related work. Section 7 presents our conclusions.

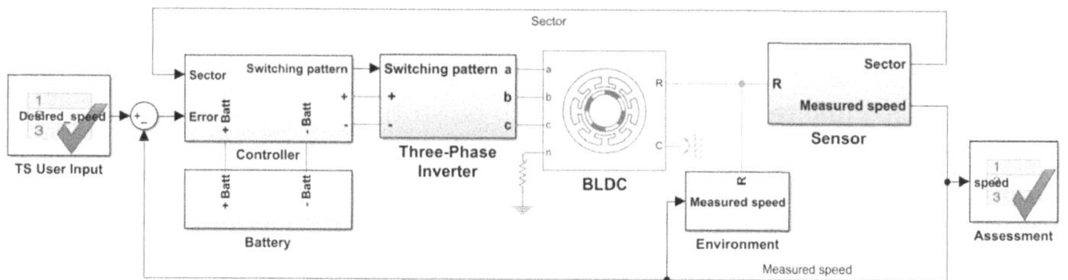

Fig. 1. simulink model for the e-Bike.

2 E-Bike Study Subject

We describe the controlled system and its requirements (Sect. 2.1), and the two controllers (Sect. 2.2).

2.1 The Controlled System

Figure 1 presents the Simulink® model of our e-Bike study subject. The controlled system consists of the following components.

The *User Inputs* component collects the inputs from the rider. Its output (*Desired Speed*) models the speed selected by the rider. The desired speed is used to compute the *Error*, i.e., the difference between the *Desired speed* and the *Measured speed*, which is one of the inputs of the *Controller* of the e-Bike.

The *Environment* component represents external forces (e.g., aerodynamic drag). The input is the *Measured speed* of the e-Bike, and the output is a signal R simulating the effects of external forces.

The *Brushless Direct Current (BLDC) Motor* component converts the electrical energy into rotational motion. The inputs of the BLDC are the currents applied to the three phases (a, b, c) and the neutral phase (n). The outputs are the torque generated by the motor for the rotor (R) and the motor case (C).

The *Sensor* component monitors the torque of the e-Bike. It returns the active *Sector* of the BLDC and the *Measured speed.*

The *Battery* component stores electrical energy. A negative (−Batt) and positive (+Batt) current recharges and accesses the energy from the battery.

The *Inverter* component converts the direct current into alternating current and regulates the electrical energy that flows from the battery to the motor. When the e-Bike decelerates (e.g., during braking), the rotor keeps rotating due to the vehicle's inertia, and the produced energy (−Batt) recharges the battery. Otherwise, it flows from the battery to the inverter to help the rider (+Batt). The inverter acts on the battery and the motor depending on a direct current (DC) signal (*Switching pattern*) received from the *Controller.*

The *Controller* component selects the *Switching Pattern* based on the *Error* signal and the active sector (*Sector*).

Engineers designed the e-Bike controller (*Controller*) to satisfy the e-Bike requirements from Table 1.

Requirement R1 is a *functional* requirement: It demands the speed of the motor not to be negative. During braking phases, the motor shall rotate in the same direction while regenerating energy to be stored in the battery: A negative speed is not considered since the e-Bike is assumed to move only forward. The braking process, therefore, reduces the positive speed of the e-Bike.

Requirement R2 is a *regulatory* requirement: It enables electric bikes to assist riders only below 25 km/h (i.e., 170 rpm wheel speed, considering a 28 *inch* wheel), as mandated by most European countries [37].

Requirement R3 is a *safety* requirement: The motor speed shall not exceed the speed requested by the rider.

Table 1. Requirements for the e-Bike.

ID	Description
R1	Motor speed shall always be positive or zero.
R2	Motor speed shall always be lower than 170 rpm.
R3	Motor speed shall not exceed that requested by the rider.

2.2 Software Controllers

In this replication study, we considered two controllers for the e-Bike: The Pulse Width Modulation (PWM) software controller and the Buck hardware controller. Experts from electrical engineering developed these controllers in a project on improving "green" mobility solutions, including e-Bikes, and involving several companies, such as Brembo [33] and Pirelli [35]. Engineers have been developing these models to determine which architecture is more efficient. The development of these models took approximately 100 h each (including testing) [10].

In this work, the e-Bike engineers provided us with two *intermediate versions* of the PWM and Buck controllers. Typically, engineers extensively test their controllers before deployment to check for failures. However, since these models are intermediate, they were only assessed by considering a limited set of test cases encoding standard profiles for the desired speed.

Step	Transition	Next
step_1 getSimTime() **speed=Hecate_sp/5*** getSimTime();	after(5,'sec')	**step_2**
step_2 **speed=Hecate_sp**	after(5,'sec')	**step_3**
step_3 **speed=Hecate_sp-Hecate_sp/5*(** getSimTime()**-10);**	after(5,'sec')	**step_4**
...	...	..
step_7 **speed=Hecate_sp-Hecate_sp/5*(** getSimTime()**-30);**	after(5,'sec')	

(a) Parameterized Test Sequence Block.

Step	Transition	Next
step_1	after(6,'sec')	**Sp_H_1**
Sp_H_1 verify(**speed<=11**)	after(4,'sec')	**step_3**
step_3	after(16,'sec')	**Sp_H_2**
Sp_H_2 verify(**speed<=11**)	after(4,'sec')	**step_1**

(b) Test Assessment Block.

Fig. 2. Test Blocks for our e-Bike model.

3 HECATE

HECATE is an SBST tool for Simulink® models. Unlike existing SBST tools, HECATE supports Simulink® Test blocks (i.e., Test Sequences and Test Assessments blocks). HECATE identifies failure-revealing test cases represented as Test Sequences using the information from Test Assessments blocks. Test blocks are embedded within the Simulink® model. For example, engineers add a Test Sequence to the model from Fig. 1 by replacing the block *User Input* with the Test Sequence block *TS User Input* that generates a *Desired speed* signal. They also add the Test Assessment block (*Assessment*) that receives the measured speed of the vehicle as input. Figure 2 details the Test Sequence (Fig. 2a) and a Test Assessment block (Fig. 2b) from Fig. 1.

A *Test Sequence* defines the test case's input. It consists of *steps* connected by *transitions*. The fragment of the Test Sequence from Fig. 2, contains four steps (i.e., `step_1`, `step_2`, `step_3`, and `step_7`). Each test step defines the values to be assumed by the output signals of the Test Sequence. For example, the `step_1` from Fig. 2 specifies that the value of the *speed* is *Hecate_sp/5*getSimTime()*. Transitions define the test steps change: They are labeled with a Boolean formula defining the condition for the transitions to be fired. When a transition is fired, the system reaches the step identified by the column **Next**. For example, the transition from the first row of the Test Sequence in Fig. 2 specifies that the test switches from `step_1` to `step_2` after 5s. When the Simulink® model is executed, the Test Sequence generates a signal for its outputs.

A *Test Assessment* follows the same structure as a Test Sequence. For example, the Test Assessment from Fig. 2b contains four steps (i.e., `step_1` and `Sp_H_1`, `step_3` and `Sp_H_2`). Unlike Test Sequences, Test Assessment blocks allow engineers to use the `verify` construct. This construct verifies whether certain conditions are met when the Test Assessment is in the corresponding step. For example, when the Test Assessment is within the test step `Sp_H_1`, the Test Assessment Block verifies whether the condition `speed` ≤ 11 holds.

A *Test Case* consists of a Test Sequence block and a Test Assessment block. The Test Sequence block specifies input signals supplied to the Simulink® simulator. The model is then run with these inputs to simulate the corresponding Test Sequence. The Test Assessment block monitors the model's output signals to determine whether any of its `verify` expressions are violated. Typically, a Test Assessment is associated with one or more system requirements. For example, the Test Assessment in Fig. 2 has been written to check the requirement R3 from Sect. 2.1. Engineers can inspect the satisfaction of these conditions using an appropriate GUI. If (at least) one of the conditions of the Test Assessment is violated, the test case is failure-revealing.

HECATE [14] extends this testing framework by supporting SBST. It enables the automatic generation of Test Sequences driven by a fitness function generated from the Test Assessment block. Specifically, HECATE requires engineers to extend their Test Sequences into Parameterized Test Sequences.

A *Parameterized Test Sequence* is a Test Sequence in which some values are parameters that are automatically assigned to values by HECATE. Figure 2a shows an example of a Parameterized Test Sequence. HECATE can assign different values to the parameter `Hecate_sp` to generate many test cases. To generate realistic Test Sequences, engineers can specify lower and upper bounds for the search parameters. For example, engineers specified that the lower and upper bounds for the values of the parameter `Hecate_sp` are 0 and 170 rpm.

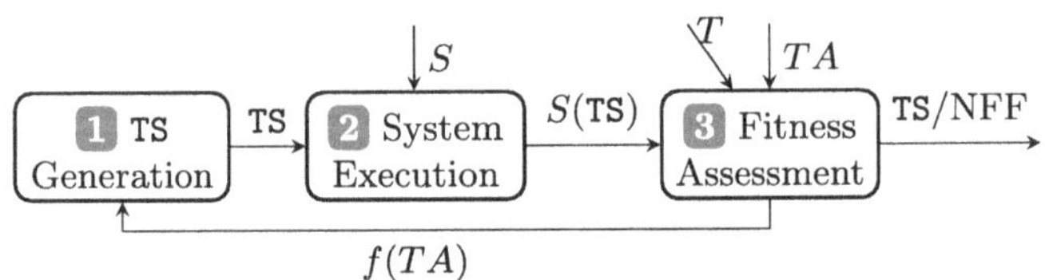

Fig. 3. Overview of the HECATE framework.

HECATE iteratively performs the steps from Fig. 3:

1 *Test Sequence Generation*: Generates a new (population of) Test Sequence (TS) by assigning values to the parameters in the Parameterized Test Sequence.

2 *System Execution*: Executes the system model S by providing the input generated from the Test Sequence (TS) and generates the output $S(\texttt{TS})$.
3 *Fitness Assessment*: Assesses a fitness function obtained from the Test Assessment w.r.t. the output $S(\texttt{TS})$. HECATE assesses if the fitness value is below a threshold level and, thus, is failure-revealing. Details on how the the fitness function is built and evaluated can be found in the corresponding publication [13]. HECATE terminates if a failure-revealing test is found or the maximum time T is reached.

Table 2. Experimental results for the e-Bike case study.

		UR									SA								
		TA_R1			TA_R2			TA_R3			TA_R1			TA_R2			TA_R3		
	PTS	**F**	$\bar{S}$	$\hat{S}$	**F**	$\bar{S}$	$\hat{S}$	**F**	$\bar{S}$	$\hat{S}$	**F**	$\bar{S}$	$\hat{S}$	**F**	$\bar{S}$	$\hat{S}$	**F**	$\bar{S}$	$\hat{S}$
PWM	*t-pyr-0*	10	1.6	1.0	10	9.6	4.0	10	1.9	1.5	10	1.8	1.5	10	8.2	7.5	10	1.8	1.0
	t-pyr-85	10	7.6	4.0	10	3.0	3.0	10	1.0	1.0	10	7.6	4.0	10	3.9	4.0	10	1.0	1.0
	t-pyr-130	10	10.6	8.5	10	1.1	1.0	10	1.0	1.0	10	4.4	3.0	10	1.8	1.0	10	1.0	1.0
	r-pulse-0	10	8.9	6.0	10	8.6	8.5	10	1.6	1.0	10	12.9	12.5	10	4.7	4.0	10	2.7	2.0
	r-pulse-85	10	14.6	12.5	10	3.0	2.5	10	1.0	1.0	10	15.2	13.5	10	2.6	2.0	10	1.0	1.0
	r-pulse-130	10	6.7	4.0	10	2.2	1.5	10	1.0	1.0	10	10.2	8.0	10	2.8	1.5	10	1.0	1.0
Buck	*t-pyr-0*	0	–	–	4	28.8	26.0	10	8.1	3.0	0	–	–	10	15.3	14.0	10	2.9	2.0
	t-pyr-85	0	–	–	5	17.6	22.0	10	4.3	4.0	0	–	–	10	19.5	18.0	10	3.1	2.5
	t-pyr-130	0	–	–	10	1.9	1.0	10	2.1	1.5	0	–	–	10	3.7	2.0	10	2.3	1.0
	r-pulse-0	0	–	–	10	2.9	2.0	10	7.3	7.5	0	–	–	10	4.1	4.0	10	7.1	8.0
	r-pulse-85	0	–	–	10	2.4	2.0	10	1.6	1.5	0	–	–	10	5.9	4.0	10	1.7	1.0
	r-pulse-130	0	–	–	10	2.7	3.0	10	1.0	1.0	0	–	–	10	2.6	2.5	10	1.0	1.0

4 Evaluation

In this replication study, we consider the following research questions:

RQ1: How *effective* is SBST in generating failure-revealing test cases?
RQ2: How *efficient* is SBST in generating failure-revealing test cases?

4.1 Experimental Setup

To assess the effectiveness of HECATE, we performed 72 experiments. Each experiment was obtained by considering one of the two models, one of the three Test Assessments, and one of the six Parameterized Test Sequences. Each experiment was repeated twice, considering two search algorithms: Uniform Random (UR) and Simulated Annealing (SA). The two models were the Simulink® models of the e-Bike obtained by considering the PWM and Buck controllers from Sect. 2.2. The three Test Assessments (TA_R1, TA_R2, TA_R3) encode the requirements (functional, regulatory, and safety, respectively) from Sect. 2.1. We considered six Parameterized Test Sequences producing truncated pyramidal and rectangular pulse behavior (*t-pyr-0*, *t-pyr-85*, *t-pyr-130*, *r-pulse-0*, *r-pulse-85*, *r-pulse-130*). We specifically designed these Parameterized Test Sequences to consider potential uses of e-Bikes in urban environments, where frequent acceleration and deceleration by riders due to traffic is common. As done in the study we replicate [15], we tested all requirements on all model versions: Each experiment was obtained by selecting one of two models, one of three requirements, one of six Parameterized Test sequences, and one of the search algorithms. Thus, we ran 72 experiments (2 models × 3 Test Assessment × 6 Parameterized Test Sequences × 2 search algorithms) in total.

For each experiment, we ran HECATE by setting the maximum number of search iterations to 50. Every run was repeated 10 times to account for the stochastic nature of the algorithms [2]. We executed experiments on an Intel(R) Core(TM) i7-9750H CPU 2.60 GHz, 6 cores, 12 MB SmartCache, 16 GB RAM. We recorded which of the 10 runs returned a failure-revealing test case.

Table 2 summarizes our results. Each row encodes the model and the Parameterized Test Sequence (**PTS**) selected for the experiment. The table is divided into two parts, containing the results for the UR and SA. The three vertical portions of the table identify the Test Assessment blocks (**TA_R1**, **TA_R2**, and **TA_R3**). For each experiment, the table reports the falsification rate (**F**), i.e., the number of runs (over a total of 10 runs) in which HECATE could find a failure-revealing test case, the average ($\hat{\mathbf{S}}$), and the median ($\bar{\mathbf{S}}$) number of iterations required to identify that test case. Cells with gray background mark scenarios in which the two search algorithms significantly differ in terms of falsification rate.

4.2 Effectiveness (RQ1)

We discuss the results (Table 2) for the PWM and Buck controllers.

Functional Requirement R1. For the *PWM controller*, HECATE could generate a failure-revealing test case for all the experiments. Therefore, the PWM controller did not ensure that the speed was always greater than or equal to zero. For the *Buck Controller*, HECATE could not generate any failure-revealing test case for all the experiments.

Regulatory Requirement R2. For both the *PWM* and the *Buck* controller, HECATE generated a failure-revealing test case for all the experiments, showing that the e-Bike violates the regulatory requirement.

Safety Requirement R3. For both the *PWM* and the *Buck* controller, HECATE generated a failure-revealing test case for all the experiments, showing that the e-Bike violates the safety requirement.

Uniform Random (UR) vs Simulated Annealing (SA). SA performed better than UR: They both showed a 10/10 falsification rate in all the experiments except in the two cases (cells marked with gray background in Table 2) where UR showed a falsification rate of 4/10 and 5/10 while SA reached 10/10.

Expert Feedback. The engineer who developed the models analyzed the results of our experiments and confirmed the failures we discovered.

For requirement R1, the engineer confirmed that the response to the reference signal is unstable: The controller (in some conditions) continuously switches between the two algorithms (i.e., for motoring and braking functions), losing stability and reaching negative speed.

For requirement R2, the engineer confirmed the limitations in the tracking speed during the acceleration and braking phases. For the acceleration phase, the PWM problem was caused by the comparison between the vehicle inertia, the motor's power, and the torque. The Buck controller reached high speed in the first step response due to some issues in the PI (Proportional Integral) controller in the speed loop. A more precise parameter tuning could fix this problem. During deceleration, the braking force was not sufficient to track the reference speed. The engineer confirmed that the e-Bike mechanical brakes were not considered in the models. They will be added in future versions of the model.

For requirement R3, the expert confirmed that the PWM speed tracking was not accurate due to the instability caused by switching between the two different algorithms for motoring and braking functions.

Our e-Bike model represents the high-level design developed to perform a preliminary comparison of the two controllers. Therefore, problems were expected.

Summary. HECATE could reveal a failure-revealing test case for all 36 experiments of the PWM controller and 24 experiments of the Buck controller. The engineer who developed the model confirmed the test cases as failure-revealing.

Effectiveness — RQ1

HECATE effectively generated failure-revealing test cases for ≈ 83% (60 out of 72) of our experiments.

4.3 Efficiency (RQ2)

To answer RQ2, we evaluated the efficiency of HECATE by analyzing the time required to detect a failure-revealing test case for each version of the model and requirement from Sect. 2.1. The boxplot from Fig. 4 reports our results of our 10 runs. It does not include the Buck controller and the requirement R1, since HECATE could not produce any failure-revealing test case. Diamonds depict the average, and lines in boxes represent the median.

For each run on the PWM controller, regardless of the algorithm, HECATE required, on average, $9'\,6''$ ($min = 1'\,2''$, $max = 45'\,2''$, $StdDev = 8'\,23''$) for R1, $6'\,14''$ ($min = 59''$, $max = 2h\,0'\,18''$, $StdDev = 12'\,57''$) for R2, and $1'\,36''$ ($min = 1'\,1''$, $max = 7'\,36''$, $StdDev = 1'\,10''$) for R3. For the Buck controller, regardless of the algorithm, it required, on average, $8'\,24''$ ($min = 1'\,4''$, $max = 56'\,59''$, $StdDev = 9'\,57''$) for R2, and $4'\,8''$ ($min = 1'\,4''$, $max = 35'\,29''$, $StdDev = 4'\,59''$) for R3.

Uniform Random (UR) vs Simulated Annealing (SA). UR and SA required on average $6'\,4''$ ($min = 1'\,1''$, $max = 2h\,0'\,18''$, std=$10'\,49''$) and $5'\,38''$ ($min = 59''$, $max = 42'\,23''$, $StdDev = 6'\,34''$) to identify the failure revealing test cases. The Wilcoxon Rank Sum Test, performed with significance level $\alpha = 5\%$, shows that there is no statistical evidence that the number of iterations required by the UR and the SA algorithms belongs to two different populations. To compute the failure-revealing test cases, HECATE required, on average, $5'\,51''$ ($min = 59''$, $max = 2h\,0'\,18''$, $StdDev = 8'\,54''$) across all failure-revealing runs.

Efficiency — RQ2

HECATE required on average $5'\,51''$ ($min = 59''$, $max = 2h\,0'\,18''$, $StdDev = 8'\,54''$) to compute failure-revealing test cases of our models.

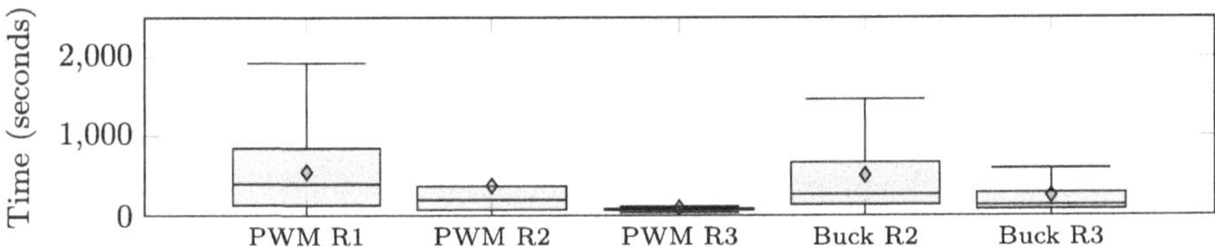

Fig. 4. Time required to generate the test cases for our benchmark.

5 Discussion

In this paper, we replicate a study performed on an automotive cruise controller [15]. We applied the same methodology to an e-Bike study subject to assess whether previously reported findings generalize beyond the original domain. We present lessons learned (Sect. 5.1) and threats to the validity (Sect. 5.2).

5.1 Lessons Learned

The four main lessons we learned from this replication study are as follows:

L1 (Modeling). E-Bike engineers typically develop tests for assessing their models by manually defining inputs and visually inspecting the models' outputs. The engineer who developed the two models confirmed that the proposed Test Sequence and Test Assessment blocks helped reflect on plausible inputs and formalize the requirements of their system. Therefore, the engineer confirmed the usefulness of the test inputs and requirements formalization.

L2 (Testing Procedure). The outputs provided by the proposed testing framework helped the engineer identify flaws within the system design (Sect. 4.2). The time required to compute the failure-revealing test cases was practical for industrial applications (Sect. 4.3). Indeed, while some runs were time-consuming, our case study pertains to safety-critical systems, where the allocated time for testing is generally significant to prevent catastrophic failures.

L3 (Comparison of Solutions). HECATE was beneficial for assessing different controllers: We could assess when the PWM and Buck worked properly. Considering these lessons, the engineer is now using HECATE to automate their testing procedure. The engineer is also interested in evaluating the failure-revealing test case on the physical platform, which they are finalizing.

L4 (Generalizability of Results). Both our results and the ones for the previous study on the automotive cruise controller [15] confirm that HECATE is effective in finding failure-revealing test cases. However, the falsification rate of the original case study ($\approx$ 67%) is lower than the one we obtained ($\approx$ 83%). This difference may derive from system maturity: The e-Bike controller is still under development, while the cruise controller model is more stable. Interestingly, despite the higher falsification rate, our experiments required more time to find failure-revealing test cases than the ones from the original work ($5'\,51''$ vs $4'\,06''$). This difference suggests that domain-specific features influence SBST performance. It indicates that while the approach generalizes conceptually, practitioners should anticipate domain-specific characteristics.

Our results are relevant for *industrial application*. Technology transfer activities require empirical studies that assess the effectiveness of different technologies. Our results confirm the effectiveness of HECATE in detecting failure-revealing test cases for a complex model from a project with industrial partners.

Our results significantly *improved the state of practice*. Before our study, engineers manually developed test cases. Additionally, during the preliminary development stage of the proposed models, engineers tested their behavior by considering profiles for smooth, limited changes in the desired speed. This project improved the state of practice by showing the benefits of search-based testing. Our results benefit other practitioners who are considering the SBST technology.

For the *generalizability of our results*, we do not expect that applying HECATE to other systems will return exactly the same percentage of failure-revealing test cases. This value depends on the model, its development stage, and the Test Blocks. However, our results are *general*: They confirm existing results from the research literature obtained in other domains (e.g., space [31], automotive [12], biomedical [4], medical [9]), and previous results on HECATE [14,15].

The goal of this work *is not* to show the superiority of HECATE compared to other techniques, and therefore compare it with a baseline, but to assess whether its use is beneficial. Comparing different search-based solutions is out of scope: An extensive comparison of SBST techniques cannot be based on a single model and should rely on a larger set to have statistically significant results.

Simulink® Design Verifier (SLDV) is the only tool that we could have used as a baseline since it is the only one that can generate test cases from Test Assessment blocks [28]. However, SLDV can not process our model since it does not support some of its blocks (e.g., the Integrator block).

HECATE can be configured with different search algorithms. Our evaluation considered UR and SA. For our case study, the effectiveness and efficiency of these two algorithms were comparable. This result confirms that random and non-random solutions are complementary [3]: Random solutions are effective when failures are not difficult to find (like early development stages), while non-random solutions (e.g., SA) are more useful when failures are difficult to find since the use of a fitness metric to guide the search process is beneficial.

Our results are based on a single case study. Yet, they are significant. First, the development of our study subjects took considerable time. Second, finding industries sharing their models is complicated since they are usually part of their core business. Third, performing the testing activity for our study subject requires significant know-how: Understanding the model and its requirements, and discussing our results with the expert took considerable time (months).

Our results are based on the opinion of a single expert. Finding knowledgeable experts, especially in niche sectors (like e-Bikes), is complicated. In our case, the expert was the model developer: This provides significant value to our findings.

5.2 Threats to Validity

The Test Blocks we considered could threaten the *external validity* of our results. However, the requirements and the Test Sequences were defined in collaboration with the engineer who developed the model. The selection of our study subject could threaten the *external validity* of our results. We acknowledge that possible missing physical elements or the maturity level of our models can impact the validity of our experiments and conclusions. However, it is a representative model developed by expert engineers in a project with industrial partners.

The values we selected for the configuration parameters of HECATE, as well as the choice of the SBST algorithm, could threaten the *internal validity* of our results. To mitigate this threat, we reused the default values provided by HECATE.

6 Related Work

Numerous studies evaluated the effectiveness of SBST in identifying failure-revealing test cases for CPS development [9,15]. In this work, we assessed the usefulness of SBST by considering the motor controller for an e-Bike, analyzing two different implementations, namely one based on a Buck converter and one controlled by using the PWM strategy.

Testing e-Bike motor controllers is of utmost importance. However, this activity is commonly performed by physically testing electric bikes or their components with different loads, pedaling profiles, roads, and scenarios [34]. Instead, in this work, we used HECATE [14] for model-in-the-loop testing.

7 Conclusion

This replication paper assesses the usefulness of HECATE in generating failure-revealing test cases for an e-Bike study subject. HECATE successfully identified failure-revealing test cases (confirmed by the engineer who developed the model) in practical time. We critically reflected on our results, presented lessons learned, and discussed their relevance for industrial applications. By repeating the original SBST experiment in a different context, this work strengthens the empirical foundation for search-based testing with Simulink® models and highlights the importance of multi-domain replication studies.

Acknowledgment. The work of Andrea Bombarda is supported by PNC - ANTHEM - PNC0000003 – CUP: B53C22006700001. The work of Nunzio Marco Bisceglia and Claudio Menghi was in part supported by the European Union – Next Generation EU. “Sustainable Mobility Center (Centro Nazionale per la Mobilitá Sostenibile - CNMS)”, M4C2 – Investment 1.4, Project Code CN_00000023. The work of Claudio Menghi was in part supported by projects SERICS (PE00000014) under the NRRP MUR program and GLACIATION (101070141).

Data Availibility Statement. A replication package with our data, results, and scripts is publicly available [16].

Disclosure of Interests. The authors have no competing interests to declare that are relevant to the content of this article.

References

1. Ali, S., Briand, L.C., Hemmati, H., Panesar-Walawege, R.K.: A systematic review of the application and empirical investigation of search-based test case generation. IEEE Trans. Softw. Eng. **36**(6), 742–762 (2010). https://doi.org/10.1109/TSE.2009.52
2. Arcuri, A., Briand, L.: A practical guide for using statistical tests to assess randomized algorithms in software engineering. In: 2011 33rd International Conference on Software Engineering (ICSE), pp. 1–10 (2011). https://doi.org/10.1145/1985793.1985795
3. Arcuri, A., Iqbal, M.Z., Briand, L.: Random testing: theoretical results and practical implications. IEEE Trans. Softw. Eng. **38**(2), 258–277 (2011)
4. Ayesh, M., Mehan, N., Dhanraj, E., et al.: Two simulink models with requirements for a simple controller of a pacemaker device. In: International Workshop on Applied Verification of Continuous and Hybrid Systems. vol. 90, pp. 18–25 (2022)

5. Badreddin, O., Lethbridge, T.C., Elassar, M.: Modeling practices in open source software. In: Open Source Software: Quality Verification, pp. 127–139. Springer (2013)
6. Boll, A., Brokhausen, F., Amorim, T., Kehrer, T., Vogelsang, A.: Characteristics, potentials, and limitations of open-source simulink projects for empirical research. Softw. Syst. Model. **20**(6), 2111–2130 (2021)
7. Boll, A., Kehrer, T.: On the replicability of experimental tool evaluations in model-based development: Lessons learnt from a systematic literature review focusing on matlab/simulink. In: Systems Modelling and Management, pp. 111–130. Springer (2020). https://doi.org/10.1007/978-3-030-58167-1_9
8. Boll, A., Vieregg, N., Kehrer, T.: Replicability of experimental tool evaluations in model-based software and systems engineering with matlab/simulink. Innov. Syst. Softw. Eng. **20**(3), 209–224 (2024)
9. Bombarda, A., Bonfanti, S., Gargantini, A.: Automatic test generation with asmeta for the mechanical ventilator milano controller. In: Testing Software and Systems, pp. 65–72. Springer International Publishing, Cham (2022). https://doi.org/10.1007/978-3-031-04673-5_5
10. Corti, F., Minervini, M., Giangrande, P., Reatti, A., Malighetti, P., Pugi, L.: Simulink-based simulation of electric bicycle dynamics and regenerative braking for battery state of charge assessment. In: Mediterranean Electrotechnical Conference (MELECON), pp. 803–808. IEEE (2024). https://doi.org/10.1109/melecon56669.2024.10608778
11. Dyba, T., Kitchenham, B.A., Jorgensen, M.: Evidence-based software engineering for practitioners. IEEE Softw. **22**(1), 58–65 (2005)
12. Fainekos, G.E., Sankaranarayanan, S., Ueda, K., Yazarel, H.: Verification of automotive control applications using S-TaLiRo. In: 2012 American Control Conference (ACC), pp. 3567–3572 (2012). https://doi.org/10.1109/ACC.2012.6315384
13. Formica, F., Fan, T., Menghi, C.: Search-based software testing driven by automatically generated and manually defined fitness functions. ACM Trans. Softw. Eng. Methodol. **33**(2) (2023). https://doi.org/10.1145/3624745
14. Formica, F., Fan, T., Rajhans, A., Pantelic, V., Lawford, M., Menghi, C.: Simulation-based testing of simulink models with test sequence and test assessment blocks. IEEE Trans. Softw. Eng. **50**(2), 239–257 (2024). https://doi.org/10.1109/tse.2023.3343753
15. Formica, F., Petrunti, N., Bruck, L., et al.: Test case generation for drivability requirements of an automotive cruise controller: an experience with an industrial simulator. In: Joint European Software Engineering Conference and Symposium on the Foundations of Software Engineering, pp. 1949–1960. ESEC/FSE, ACM (2023). https://doi.org/10.1145/3611643.3613894
16. FOSELAB: Experimental Results. https://github.com/foselab/HECATE-Bikes (2024), Accessed 21 July 2025
17. Harman, M., Jia, Y., Zhang, Y.: Achievements, open problems and challenges for search based software testing. In: IEEE International Conference on Software Testing, Verification and Validation (ICST), pp. 1–12 (2015). https://doi.org/10.1109/ICST.2015.7102580
18. Harman, M., Jones, B.F.: Search-based software engineering. Inf. Softw. Technol. **43**(14), 833–839 (2001). https://doi.org/10.1016/s0950-5849(01)00189-6
19. Inc., M.: Design. Simulate. Deplo. https://www.mathworks.com/help/matlab/add-ons.html (2024), Accessed 21 July 2025

20. Inc., M.: Simulink test develop, manage, and execute simulation-based tests. https://www.mathworks.com/products/simulink-test.html (2024), Accessed 21 July 2025
21. Inc., M.: Test assessment. https://www.mathworks.com/help/sltest/ref/testassessment.html (2024), Accessed 21 July 2025
22. Inc., M.: Test sequence basics. https://www.mathworks.com/help/sltest/ug/introduction-to-test-sequences.html (2024), Accessed 21 July 2025
23. Insights, F.B.: E-bike drive unit market size, share & covid-19 impact analysis, by product type (mid-drive motors and hub motors), by application (oem and aftermarket), and regional forecasts, 2023-2030. https://www.fortunebusinessinsights.com/e-bike-drive-unit-market-107520 (2024), Accessed 21 July 2025
24. Juristo, N., Gómez, O.S.: Replication of software engineering experiments. In: Empirical Software Engineering and Verification: International Summer Schools, LASER 2008-2010, Revised Tutorial Lectures, pp. 60–88 (2012)
25. Khandait, T., Formica, F., Arcaini, P., et al.: Arch-comp 2024 category report: Falsification. In: International Workshop on Applied Verification for Continuous and Hybrid Systems. EPiC Series in Computing, vol. 103, pp. 122–144. EasyChair (2024). https://doi.org/10.29007/hgfv
26. Kitchenham, B., Dyba, T., Jorgensen, M.: Evidence-based software engineering. In: International Conference on Software Engineering, pp. 273–281 (2004). https://doi.org/10.1109/ICSE.2004.1317449
27. Liebel, G., Marko, N., Tichy, M., Leitner, A., Hansson, J.: Model-based engineering in the embedded systems domain: an industrial survey on the state-of-practice. Softw. Syst. Model. **17**, 91–113 (2018)
28. MathWorks: Generate and Export Tests from Requirements Table Blocks (2024). https://www.mathworks.com/help/slrequirements/ug/export-generated-tests-from-requirements-table.html
29. Matinnejad, R., Nejati, S., Briand, L.C., Bruckmann, T.: Automated test suite generation for time-continuous simulink models. In: International Conference on Software Engineering, pp. 595–606. ICSE, ACM (2016). https://doi.org/10.1145/2884781.2884797
30. Melo, S.M., Carver, J.C., Souza, P.S., Souza, S.R.: Empirical research on concurrent software testing: a systematic mapping study. Inf. Softw. Technol. **105**, 226–251 (2019)
31. Menghi, C., Nejati, S., Briand, L., Parache, Y.I.: Approximation-refinement testing of compute-intensive cyber-physical models: an approach based on system identification. In: International Conference on Software Engineering, pp. 372–384. ICSE, ACM/IEEE (2020). https://doi.org/10.1145/3377811.3380370
32. Mezhuyev, V., Al-Emran, M., Ismail, M.A., Benedicenti, L., Chandran, D.A.P.: The acceptance of search-based software engineering techniques: an empirical evaluation using the technology acceptance model. IEEE Access **7**, 101073–101085 (2019). https://doi.org/10.1109/ACCESS.2019.2917913
33. N.V., B.: Brembo homepage. https://www.brembo.com/en/ (2024), Accessed 21 July 2025
34. Parastiwi, A., Al-Akbary, P.C.M., Safitri, H.K.: Analysis and testing of DC motor control system for electric bike. Conf. Seri. Mater. Sci. Eng. **732**(1), 012055 (2020). https://doi.org/10.1088/1757-899x/732/1/012055
35. Pirelli: Pirelli homepage. http://www.pirelli.com (2024), Accessed 21 July 2025

36. Sayyad, A.S., Goseva-Popstojanova, K., Menzies, T., Ammar, H.: On parameter tuning in search based software engineering: a replicated empirical study. In: International Workshop on Replication in Empirical Software Engineering Research, pp. 84–90. RESER, IEEE (2013). https://doi.org/10.1109/RESER.2013.6
37. Schepers, P., Wolt, K.K., Fishman, E.: The safety of e-bikes in the netherlands. International Transport Forum Discussion Paper 2018-02, Paris (2018). https://doi.org/10.1787/21de1ffa-en
38. Shepperd, M., Ajienka, N., Counsell, S.: The role and value of replication in empirical software engineering results. Inf. Softw. Technol. **99**, 120–132 (2018)
39. Shrestha, S.L., Chowdhury, S.A., Csallner, C.: Replicability study: corpora for understanding simulink models & projects . In: ACM/IEEE International Symposium on Empirical Software Engineering and Measurement (ESEM), pp. 1–12. IEEE (2023). https://doi.org/10.1109/ESEM56168.2023.10304867
40. Stories, M.C.: Bosch ebike systems develops electric bike controller with model-based design. https://www.mathworks.com/company/user_stories/bosch-ebike-systems-develops-electric-bike-controller-with-model-based-design.html (2024), Accessed 21 July 2025
41. Times, E.: Software takes ebikes to new heights. https://www.eetimes.eu/software-takes-ebikes-to-new-heights/ (2024), Accessed 21 July 2025

Challenge Track

Fuzz Smarter, Not Harder: Towards Greener Fuzzing with GreenAFL

Ayse Irmak Ercevik[1], Aidan Dakhama[1](✉), Melane Navaratnarajah[1], Yazhuo Cao[1], and Leo Fernandes[2]

[1] King's College London, London, UK
{ayse.ercevik,aidan.dakhama,melane.navaratnarajah,yazhuo.cao}@kcl.ac.uk
[2] The Federal Institute of Education, Science, and Technology of Alagoas, Alagoas, Brazil
leonardo.fernandes@ifal.edu.br

Abstract. Fuzzing has become a key search-based technique for software testing, but continuous fuzzing campaigns consume substantial computational resources and generate significant carbon footprints. Existing grey-box fuzzing approaches like AFL++ focus primarily on coverage maximisation, without considering the energy costs of exploring different execution paths. This paper presents GreenAFL, an energy-aware framework that incorporates power consumption into the fuzzing heuristics to reduce the environmental impact of automated testing whilst maintaining coverage. GreenAFL introduces two key modifications to traditional fuzzing workflows: energy-aware corpus minimisation considering power consumption when reducing initial corpora, and energy-guided heuristics that direct mutation towards high-coverage, low-energy inputs. We conduct an ablation study comparing vanilla AFL++, energy-based corpus minimisation, and energy-based heuristics to evaluate the individual contributions of each component. Our evaluation shows up to 7.4% lower energy usage and 7.1% lower throughput while maintaining or improving coverage, with best-case coverage gains of 2.6%.

Keywords: software sustainability · fuzzing · green computing · AFL++

1 Introduction

Fuzzing has emerged as a powerful greedy search-based technique for discovering bugs in complex software systems, serving as a common search-based technique in industrial testing pipelines; however, it comes with significant computational and energy costs. Systems such as OSS-Fuzz [11] run continuous fuzzing campaigns using substantial resources, consequently producing large carbon footprints. Similarly, fuzzing is increasingly applied to large-scale and energy-intensive systems such as operating systems [3,13], quantum system simulators [2], and system simulators [5,6,8]. As automated testing scales, it becomes

M. Wagner and M. Zhang (Eds.): SSBSE 2025, LNCS 16228, pp. 133–139, 2026.
https://doi.org/10.1007/978-3-032-24839-8_9

increasingly important to manage the energy usage of such systems. Grey-box fuzzing techniques such as AFL++ use coverage feedback to guide input mutation towards more effective test cases. Whilst this coverage-guided approach improves the efficiency of discovering new execution paths, it fails to consider the energy consumption associated with exploring these paths. Consequently, running fuzzing campaigns remains an energy-intensive process. Much of the existing work on reducing the emissions of fuzzing focuses on stopping criteria [9], or in the case of `GreenBench`, improving the emissions of the benchmarks used to evaluate fuzzers [12]. Yue et al.'s EcoFuzz reduces redundant test case generation through optimised scheduling with an Adversarial Multi-Armed Bandit model, achieving higher coverage from fewer executions [14]. Similarly, Lyu et al.'s SLIME introduces program-sensitive energy allocation to adaptively distribute fuzzing effort across seeds rather than measuring actual power use [10]. Unlike our approach, neither EcoFuzz nor SLIME measure actual energy usage, but instead optimise seed scheduling to indirectly reduce waste.

We propose GreenAFL, a modification to `afl-cmin` that considers the system energy usage of each input when minimising the initial corpus. Further, we extend the heuristics used by AFL++ to guide fuzzing towards inputs that achieve high coverage whilst maintaining low CPU and memory energy consumption. To the best of our knowledge, this is the first work that directly incorporates energy usage into fuzzing and minimisation heuristics. In our evaluation, energy-aware corpus minimisation consistently delivered the best balance of reduced energy (up to 7.4%) and maintained or improved coverage (up to 2.6%), while energy-guided fuzzing heuristics showed promising benefits but require further refinement. Together, these results demonstrate that direct integration of energy awareness into fuzzing workflows is both feasible and impactful. Beyond sustainability, reducing energy translates directly into lower infrastructure costs, making greener fuzzing attractive for industrial-scale deployments.

Availability. GreenAFL, and documentation demonstrating its generalisability, reproducibility materials, and experimental results, are available at [1].

2 GreenAFL

GreenAFL extends the AFL++ fuzzing framework by integrating energy awareness into corpora minimisation (`green-cmin`) and energy-aware fuzzing heuristics (`green-afl`). Our approach leverages Intel's hardware-based power monitoring via `cppjoules` [4]. Our implementation is generic and modular, utilising the `LD_PRELOAD` library that wraps the system under test to record energy usage to ensure portability. While our implementation is Intel-specific, the preload-based mechanism can be adapted to other architectures (e.g. AMD or ARM CPUs) and extended to NVIDIA GPUs, where `cppjoules` already provides support [4].

2.1 Energy-Aware Corpus Minimisation

AFL's `cmin` reduces the initial corpus by discarding redundant inputs, keeping only those that contribute new coverage. GreenAFL augments this process by also considering the energy consumption of each input. Specifically, we retain inputs that maximise coverage while minimising power cost – balancing effectiveness with efficiency; this can reduce the emissions required for a test, as well as serve to reduce running costs, especially in the context of large scale long running campaigns. This ensures that the subsequent fuzzing loop operates on inputs that are both coverage-rich and energy-efficient. GreenAFL runs **`afl-showmap`** once per seed to record which program edges the seed reaches, while measuring the total energy for that run. For each edge, we keep the seed that has the lowest energy cost. It is important to note that this measurement reflects the energy consumed during the execution of each seed by the fuzzer, rather than the long-term cost of the resulting test archive.

2.2 Energy-Guided Fuzzing Loop

In traditional AFL++, the fuzzing loop schedules mutant generation according to new coverage. GreenAFL extends this loop with energy-aware heuristics that modify the allocation of mutation cycles. These heuristics aim to bias the search towards executions with higher "coverage-per-watt".

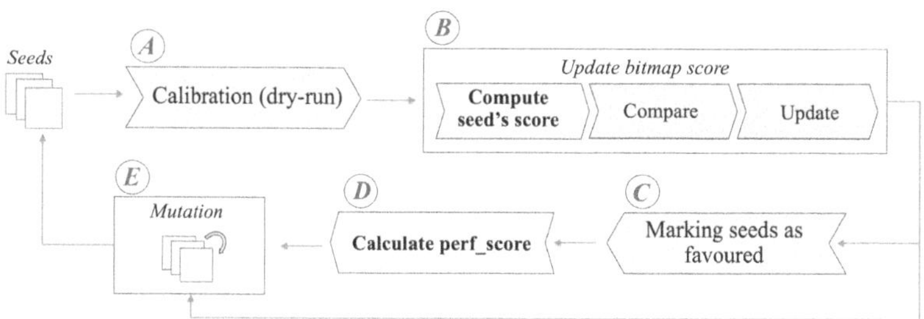

Fig. 1. Overview of GreenAFL's energy-guided fuzzing loop. The **green boxes with bold text** highlight where our energy-aware heuristics are applied, ((B), energy-aware score computation) and ((D), airtime scheduling).

Airtime Scheduling via Energy-Scaled Performance Score . In the AFL++ fuzzing loop (Fig. 1, (D)) each seed has a `perf_score` computed which determines how much fuzzing effort is allocated and represents a combination of factors – such as execution speed and input size – which is used to determine the number of mutation cycles. We modify `perf_score` to be energy-aware by applying a scale factor inversely proportional to the energy used during the execution of the seed. The multipliers are derived from each seed's CPU and memory energy relative to the campaign's global minimum and maximum energy cost, which we map to the range of $5\times$ to $\frac{1}{5}\times$. This prioritises low energy seeds, allowing for more mutation cycles (Fig. 1, (E)).

Energy-Aware Favoured Seed Selection. AFL++ assigns a single champion seed to each edge transition in the coverage bitmap (Fig. 1, (B)). Whenever a seed is executed and hits an instrumented edge, its score is compared against the current champion's score. If the new seed has a lower score, it replaces the current champion for that edge. We make this selection energy-aware by applying an energy-based scale factor in the range of $\frac{4}{5}\times$ to $\frac{5}{4}\times$. The multiplier is obtained by a logarithmic normalisation of the seed's total energy cost relative to the campaign's minimum and maximum energy costs. This prioritises low-energy seeds and penalises high-energy seeds, marking low-energy seeds as favoured (Fig. 1 stage (C)). Favoured seeds are then prioritised in the fuzzing schedule and selected more often for mutation.

Table 1. Results from 3 repetitions of fuzzing campaigns across all three targets, showing the mean ± variance. **Energy** (as reported by `perf`) combines CPU and RAM package power. **Throughput** represents executions per second. **Bold** marks the best per target, ***bold italics*** the best overall.

Config		Throughput			Energy (kJ)			Coverage (%)		
cmin	**fuzz**	*libpng*	*zlib*	*jsoncpp*	*libpng*	*zlib*	*jsoncpp*	*libpng*	*zlib*	*jsoncpp*
afl	afl	3135 ± 15.6	2845 ± 54	2001 ± 170	2122 ± 1.74	2029 ± 7.12	2021 ± 6.31	0.2 ± 0	50.1 ± 0.28	38.9 ± 0
green	afl	1110 ± 871	2947 ± 43.2	2133 ± 59.1	**2120** ± 40.2	2153 ± 10.2	***1872*** ± 4.73	39.5 ± 0.01	***51.4*** ± 0	**39.1** ± 0
afl	green	2101 ± 11.9	**1867** ± 91.9	**1826** ± 37.4	2167 ± 1.22	2211 ± 3.29	2211 ± 10.2	0.2 ± 0	50.3 ± 0.55	38.9 ± 0
green	green	***969*** ± 200	1981 ± 28.4	1858 ± 2.65	2421 ± 7.41	**1971** ± 3.58	2252 ± 3.09	**39.6** ± 0.01	***51.4*** ± 0	**39.1** ± 0

2.3 Experimental Setup

We evaluate GreenAFL through an ablation study with two toggles: corpus minimisation (`green-cmin`, `afl-cmin`) and energy-guided fuzzing (`green-fuzz`, `afl-fuzz`). We run four configurations âĂŞ neither, each individually, and both. The impact of each setting is measured in terms of total energy consumption, as reported by `perf stat`. The fuzzing targets come from OSS-Fuzz [11], specifically we explore `libpng`, `zlib`, and `jsoncpp` with the corpora and test harnesses provided by OSS-Fuzz. We run this evaluation over three repetitions across each configuration and each target, with 24 h campaigns. We perform this evaluation on an Intel Xeon D-1548 CPU (2.0 GHz, 8 cores), with 64 GB RAM, 8 GB swap, and running Ubuntu 22.04.5 LTS (x86_64), ensuring only one campaign is run at a given time to minimise external effects on power usage.

3 Results

RQ1: *To what extent can energy-aware corpus minimisation and fuzzing reduce energy use whilst maintaining or improving coverage across different targets?*

We compare the impact of our `green-fuzz` and `green-cmin` fuzzing campaigns by highlighting their distinctive contributions in Table 1. Incorporating `green-cmin` was found to consistently maintain or improve coverage across all targets whilst having the lowest energy usage. For example, `jsoncpp`, `green-cmin` achieved 39.1% coverage compared to the baseline 38.9% coverage while consuming 1872kJ (vs 2021kJ), resulting in a statistically significant reduction in energy consumption (Welch's t-test, $p < 10^{-4}$). `zlib` achieved the highest coverage (51.4%), which is also statistically significant compared to the baseline (Welch's t-test, $p < 0.02$), and 3% less energy than the baseline with both modifications. However, `green-fuzz` produces coverage that is often comparable to the baseline but can sometimes increase the overall energy usage. In all cases, the best performing configuration included at least one of our modifications; showing that prioritising inputs by energy usage can also result in higher fuzzing performance and yield tangible savings in energy. Additionally, the configurations that explicitly resulted in the lowest energy consumption often reached the highest coverage.

`green-Fuzz`, reduces the execution throughput (execs/s) considerably. For `libpng` there is a 69.2% reduction in executions from the baseline, yet achieving better coverage. This shows that less effort is needed for comparable results to the baseline coverage results. A deeper analysis is required to determine whether `green-fuzz`'s higher total energy stems from increased energy per execution, overhead in measurement, or the heuristic calculations. However, the fact that `green-fuzz` reaches comparable results with fewer executions suggests potential efficiency gains if this issue can be resolved.

`Libpng` was found to have an unexpected anomaly in the configurations that used the standard corpus minimisation, where it produced an extremely low coverage – this was found to be a consequence of the over-aggressive minimisation of `afl-cmin`, reducing the initial corpus to 1 seed.

(RQ2) *To what extent can energy-aware corpus minimisation and energy-guided heuristics improve the rate of convergence?*

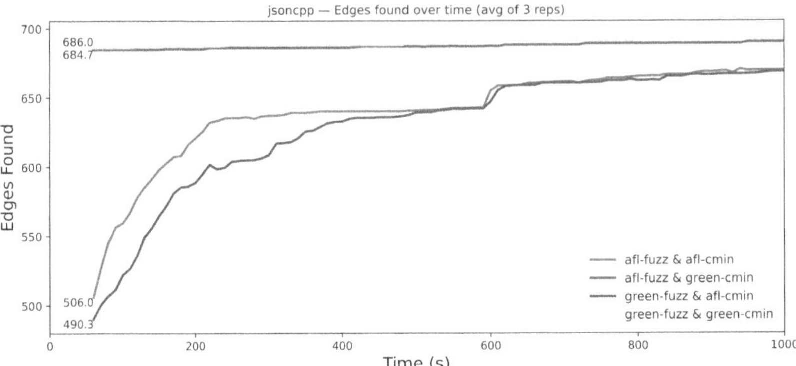

Fig. 2. Edges found over time for `jsoncpp`. Each curve shows the mean across three repetitions for a given configuration.

Figure 2 highlights that runs with `green-cmin` have an early advantage; the energy-aware seeds find unique edges sooner than `afl-cmin`. For instance, `jsoncpp`'s first 680 unique edges were found within 60 s, whereas this took more than 1200 s with `afl-cmin`. This pattern is present across all configurations and targets that include `green-cmin`, demonstrating the effectiveness of this modification. During the actual fuzzing for `green-cmin`, the coverage/edges only slowly increase, likely due to being closer to saturation of the targets. However, after the 24-hour runs, `afl-cmin` is still not surpassed by the baseline. Although we do not have the time series for energy consumption, we can use throughput as a proxy. Inspection using throughput over time reveals that `green-fuzz` consistently reduces the execution throughput (execs/s) throughout the entire run, indicating that `green-fuzz` likely uses less energy in the actual execution of seeds despite the higher overall energy usage.

4 Discussion and Conclusion

In this work, we introduce GreenAFL, an energy-aware extension of AFL++ that integrates energy costs into corpus minimisation and fuzzing heuristics. Our evaluation across a subset of industry standard OSS-Fuzz benchmarks demonstrates that integrating energy-guided heuristics into corpus minimisation (`green-cmin`) is an effective method to increase coverage and reduce energy usage. `green-cmin` tends to preserve cheaper, coverage-rich seeds, giving an early advantage and preventing over-pruning.

While we did not find the energy-aware heuristic (`green-fuzz`) to reduce the energy cost of fuzzing, it showed promise in maintaining comparable coverage while executing fewer seeds. This shows that the bottleneck to lower energy usage is likely in the implementation and parameters of our heuristic. Further, we found a high fluctuation in the rate of execution when using `green-fuzz`, showing that the relationship between seed energy usage of mutants is not strictly linear. As such, future work includes tuning these parameters to a general range, exploring dynamically adjusting these parameters during the fuzzing process, and optimising the efficiency of the heuristic measurements and implementation.

Overall, our results show that energy-based heuristics can improve coverage-per-watt in fuzzing and help reduce the environmental impact of large-scale campaigns. Given the widespread use of fuzzing in industry (e.g., OSS-Fuzz [11]), these results indicate that energy-aware extensions could offer immediate relevance for practical continuous testing pipelines, reducing the environmental footprint of large-scale fuzzing while improving efficiency.

Acknowledgments. We thank CloudLab [7] for providing the platform and infrastructure that enabled our experiments.

References

1. Artifact of Greenafl (2025). https://doi.org/10.5281/zenodo.17172496
2. Blackwell, D., et al.: Fuzzing-based differential testing for quantum simulators. In: SSBSE Conference, pp. 63–69. Springer (2024)
3. Bursey, J., et al.: Syzretrospector: a large-scale retrospective study of syzbot. arXiv preprint arXiv:2401.11642 (2024)
4. Chattaraj, R., et al.: Cppjoules: an energy measurement tool for c++. arXiv preprint arXiv:2412.13555 (2024)
5. Dakhama, A., et al.: Searchgem5: Towards reliable gem5 with search based software testing and large language models. In: SSBSE Conf, pp. 160–166 (2023)
6. Dakhama, A., et al.: Enhancing search-based testing with LLMs for finding bugs in system simulators. Autom. Softw. Eng. **32**(2), 1–45 (2025)
7. Duplyakin, D., et al.: The design and operation of CloudLab In: USENIX ATC 19 Conf, pp. 1–14 (2019)
8. Even-Mendoza, K., et al.: Search+ LLM-based testing for arm simulators. In: 2025 ICSE-SEIP Conf, pp. 469–480. IEEE (2025)
9. Lipp, S., et al.: Green fuzzing: a saturation-based stopping criterion using vulnerability prediction. In: ISSTA 2023 Conf, pp. 127–139 (2023)
10. Lyu, C., et al.: Slime: program-sensitive energy allocation for fuzzing. In: Proceedings of the 31st ACM SIGSOFT International Symposium on Software Testing and Analysis, pp. 365–377 (2022)
11. Oss-fuzz: Continuous fuzzing for open source software (2016). https://google.github.io/oss-fuzz/
12. Ounjai, J., et al.: Green fuzzer benchmarking. In: ISSTA, pp. 1396–1406 (2023)
13. Shi, H., et al.: Industry practice of coverage-guided enterprise Linux kernel fuzzing. In: ESEC/FSE 2019, pp. 986–995 (2019)
14. Yue, T., et al.: EcoFuzz : Adaptive Energy-Saving Grey box fuzzing as a variant of the adversarial Multi-Armed bandit. In: USENIX Security 20 Conf, pp. 2307–2324 (2020)

GA4GC: Greener Agent for Greener Code via Multi-objective Configuration Optimization

Jingzhi Gong[1], Yixin Bian[2], Luis de la Cal[3], Giovanni Pinna[4], Anisha Uteem[5], David Williams[6], Mar Zamorano[6], Karine Even-Mendoza[5], W. B. Langdon[6], Hector D. Menendez[5], and Federica Sarro[6](✉)

[1] University of Leeds, Leeds, UK
j.gong@leeds.ac.uk
[2] Harbin Normal University, Harbin, China
bianyixin@hrbnu.edu.cn
[3] Universidad Politécnica de Madrid, Madrid, Spain
l.delacal@upm.es
[4] University of Trieste, Trieste, Italy
giovanni.pinna@phd.units.it
[5] King's College London, London, UK
{anisha.uteem,karine.even_mendoza,hector.menendez}@kcl.ac.uk
[6] University College London, London, UK
{ucabdjj,maria.lopez.20,w.langdon,f.sarro}@ucl.ac.uk

Abstract. Coding agents powered by Large Language Models (LLMs) face critical sustainability and scalability challenges in industrial deployment, often incurring costs that may exceed optimization benefits. We introduce GA4GC, the first framework to optimize coding agent runtime (greener agent) and code performance (greener code) trade-offs by discovering Pareto-optimal agent hyperparameters and prompt templates. Evaluation on the SWE-Perf benchmark demonstrates up to 135-fold hypervolume improvement, reducing agent runtime by 37.7% while improving correctness. Baseline comparisons and influence analysis confirm the effectiveness of GA4GC, identify temperature as the most influential hyperparameter, and provide actionable strategies to balance agent and code sustainability in industrial deployment.

Keywords: SBSE · GenAI · Coding Agents · Green SE · AI4SE

1 Introduction

Code performance optimization is fundamental to software development, directly impacting system scalability, resource consumption, and user experience [15]. While Large Language Models (LLMs) show promise in automating this process [10], current approaches focus on simple benchmarks like HumanEval [6] that do not capture real-world software engineering complexity [12].

M. Wagner and M. Zhang (Eds.): SSBSE 2025, LNCS 16228, pp. 140–146, 2026.
https://doi.org/10.1007/978-3-032-24839-8_10

To address this limitation, researchers and practitioners have increasingly turned to agentic workflows, where LLMs operate as autonomous agents capable of iterative reasoning, tool use, and complex decision-making [3]. These approaches have shown promising results in realistic software engineering (SE) benchmarks such as SWE-Perf [13], which provides code optimization tasks reflecting the complexity that agents face in industry deployments.

Unlike single-shot code LLMs, coding agents operate through iterative reasoning processes that require multiple LLM calls, each consuming significant computational resources [4]. Although these agents can successfully solve complex real-world coding tasks, a single agent running on real-world SE problems can consume over 100,000 tokens [1]. Moreover, without careful tuning, the energy consumed by an optimization agent can require hundreds of thousands of code executions to reach an energetic "break-even" point, making some optimizations a net energy loss [7]. As organizations scale deployments, this creates prohibitive costs and threatens environmental sustainability, directly conflicting with Green Software Engineering principles and Net Zero targets [8].[1]

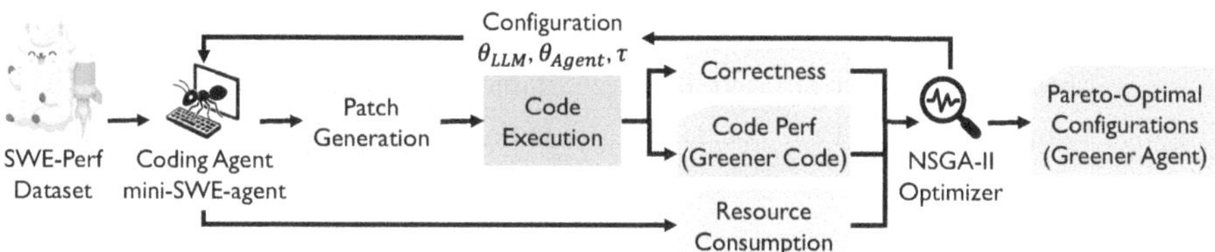

Fig. 1. toolName workflow of multi-objective configuration optimization.

We address these challenges by proposing `GA4GC` (Greener Agent for Greener Code), which optimizes the trade-off between resource consumption of the coding agent and performance of the generated code. Our key insight is that the vast configuration space of coding agents, including prompt templates, LLM- and agent-specific hyperparameters, is too complex for manual exploration. Therefore `GA4GC` uses NSGA-II Multi-Objective Genetic Algorithm (MOGA) optimization to discover Pareto-optimal agent configurations. **Our contributions are**:

- `GA4GC`, a MOGA framework that discovers Pareto-optimal coding agent configurations that are up to 37.7% faster (943 vs 1513 s) while improving correctness, with up to 135 times improved hypervolume over the default.
- Configuration influence analysis via Random Forest reveals that temperature has the highest overall influence. LLM hyperparameters primarily impact task effectiveness, while agent constraints affect resource consumption.
- Actionable suggestions for coding agent practitioners across three scenarios: runtime-critical (low temperature with restrictive top_p), performance-critical (moderate temperature with balanced top_p), and context-specific optimization via `GA4GC`.

[1] https://www.un.org/en/climatechange/net-zero-coalition.

Related Work. Recent green GenAI research has applied reinforcement learning for energy-efficient code generation [14], compared energy efficiency of LLM versus human-written code [2], and optimized GenAI hyperparameters for domain modeling [5] and text-to-image generation [9,11]. These approaches, however, focus on single-shot generative tasks. By contrast, we address the challenges of complex, multi-turn agentic workflows, mitigating the substantial computational costs of deploying coding agents in real-world software engineering.

Table 1. Configuration search space. Decimal range = any value within the range; integer range = only integer values; {set} = only specified values.

Category	Hyperparameter	Abbr.	Range/Values	Description
LLM	Temperature	Temp	[0.0, 1.0]	Controls randomness in token selection
	Top_p	TopP	[0.1, 1.0]	Limits sampled token vocabulary size
	Max_tokens	Token	[512, 4096]	Constrains maximum response length
Agent	Step_limit	Step	[10,40]	Limits number of LLM calls
	Cost_limit ($)	Cost	[3.0, 10.0]	Constrains total cost of LLM usage
	Env_timeout (s)	ETi	[40, 60]	Timeout for environment operations
	LLM_timeout (s)	LTi	[40, 60]	Timeout for individual LLM calls
Prompt	Template Variant	Pr	{1,2,3}	Different template configurations

2 Methodology and Experimental Setup

MOGA Optimization. Figure 1 illustrates GA4GC's workflow, where we employ NSGA-II to explore the agent configuration space defined by $\mathcal{C} = (\theta_{LLM}, \theta_{agent}, \tau)$, where θ_{LLM} represents LLM-specific hyperparameters, θ_{agent} represents agent-specific operational constraints, and τ represents the prompt template variant[2]. Table 1 details the configuration search space.

We define three fitness functions: $f_1(\mathcal{C})$ = correctness (passes all test cases), $f_2(\mathcal{C})$ = performance gain (code speedup), and $f_3(\mathcal{C})$ = agent runtime (minimize). For each candidate configuration, the agent receives a code optimization task and generates patches through iterative reasoning, during which we measure f_3. Generated patches are executed in isolated Docker environments to measure f_1 and f_2, and the output is a Pareto front of non-dominated configurations.
Research Questions. We address three research questions (RQs):

➤**RQ1. To what extent can GA4GC improve the resource consumption and performance trade-offs of coding agents compared to default configurations?**

➤**RQ2. How do different hyperparameters influence agent resource consumption and task performance in the optimization process?**

[2] Details on the prompt templates we used can be found on GA4GC's GitHub page.

➤RQ3. What actionable strategies can be derived from the Pareto-optimal configurations for sustainable coding agent deployment?

Experimental Setup. We implement mini-SWE-agent[3] with Gemini 2.5 Pro as the base LLM. Our evaluation uses SWE-Perf [13], a benchmark for code optimization tasks in real-world repositories where the goal is to improve code runtime while maintaining functionality. Given the extensive evaluation time required for each candidate configuration, we focus on the astropy project[4], using 9 instances for training and 3 instances for validation.

We use `pymoo`'s default NSGA-II setup[5] with a population of 5 and 5 generations, giving 25 configurations. Each configuration is evaluated by running the agent on all 9 training instances and measuring the three objectives (f_1, f_2, f_3). After optimization, we extract the Pareto-optimal configurations and, to assess generalization, validate them on 3 held-out instances. In total, each run took between 25 and 35 h and cost \$50 to \$150 for LLM API calls.

All experiments are conducted on an isolated Google Cloud Platform server with 4 CPUs, 16 GB RAM, running Ubuntu 25.04. Performance gains for each SWE-Perf instance are measured 20 times, and statistical significance is evaluated using the Mann-Whitney U test with $p < 0.1$ [13].

Table 2. Default vs. `GA4GC`-optimized configurations. Corr = Correctness, Perf = performance gain (%), Runt = runtime (s), HV = hypervolume, VHV = validation hypervolume. See Table 1 for other definitions. Green cells indicate improvements over default.

Config	Temp	TopP	Token	Step	Cost	ETi	LTi	Pr	Corr	Perf	Runt	HV (%)	VHV (%)
Default	0.000	1.000	4096	240	3.00	60	60	-	2/9	0.00	1513.3	0.52	1.1
#4	0.085	0.135	1120	36	9.26	41	57	2	4/9	0.00	943.1	5.82	4.1
#5	0.692	0.384	2972	38	6.73	40	56	3	8/9	6.43	984.8	70.28	14.9
#9	0.725	0.412	2972	22	6.73	43	41	3	7/9	0.00	958.1	9.25	21.6
#15	0.657	0.384	2972	38	6.73	40	56	2	7/9	10.67	1400.1	33.42	2.7
#16	0.085	0.131	1120	36	6.91	41	57	2	0/9	0.00	853.3	1.10	21.6

3 Results and Analysis

RQ1 Results. Table 2 shows the results of RQ1, where NSGA-II identifies five Pareto-optimal configurations: Config#4 achieves 37.7% runtime reduction (943.1 s vs 1513.3 s) while doubling correctness, Config#15 achieves 10.67% code performance gain with similar runtime overhead, and Config#5 delivers 4 times

[3] https://github.com/pppyb/mini-swe-agent.

[4] https://github.com/astropy/astropy.

[5] Detailed NSGA-II setup and complete methodology can be found on GitHub.

better correctness (8/9 vs 2/9) while simultaneously improving performance by 6.43%. Notably, **4 out of 5 configurations dominate default in multiple objectives**, addressing both greener agent and greener code requirements.

We computed the hypervolume indicator using `pymoo` with objectives normalized to [0, 1] and reference point [−0.1, [−0.1, [−0.1] (runtime inverted). **Each optimized configuration substantially outperforms the default**: Config#5 achieves 135 × higher hypervolume (70.28% vs 0.52%), Config#15 achieves 64× improvement (33.42% vs 0.52%), and even the lowest-performing Config#16 achieves 2× improvement (1.10% vs 0.52%). Validation on three held-out instances confirms generalization, with all optimized configurations maintaining superior hypervolume. Moreover, NSGA-II outperforms the random search baseline (83.0% vs 53.1% cumulative hypervolume, 5 vs 3 Pareto solutions), confirming directed optimization rather than random exploration[6].

RQ1: `GA4GC` achieves 135 times higher hypervolume, 37.7% faster runtime while improving correctness, and 4/5 Pareto front configurations dominating the default while all maintaining superior hypervolume on unseen tasks.

Table 3. Random Forest feature importance for hyperparameters on optimization objectives. Colors indicate importance: Low (0.0-0.1) , Medium (0.1-0.2) , High (>0.2) .

Category	Hyperparameter	Correctness Impact	Performance Impact	Runtime Impact
LLM	Temperature	0.152	0.392	0.199
	Top_p	0.199	0.051	0.097
	Max_tokens	0.057	0.090	0.089
Agent	Step_limit	0.140	0.119	0.049
	Cost_limit	0.199	0.076	0.128
	Env_timeout	0.060	0.034	0.298
	LLM_timeout	0.120	0.109	0.102
Prompt	Template Variant	0.072	0.130	0.038

RQ2 Results. Table 3 shows the hyperparameter influence analysis. We train a Random Forest for each objective using all 25 evaluated configurations to measure influence magnitudes [11]. Among others, **temperature emerges as the most critical hyperparameter**, with high-performing Config#5 and #15 using moderate temperatures (0.66–0.69) while low-temperature Config#4 and #16 achieve faster runtime but no performance gain, indicating its role in balancing exploration versus exploitation during token generation.

Top_p shows correctness influence (0.199) with successful configurations using mid-range values (0.38–0.41), indicating that balanced vocabulary sampling avoids both overly restrictive and chaotic token selection. Cost_limit exhibits influence across correctness (0.199) and runtime (0.128), with Pareto-optimal

[6] Complete baseline comparison and Pareto front visualizations are available here.

configurations using higher budgets ($6.73–$9.26 vs $3.0 default) to enable more thorough exploration without timeout constraints. Prompt template variants show moderate performance influence (0.130), with templates 2 and 3 dominating the Pareto front, suggesting that task-specific prompt engineering significantly impacts optimization effectiveness.

RQ2: Temperature shows highest overall influence, LLM hyperparameters primarily impact task effectiveness while agent constraints affect resource consumption, confirming the need for MOGA in green coding agent deployment.

RQ3 Results. Based on the hyperparameter influence analysis, we derive three actionable strategies for green SBSE practitioners across different optimization scenarios: **For runtime-critical scenarios:** Use low temperature (0–0.1) with restrictive top_p (0.13–0.14) to minimize exploration overhead, combined with moderate max_tokens (1120–2000) and step limits (20–36). **Performance-critical scenarios:** Use moderate temperature (0.65–0.70) with balanced top_p (0.38–0.41) to enable creative optimization strategies, combined with higher cost budgets ($6.5–$9.5) and prompt templates optimized for performance tasks. **For most accurate optimization:** For practitioners with specific requirements, we recommend applying `GA4GC` to discover context-specific Pareto-optimal configurations tailored to their deployment priorities.

RQ3: We provide scenario-specific actionable suggestions for greener coding agent deployment. For more accurate optimization, practitioners can apply `GA4GC` to discover context-specific Pareto-optimal configurations.

Threats to Validity. Our evaluation focuses on the astropy project (12 instances) from SWE-Perf and is specific to mini-SWE-agent with Gemini 2.5 Pro due to computational constraints, which may limit generalizability. The limited search budget may prevent full Pareto front convergence. The stochastic nature of NSGA-II and LLM inference means results may vary across runs. All limitations reveal opportunities for future studies.

4 Conclusion

We introduced `GA4GC`, a framework to optimize coding agent resource-performance trade-offs via multi-objective optimization. On SWE-Perf, it achieves 135-fold hypervolume improvement and 37.7% runtime reduction while improving correctness. Our analysis reveals temperature is the most important LLM parameter and other insights and actionable guidelines to address both green concerns and use by industry.

Availability. Code and results are available at GitHub & https://doi.org/10.5281/zenodo.17177692.

References

1. Anthropic: Raising the bar on SWE-bench Verified with Claude 3.5 Sonnet (2025). https://www.anthropic.com/research/swe-bench-sonnet
2. Apsan, R., et al.: Generating energy-efficient code via large-language models–where are we now? arXiv preprint arXiv:2509.10099 (2025)
3. Ashiga, M., et al.: Industrial LLM-based code optimization under regulation: a mixture-of-agents approach. arXiv preprint arXiv:2508.03329 (2025)
4. Belcak, P., et al.: Small language models are the future of Agentic AI (2025). https://arxiv.org/abs/2506.02153
5. Bulhakov, V., et al.: Investigating the role of LLMs hyperparameter tuning and prompt engineering to support domain modeling. In: SEAA 2025, pp. 349–366 (2025)
6. Chen, M., Tworek, J., et al.: Evaluating large language models trained on code (2021). https://arxiv.org/abs/2107.03374
7. Coignion, T., Quinton, C., Rouvoy, R.: When faster isn't greener: the hidden costs of LLM-based code optimization. In: ASE 2025
8. Cruz, L.E.A.: Greening AI-enabled systems with software engineering: a research agenda for environmentally sustainable AI practices. ACM SIGSOFT Softw. Eng. Notes **50**(3), 14–23 (2025). https://doi.org/10.1145/3743095.3743099
9. d'Aloisio, G., Fadahunsi, T., Choy, J., Moussa, R., Sarro, F.: SustainDiffusion: optimising the social and environmental sustainability of stable diffusion models. In: 2025 IEEE/ACM ICSE (2025). https://arxiv.org/abs/2507.15663
10. Gong, J., Giavrimis, R., Brookes, P., et al.: Tuning LLM-based code optimization via meta-prompting: an industrial perspective. arXiv:2508.01443 (2025)
11. Gong, J., Li, et al.: GreenStableYolo: optimizing inference time and image quality of text-to-image generation. In: SSBSE, pp. 70–76. Springer (2024)
12. Gong, J., et al.: Language models for code optimization: Survey, challenges and future directions (2025). https://arxiv.org/abs/2501.01277
13. He, X., et al.: SWE-PERF: can language models optimize code performance on real-world repositories? (2025). https://arxiv.org/abs/2507.12415
14. Ilager, S., Briem, L.F., Brandic, I.: Green-code: learning to optimize energy efficiency in LLM-based code generation. In: CCGrid 2025, pp. 559–569. IEEE (2025)
15. Shypula, A.G., et al.: Learning performance-improving code edits. In: ICLR (2024)

GreenMalloc: Allocator Optimisation for Industrial Workloads

Aidan Dakhama[1], W. B. Langdon[2(✉)], Hector D. Menendez[1], and Karine Even-Mendoza[1]

[1] King's College London, London, UK
{aidan.dakhama,hector.menendez,karine.even_mendoza}@kcl.ac.uk
[2] University College London, London, UK
w.langdon@ucl.ac.uk

Abstract. We present GreenMalloc, a multi-objective search-based framework for automatically configuring memory allocators. Our approach uses NSGA-II and rand_malloc as a lightweight proxy benchmarking tool, we efficiently explore allocator parameters from execution traces and transfer the best configurations to gem5, a large system simulator, in a case study on two allocators: the GNU C/C++ compiler's glibc malloc and Google's TCMalloc.Across diverse workloads, our empirical results show up to 4.1% reduction in average heap usage without loss of runtime efficiency,indeed we get a 0.25% reduction.

1 Introduction

Efficient memory management remains a challenge in modern computing, with empirical studies showing that allocator choice and configuration significantly affect performance and resource use [3,12], and consequently influence energy consumption [11]. Memory allocators such as the GNU allocator (glibc malloc) [9] and Google's TCMalloc [6] are widely deployed, but tuning their runtime parameters, which allows fine-grained control of their operation, is difficult since optimal settings vary substantially with workload and system behaviour. As a result, production systems often rely on default configurations, which can waste memory, increase energy use, and degrade performance.

The gem5 simulator has become a de facto standard for hardwareâĂŞsoftware co-design evaluation in academia and industry [1]. gem5 is a large, complex codebase with unusual allocation patterns. Simulations are notoriously slow, often lasting minutes to days, magnifying the impact of allocator efficiency while making manual parameter tuning infeasible. Even modest improvements in heap usage or allocation overhead can shorten runtimes, reduce computational costs, and lower the energy footprint of repeated experiments. Among the many potential optimisation targets, allocator parameters represent a promising but underexplored opportunity to improve runtime and memory consumption in gem5. Yet, allocator optimisation in realistic workloads is challenging: exploration is costly due to long execution times and high memory demands, and results shall be relevant to system behaviour in the wild.

M. Wagner and M. Zhang (Eds.): SSBSE 2025, LNCS 16228, pp. 147–153, 2026.
https://doi.org/10.1007/978-3-032-24839-8_11

We show it is possible to automatically tune memory allocator parameters to reduce heap usage and energy consumption in industrial workloads. By targeting both memory and runtime, we identify allocator configurations that yield practical improvements across different contexts. We employ a search-based optimisation approach to tune allocator parameters and evaluate their impact on heap usage and runtime in GEM5's System Emulation (SE) mode [1]. To avoid the prohibitive cost of optimising directly on full simulations, we use RAND_MALLOC [8] as a lightweight proxy benchmark, enabling efficient exploration of the parameter space before deploying promising configurations in GEM5.

Experimental results demonstrate that while peak heap usage remained largely unchanged, GLIBC MALLOC tuning yields consistent reductions in average memory (≈4% improvement), a big improvement in free rate (≈2.4× faster release of memory), and a small but measurable reduction in instructions (≈0.25% less). TCMALLOC shows more modest improvements in stability and predictability, with small gains in memory free rate and instruction count. These findings suggest that automated allocator tuning significantly reduces computational and energy footprints of long-running industrial simulations keeping reliability and performance. This paper makes the following key contributions:

- A novel search-based optimisation methodology for configuring memory allocators to improve performance and energy efficiency.
- GREENMALLOC, a prototype implementation of this approach, designed to be generalisable beyond the allocators studied in this paper.
- A systematic study of allocator tuning using GREENMALLOC, applied to two widely used allocators, GLIBC MALLOC and TCMALLOC, in the context of GEM5, a complex and industrially relevant system.

Availability. GREENMALLOC and all artifacts are at DOI 10.5281/zenodo.17182847.

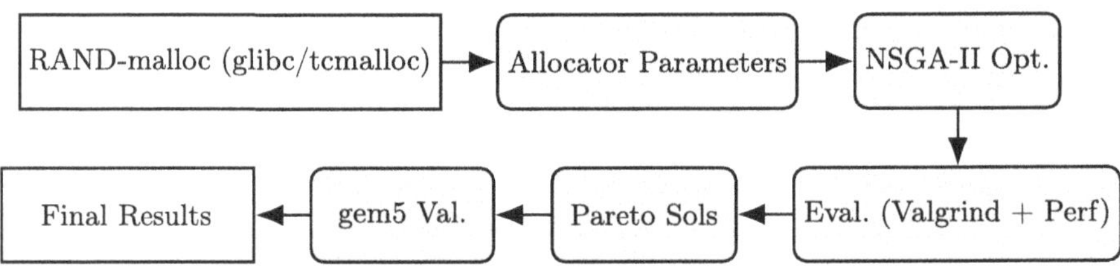

Fig. 1. General GREENMALLOC workflow: starting with RAND_MALLOC optimisation to identify efficient allocation parameters, ended by validation on GEM5 to assess improvements in memory usage and runtime.

2 Methodology

Figure 1 shows the whole system workflow. First, we optimise over a synthetic benchmark RAND_MALLOC [8] to explore the parameter search space efficiently;

next, we run the resulting optimal parameters on GEM5 simulator to evaluate the transferability to the real system under complex running conditions.

2.1 Heap Memory Allocator Parameters

Both allocators expose several tunable parameters that govern allocation behaviour. For GLIBC MALLOC, parameters including thresholds for switching between `mmap` and `sbrk` allocation, trimming and padding behaviour, and arena limits, all of which were extracted from the GLIBC MALLOC manual [9]. For TCMALLOC, there is a range of tunable parameters, such as release rates, thread cache size, page size overrides, and heap limits and were extracted from Google's TCMALLOC documentation [5]. These parameters form a high-dimensional, mixed discrete-continuous search space with non-trivial interactions, making manual tuning impractical. A summary of these parameters is in our artifact [7].

2.2 Genetic Algorithm Optimisation with `pymoo`

We employ the genetic algorithm (GA), `NSGA-II`, implemented using `pymoo`, selected for its effectiveness in multi-objective optimisation. Each candidate encodes a *configuration of allocator parameters*, which are passed as environment variables to the allocator implementation (`glibc malloc` or `tcmalloc`). Standard GA operators (mutation, crossover, and elitism) are applied to evolve the population towards better-performing configurations.
We formulate the optimisation as a multi-objective problem, jointly targeting *peak heap usage* and *execution time* to balance sustainability and performance:

- *Green Allocation.* Peak heap usage, measured using `valgrind`'s `massif` tool to minimise the total memory consumed by GEM5 at any given point. Lowering peak memory has two sustainability benefits: it reduces hardware requirements, and enables better workload co-location. Whilst average heap usage may correlate with runtime energy consumption, peak heap determines the minimal system configuration required. Our evaluation measures both metrics.
- *Performance.* Execution time, measured with the `time` utility to balance memory efficiency against performance. This ensures that improvements do not come at the cost of excessively slow executions.

For each generation, `NSGA-II` evaluates candidate parameter vectors by executing RAND_MALLOC and recording the two optimisation objectives. This yields a Pareto front of non-dominated solutions balancing memory usage and runtime. From this front, we select representative candidates: the one minimising runtime, the one minimising memory, and a balanced solution near the centre of the trade-off curve.

2.3 Case Study: Allocator Optimisation for GEM5

Allocator optimisation in realistic workloads is challenging: exploration is expensive, and results must align with system behaviour in the wild. We investigate the potential of memory allocator optimisation through a case study on GEM5, a large and complex system simulator.

Synthetic Benchmarking withRAND_MALLOC. Direct optimisation against the full GEM5 system would be prohibitively expensive, as a single run may take hours or days. We therefore employ RAND_MALLOC [8] as a proxy benchmark to effectively explore the allocator parameter space. RAND_MALLOC provides a synthetic workload, generated from a seed trace of the real system, to exercise the memory allocation behaviour while remaining representative of the memory behaviour observed in GEM5. This can also be used to measure and emulate the workload patterns of other systems, in order to provide a proxy to optimise over.

Evaluation onGEM5 To assess the effectiveness of our approach, we transfer the best-performing parameter configurations to GEM5. We evaluated GEM5's system emulation (SE) mode. For the SE mode, we rely on benchmark programs from previous work on fuzz testing of GEM5 [2,4].

3 Evaluation

We evaluated GREENMALLOC on GEM5 using 50 C test programs from SEARCH-SYS's datasets [2,4]. The study analyses GREENMALLOC's impact on peak and average heap size, memory release rate, and instruction counts under four configurations:

- **(1) Def `glibc`:** unmodified GLIBC MALLOC (baseline)
- **(2) Opt `glibc`:** GLIBC MALLOC tuned with GREENMALLOC
- **(3) Def `tcmalloc`:** unmodified TCMALLOC (baseline)
- **(4) Opt `tcmalloc`:** TCMALLOC tuned with GREENMALLOC

We then ask the following research questions (RQ):

RQ1: *What are the trade-offs between runtime performance and memory efficiency along the Pareto front of configurations discovered byGREENMALLOC?*
RQ2: *How effective is GREENMALLOC 's optimisation in reducing memory consumption and execution time in industrial simulation workloads?*

For each case study, we compiled our generated C test inputs for use in GEM5's SE mode, executed them under the four configurations, and measured memory usage with Valgrind [10] and instruction counts with perf. We use a population size of 24, and run for 500 generations before stopping across all repetitions. We used Valgrind 3.18.1 and perf 5.15.184, running on an Intel Xeon D-1548 (2.0 GHz, 8 cores) with 64 GB RAM, 8 GB swap, and Ubuntu 22.04.5 LTS (x86_64).

Results: RQ1. The hypervolume and Pareto front reveal trade-offs between the two allocators. For glibc, we achieve a mean hypervolume of 9.37×10^{16}. The

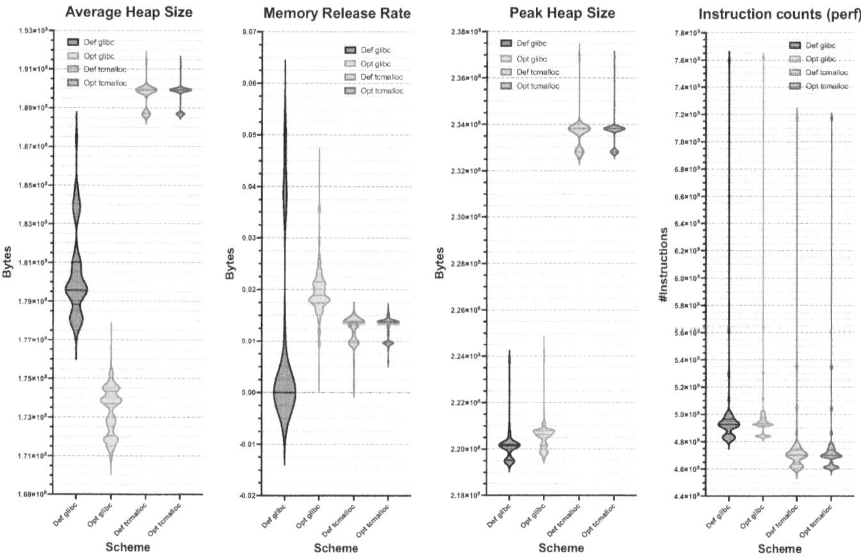

Fig. 2. Comparison of default and GreenMalloc-optimised configurations of glibc malloc (`glibc`) and TCMalloc (`tcmalloc`). From left to right: average heap size, Memory release Rate, peak heap size, and instruction counts, as measured with Valgrind, perf, and gem5. Values are all pareto optimal values.

Pareto fronts average 3 solutions per run, across 0.095% of the instruction space and 0.162% of the peak-heap space relative to the best-performing configuration on the front, with a trade-off slope of -0.216. While TCMalloc achieves a mean hypervolume of 5.46×10^{16}, with smaller Pareto fronts averaging 1.6 solutions per run. While its instruction span is constrained to just 0.005%, it offers greater potential with a 0.259% peak-heap span; however, it also has a much steeper trade-off of -3.17. This demonstrates glibc malloc's default configuration allows for more gradual trade-offs, while TCMalloc operates closer to optimal performance boundaries, constraining the search space but requiring more aggressive trade-offs between objectives. Full RQ1 results are provided in the zip file at [7].

Results: RQ2. For **average heap usage**, `glibc` shows a clear improvement: Tuning reduced the mean from 180 428 315 to 173 293 862, with a tighter standard deviation (2.2M to 1.6M). This indicates both greener execution – due to a lower memory footprint – and greater performance stability. For `tcmalloc`, the mean remains nearly unchanged, though the density distribution in Fig. 2 shows less variance around hotspots, improving predictability. Neither allocator shows reductions in **peak heap usage**. `glibc`'s average slightly increases (220 104 049 to 220 523 190), while `tcmalloc` remains stable. This shows **peak heap usage** is close to its minimum. `glibc` benefits significantly in **memory release rate**: The free rate rises from 0.0080 to 0.0196, reducing retention. `tcmalloc` also improves, with both average release and minimum release increasing. For **instructions executed**, `glibc` improves from 4.992×10^9 to 4.990×10^9, with standard deviation tightened. `tcmalloc` shows a clearer benefit: reducing average instructions from 4.77×10^9 to 4.76×10^9, with variance shrinking as well. These reductions translate into greener execution and improved efficiency.

In best-case runs, we found a single instance of TCMALLOC achieved a significant improvement over the unoptimised baseline: specifically, a 4.65% reduction in instruction count as well as a simultaneous 2.06% reduction in peak heap usage. In contrast, the best case run for `glibc` demonstrated a tradeoff between the two optimisation parameters, though it achieved a larger improvement in each metric individually. This suggests that while the transferability from the synthetic benchmark is sufficient, it could benefit from further tuning.

Overall, allocator tuning reduces memory usage and instruction count in `glibc`, while improving consistency in both `glibc` and `tcmalloc`, demonstrating tangible gains in both sustainability and performance. The improvements found by the synthetic benchmark could effectively translate to real workloads. In `glibc`, the tuned parameters reduced average memory and instructions and increased release rate significantly – matching synthetic predictions of greener, more efficient behaviour. In `tcmalloc`, while mean values remained largely stable, the improved consistency of both heap usage and instruction counts mirrors the synthetic outcomes. Full RQ2 results are provided in the zip file at [7].

4 Conclusion

We introduced GREENMALLOC, a search-based framework for memory allocator parameter optimisation using lightweight benchmarking. With GEM5 we observed reductions in heap usage and instruction counts for both GLIBC and TCMALLOC, highlighting malloc parameter optimisation as a practical approach for efficient and greener systems. The combination of search-based optimisation with lightweight benchmarking opens the door to investigating other aspects of complex software using this strategy, such as GEM5's full system (FS) mode, and broader targets including VMs, simulators, emulators, and interpreters.

References

1. Binkert, N., et al.: The gem5 simulator. SIGARCH Comput. Archit. News **39**(2), 1–7 (2011). https://doi.org/10.1145/2024716.2024718
2. Dakhama, A., et al.: Enhancing search-based testing with LLMs for finding bugs in system simulators. Autom. Softw. Eng. **32**(2) (2025)
3. Durner, D., et al.: On the impact of memory allocation on high-performance query processing. In: DaMoN (2019). https://doi.org/10.1145/3329785.3329918
4. Even-Mendoza, et al.: Search+LLM-based testing for ARM simulators. In: ICSE-SEIP, pp. 469–48 (2025). https://doi.org/10.1109/ICSE-SEIP66354.2025.00047
5. Ghemawat, S.: TCMalloc: thread-caching malloc (2024). https://gperftools.github.io/gperftools/tcmalloc.html. Accessed Sep 2025

6. Google: TCMalloc (2025). https://github.com/google/tcmalloc
7. GreenMalloc: this paper's artifact (2025). https://doi.org/10.5281/zenodo.17171047
8. Langdon, W.B.: A genetic improvement parameter benchmark: rand_malloc.c. In: UKCI (2025). https://gpbib.cs.ucl.ac.uk/gp-html/Langdon_2025_UKCI.html
9. Loosemore, S., et al.: The GNU C library reference manual. GNU Project (2025). https://sourceware.org/glibc/manual/latest/pdf/libc.pdf
10. Nethercote, N., et al.: Valgrind: a framework for heavyweight dynamic binary instrumentation. In: PLDI , pp. 89–100 (2007)
11. Pereira, R., et al.: Energy efficiency across programming languages: how do energy, time, and memory relate? In: SLE, pp. 256–267. ACM (2017)
12. Zhou, Z., et al.: Characterizing a memory allocator at warehouse scale. In: ASPLOS (2024), pp. 192–206 ACM. https://doi.org/10.1145/3620666.3651350

HotCat: Green and Effective Feature Selection toward Hotfix Bug Taxonomy

Luis de la Cal[1], Yazhuo Cao[2], Ayse Irmak Ercevik[2], Giovanni Pinna[3], Lukas Twist[2], David Williams[4], Karine Even-Mendoza[2], W. B. Langdon[4], Hector D. Menendez[2], and Federica Sarro[4(✉)]

[1] Universidad Politécnica de Madrid, Madrid, Spain
l.delacal@upm.es
[2] King's College London, London, UK
{yazhuo.cao,ayse.ercevik,lukas.twist,karine.even_mendoza, hector.menendez}@kcl.ac.uk
[3] University of Trieste, Trieste, Italy
giovanni.pinna@phd.units.it
[4] University College London, London, UK
{david.williams.22,w.langdon,f.sarro}@ucl.ac.uk

Abstract. HotBugs.jar is a novel benchmark targeting time-critical (a.k.a. hot) fixes. We propose an approach to analyze the taxonomy of the bugs in HotBugs.jar by extending *PatchCat* into *HotCat*, integrating hotfix metadata with multi-objective optimization. Using NSGA-II, we evolve bitmask-based feature subsets that balance accuracy, Normalized Mutual Information (NMI), and runtime. On 88 records across 17 categories, *HotCat* achieved 0.59 accuracy and 0.58 NMI in 129 s, with maximum accuracy of 0.63 in 132 s, demonstrating accuracy improvements without additional resource use, thus supporting sustainability. Future work will expand and augment the dataset, refine optimization objectives, and improve semantic categorization, robustness, and cluster balance.

Keywords: Genetic Algorithm · LLM · SSBSE · Time-critical Apache Java Software Errors · Hotfix · HotBugs-dot-jar · PatchCat · Jira issue

1 Introduction

Hotfixes represent a critical category of software patches that address time-sensitive issues requiring immediate deployment to production systems [9]. These patches aim to minimize system downtime while fixing urgent vulnerabilities.

Recently, Even-Mendoza et al. [6] introduced *PatchCat*, which leverages Sentence-BERT embeddings with short-text clustering [12,13] as a lightweight machine learning approach to approximate patch edits based on descriptions synthesized by *Large Language Models* (LLMs). *PatchCat* demonstrated the feasibility of semantic-aware patch classification, capturing edit intent (e.g., "added

M. Wagner and M. Zhang (Eds.): SSBSE 2025, LNCS 16228, pp. 154–160, 2026.
https://doi.org/10.1007/978-3-032-24839-8_12

dead code", "duplicated code") and integration with issue-tracking systems for analysis.

We extend *PatchCat* from patch clustering to classifying and organizing hotfixes into coherent semantic categories, combining clustering results with project metadata, such as Jira issue reports, to derive a taxonomy that reflects real-world maintenance practices. This taxonomy enables systematic analysis of urgent patches and opportunities for automated reasoning in software maintenance while targeting challenges: 1) Hotfix data is typically sparse and imbalanced, limiting the effectiveness of traditional classification approaches [4]; and 2) balancing accuracy with the high computational cost of large-scale LLM-based analyses is crucial, motivating the integration of *Search-Based Software Engineering* (SBSE) techniques, where multi-objective optimization has proven effective in feature selection under competing objectives.

Our Contribution. We propose an automated pipeline that adapts and extends *PatchCat* [6] for hotfix analysis of the HotBugs.jar [7] SSBSE'25 Challenge Case:

- We adapt *PatchCat* to operate directly on hotfix patches from the HotBugs.jar dataset [7], integrating project metadata and LLM-based summarization.

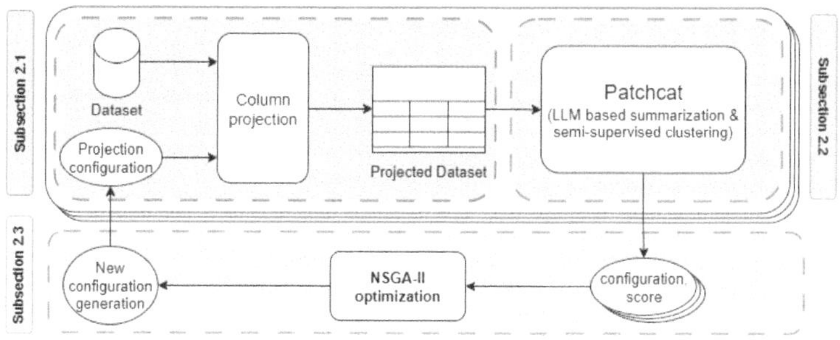

Fig. 1. Architecture diagram of *HotCat*.

- We address sparsity and imbalance by combining centroid-based description, LLM-generated augmentation, and semantic enrichment [4,9].
- We use NSGA-II for feature selection, balancing quality with computational efficiency, and green responsible resource usage.
- We empirically demonstrate that extending *PatchCat* with search-based optimization is a step toward an automatically extracted hotfix bug taxonomy.

Related Work. Hotfixes require immediate deployment and must balance urgency with system stability [9]. This urgency has motivated advances in semantic patch analysis, where approaches such as SemFix [10] and CapGen [15] showed that capturing edit intent yields better results than syntactic methods.

In parallel, bug taxonomies have progressed from manual schemes like Orthogonal Defect Classification [3] to machine learning approaches [2]. However, a key challenge lies in the sparse and imbalanced nature of hotfix data. To tackle this, data augmentation has shown promise, improving classification accuracy to 88% in imbalanced settings [4]. Yet, despite advances with *PatchCat* [6] and *Gin* [11], the combination of semantic clustering and multi-objective optimization for hotfix taxonomy construction remains unexplored.

Availability. *HotCat* and all artifacts are available at DOI: 10.5281/zenodo.17170205.

2 Methodology

Our objective is to leverage *PatchCat* [6] to classify Jira issues based on the features in the SSBSE hotfix dataset [7]. *PatchCat* [6] was originally designed to classify software patches in Gin: given a code diff, it generates a short natural language summary via an LLM, applies semi-supervised clustering via K-Means and Sentence-BERT embeddings [13] refined by iterative classification [12] to assign patches to semantic categories, and outputs accuracy and *Normalized Mutual Information* (NMI) scores, indicating clustering performance.

Table 1. Bug taxonomy description & data sources for categories 1–17

#	Description	Hotfix	Centroids	Le Chat	PatchCat
1	Test suite, tests, test folder	✓	✓		
2	Crash or Hang	✓	✓		
3	Missing Code or Components, or Incomplete	✓	✓	✓	14,3
4	Start, Access, or Availability of Service Issues	✓	✓		
5	Security Vulnerability or Permission Issues	✓	✓		
6	Configuration Dependency, Versioning or Deprecation	✓	✓	✓	
7	Configuration Build or CI Failures	✓	✓	✓	
8	Buggy Configuration or Broken Config Files	✓	✓		
9	Database	✓	✓	✓	
10	API / Parsing / Syntax errors	✓	✓		
11	Exceptions, Error Handling, or Missing Checks	✓✓	✓		
12	unsupported, Undefined or unspecified behavior	✓	✓	✓	18
13	Network	✓	✓		
14	Performance	✓	✓	✓	11,14
15	Permission Deprecation, Access Control or Policy Issues	✓	✓	✓	
16	Functionality issue (Logical Bugs)	✓✓✓	✓		
17	Concurrency or Race Conditions	✓	✓	✓	11

We adapt *PatchCat* to operate not only on patch diffs but on selected subsets of attributes from the hotfix dataset, thereby extending its scope from categorizing code-level edits to classifying hotfix issues using a richer representation of metadata. Using all features is neither sustainable nor effective. Larger prompts increase energy use and costs [14], while some features add more noise than value. We employ NSGA-II to identify feature subsets that strike a balance between predictive accuracy and efficiency. The overall process is illustrated in Fig. 1: subset selection produces a projected dataset (§2.1), each projection is evaluated with *PatchCat* to assess performance (§2.2), and resulting fitness scores are fed into NSGA-II to evolve improved generations of feature subsets (§2.3).

2.1 Dataset, Projected Dataset and Configuration Definition

The HotBugs.jar dataset [7] contains **88 entries** and provides metadata per hotfix instance, like project name, Jira reference, build configuration, assigned bug category, and rationale for classifying it as a hotfix. We further enrich the dataset with code diffs and additional information, such as time-to-fix and the number of participants, gathering information from multiple sources listed in Table 1. The **enriched and augmented dataset** comprises **155 records**, each with **18 features** (i.e., bitmask vector size) across **17 categories** (Table 1). We applied two-stage **data augmentation**: 1) balancing category sizes so no category contained fewer than three records (yielding 155 records), and 2) adding 50 records per category *post-optimization* to evaluate if augmentation improves quality (yielding an additional 17×50 records, used in RQ2 only). Features span hotfix data, bug details, and code commit diffs detailed at [8].

We load the dataset and apply a *bitmask* to project onto selected features, where, per feature, 1 denotes inclusion and 0 exclusion. The projected dataset (referred to as "hotfix"), together with its *bitmask*, is then passed to *PatchCat* for fitness evaluation. In this setting, the *configuration* is the *bitmask*.

2.2 PatchCat and Fitness Function

We modify *PatchCat* in two ways: 1) extending it to incorporate additional hotfix fields, specified through the *configuration* bitmask, as opposed to code diffs alone, and 2) automating its operation within the optimization loop to serve as the NSGA-II fitness function. We then, per configuration, employ modified *PatchCat* as a black box, taking the projected dataset as input and returning category-quality metrics that directly serve as fitness values.

Hotfix projected records are passed to an LLM (via Ollama or similar interfaces) to generate short, clean summaries of each hotfix. Prompting is altered to include two prompts in sequence. The first sets the LLM's role, and the second defines the concrete task. Prompts templates are at [8]. Bug category IDs are fixed: While projections yield different summaries, labels remain constant as defined by the original hotfix dataset's expert as ground truth.

2.3 Optimization

Determining the right balance between too much and too little information is an open question in the context of hotfixes and bug reports, which we begin to investigate in this work. We define the *bitmask* pattern as a configuration in our optimization setting: each bit encodes whether a dataset field is included or excluded (1 or 0, respectively). Searching for bitmasks corresponds to exploring different projections of the dataset, with optimization aiming to identify those projections that yield the most meaningful summaries and category performance.

NSGA-II Optimization. Using NSGA-II [1,5], we evolve new generations of candidate configurations, keep those that strike the best balance across objectives, promote diversity via binary crossover and occasional bit flip mutations, and discard duplicates. Since our problem is multi-objective, we will produce an approximation to the Pareto front, representing the set of non-dominated configurations that characterize the trade-offs between classification performance and computational efficiency for hotfix analysis.

3 Evaluation

Research Questions. We ask the following research questions (RQ):

RQ1: *What is the trade-off between classification performance and runtime when classifying hotfixes using HotCat?*
RQ2: *Do our predicted bug categories improve real maintenance workflows?*

Setup. We implemented *HotCat* in Bash and Python, with performance assessed by execution time. Configurations were evaluated using PatchCat. *Optimization* used the NSGA-II algorithm [5] from `pymoo` library v0.6.1.5 [1], with a population size of 20 over 20 generations, which balances exploration and exploitation. Objectives minimized runtime and maximized accuracy (labelâĂŞground truth alignment), and NMI, yielding a Pareto front of non-dominated configurations, capturing the best trade-offs. *Post-optimization*, Pareto-front configurations train PatchCat models to classify manually labeled unclassified hotfix entries.

indiv.	accuracy	NMI	seconds
1.1	0.59	**0.58**	129
1.2	0.55	0.56	125
1.3	0.54	0.50	119
1.4	0.56	0.56	125
2	0.59	0.55	125
3	**0.63**	0.57	132
4.1	0.58	0.53	121
4.2	0.54	0.52	120
5.1	0.52	0.48	**116**
5.2	0.54	0.49	119
6	0.57	0.54	123
7	0.51	0.49	118
8.1	0.57	0.53	121
8.2	0.55	0.55	124
9	0.52	0.48	118

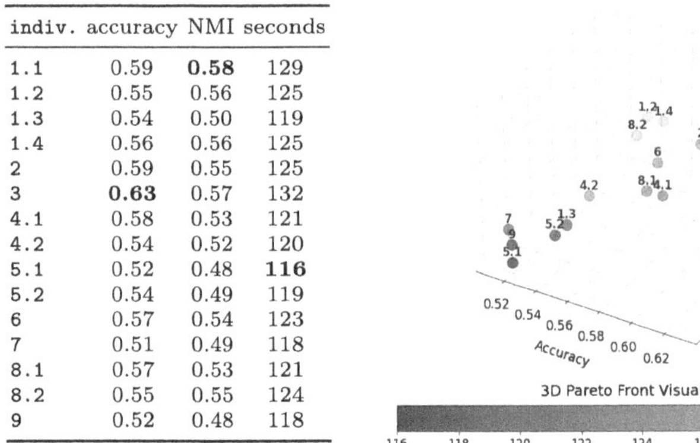

Fig. 2. Pareto Front individuals and visualization.

Results. Our optimization process focused on three specific objectives using the NSGA-II algorithm: accuracy, NMI, and execution time. It also accounts for the non-deterministic behavior of the bug categorization process, which may yield repeated solutions with different fitness values. These solutions are denoted as $X.Y$, where X is the individual number and Y is the repetition identifier. In Fig. 2 (left side, table), we present the Pareto-optimal individuals obtained after running the algorithm with these objectives. Individual 3 is the slowest (132 s) and the fastest is 5.1 (116 s). Individual 3 achieves the highest accuracy (0.63), whereas individual 7 records the lowest (0.51). The best NMI value is obtained by individual 1.1 (0.58), while the lowest is found in individual 5.1 (0.48). Individual 6 combines solid accuracy (0.57) and NMI (0.54), with a competitive runtime (123 s), making it a reasonable candidate. The most *balanced solution* is individual 1.1.

RQ1 Answer. The best trade-off (individual 1.1) identified by NSGA-II achieved high accuracy (0.59), the best NMI (0.58), and a runtime close to the median (129 s), representing a strong balance across the three objectives.

To evaluate generalization, we manually annotated 51 challenging bug reports that were tagged in the dataset but excluded from `HotBugs.jar` [7] to test our Pareto-optimal models with five repeats per configuration, obtaining average accuracy/NMI of 0.55/0.52 on the original dataset and 0.72/0.75 on the augmented dataset. Each model was provided with the corresponding Jira ticket (including description and metadata), and final labels were assigned by a majority vote across the ensemble. The ensemble underperformed relative to training results, likely due to the small, imbalanced training set (88 records across 17 classes) and vocabulary overlap that blurs fine-grained boundaries, tending to collapse predictions into a few dominant categories (notably 13 and 16).

RQ2 Answer. On 51 specially hard hotfixes, the ensemble underperformed. Labels collapsed into a few classes due to a tiny, imbalanced training dataset of 88 records across 17 categories and a strong vocabulary overlap. Improvements are likely with data augmentation techniques and class balancing.

4 Conclusion

We propose an initial taxonomy for classifying hot fixes. We showed that multi-objective optimization improves accuracy while maintaining sustainability: the best-balanced solution (1.1) reached 0.59 accuracy and 0.58 NMI at 129 s runtime, while the maximum accuracy (0.63) required only slightly longer runtime (132 s). These results demonstrate that higher accuracy can be achieved without increasing resource use.

During optimization, we used runtime as a proxy for efficiency and measured energy and emissions post hoc; future work should make these first-class objectives and mitigate LLM run-to-run variance. Our results are limited by a small, imbalanced dataset (88 records across 17 categories) and overlapping vocabularies that blur class boundaries (e.g., memory leaks vs. performance vs. concurrency), which led to overprediction of a few bug categories (13, 16). We also evaluated on harder, previously excluded records. Expanding the dataset and refining the objectives should improve robustness, avoid local optima, and yield better accuracy-efficiency trade-offs.

References

1. Blank, J., Deb, K.: Pymoo: multi-objective optimization in python. IEEE Access **8**, 89497–89509 (2020)
2. Catolino, G., et al.: Not all bugs are the same: understanding, characterizing, and classifying bug types. J. Syst. Softw. **152**, 165–181 (2019)
3. Chillarege, R., et al.: Orthogonal defect classification-a concept for in-process measurements. IEEE TSE **18**(11), 943–956 (1992)
4. Ciborowska, A., Damevski, K.: Too few bug reports? Exploring data augmentation for improved changeset-based bug localization. arXiv:2305.16430 (2023)
5. Deb, K., Pratap, A., Agarwal, S., Meyarivan, T.: A fast and elitist multiobjective genetic algorithm: NSGA-II. IEEE TEVC **6**(2), 182–197 (2002)
6. Even-Mendoza, K., et al.: LLM-guided genetic improvement: envisioning semantic aware automated software evolution. In: ASE NIER (2025)
7. Hanna, C., Sarro, F., Harman, M., Petke, J.: Hotbugs.jar: a benchmark of hot fixes for time-critical bugs (2025). https://arxiv.org/abs/2510.07529
8. HotCat: The paper's artifact (2025). https://doi.org/10.5281/zenodo.17170205
9. Islam, C., Prokhorenko, V., Babar, M.A.: Runtime software patching: taxonomy, survey and future directions. J. Syst. Softw. **200**, 111652 (2023)
10. Nguyen, H.D.T., Qi, D., Roychoudhury, A., Chandra, S.: Semfix: program repair via semantic analysis. In: ICSE, pp. 772–781. IEEE (2013)
11. Petke, J., et al.: Program trans... using Gin. ESE **28**, 104 (2023)
12. Rakib, M.R.H., Zeh, N., Jankowska, M., Milios, E.: Enhancement of short text clustering by iterative classification. In: Métais, E., Meziane, F., Horacek, H., Cimiano, P. (eds.) NLDB 2020. LNCS, vol. 12089, pp. 105–117. Springer, Cham (2020). https://doi.org/10.1007/978-3-030-51310-8_10
13. Reimers, N., Gurevych, I.: Sentence-BERT: sentence embeddings using siamese BERT-networks (2019). https://arxiv.org/abs/1908.10084
14. Robinson, J., Kummerfeld, J.K.: Simple and effective baselines for code summarisation evaluation. arXiv:2505.19392 (2025)
15. Wen, M., Chen, J., Wu, R., Hao, D., Cheung, S.C.: Context-aware patch generation for better automated program repair. In: ICSE (2018)

Author Index

M. Wagner and M. Zhang (Eds.): SSBSE 2025, LNCS 16228, p. 161, 2026.
https://doi.org/10.1007/978-3-032-24839-8

The manufacturer's authorised representative in the EU is Springer Nature Customer Service Centre GmbH, Europaplatz 3, 69115 Heidelberg, Germany. If you have any concerns regarding our products, please contact ProductSafety@springernature.com

Printed and bound by CPI Group (UK) Ltd, Croydon, CR0 4YY
07/07/2026
02160917-0001